The Linguistics of American Sign Language

The Linguistics of American Sign Language

by

John O. Isenhath

McFarland & Company, Inc., Publishers
Jefferson, North Carolina, and London

HV
2474
.I84
1990
15·1929
may 1991

British Library Cataloguing-in-Publication data are available

Library of Congress Cataloguing-in-Publication Data

Isenhath, John O., 1951–
   The linguistics of American sign language / by John O. Isenhath.
      p.   cm.
   Includes bibliographical references (p. 245) and index.
   ISBN 0-89950-493-0 (lib. bdg.: 50# alk. paper) ∞
   1. Sign language.   2. Deaf—United States—Means of communication.
I. Title.
HV2474.I84   1990
419—dc20   89-43653
                                                                CIP

Manufactured in the United States of America

McFarland & Company, Inc., Publishers
  Box 611, Jefferson, North Carolina 28640

I dedicate this book with love to my wife Kaye,
who communicates so well herself—in many languages—
and to the late Milton H. Erickson, M.D.,
whose teachings have had an impact on my own communications

Contents

Preface

The Linguistics of American Sign Language investigates the natural transition that takes place when a person moves from one language, English, to another language, ASL. The material it presents extends far beyond a sign vocabulary. By approaching ASL from a variety of perspectives, it forms a much-needed bridge between theory and practical ASL–based communications.

The book's foremost goal is to serve as a practical guide for students to understand ASL as a communication system. Students achieve the transition from English to ASL in a series of steps. The book organizes its material systematically from simple to complex. Students can begin at the level of the sign and progress at their own pace until they have acquired a working understanding of how to convey a compound sentence in ASL.

Presenting the various elements of the language in an easy-to-learn format does not mean that the material is oversimplified. Rather, the various linguistic complexities are unraveled in order to provide a clear learning process. As a result, this book is appropriate for both group and individual learning.

The Linguistics of American Sign Language approaches the transition from English structure and philosophy to ASL in two main parts, each reflecting a different perspective. In the first part ASL is investigated from a communication viewpoint. Each chapter contributes to form a balanced presentation of how this manual language enables signers to communicate their thoughts, ideas, or feelings through a gestural/visual modality rather than a speech-auditory pathway. In the second part the book concentrates on the technical aspects of the language, its grammatical structure. Students learn how signs are modified in actual content and how signs can become so interrelated that one sign may affect the composition and occurrence of another sign within a sentence. This latter section highlights sentence construction and discusses the many different sentence patterns and how each pattern is influenced by linguistic and situational constraints.

The book is an introductory text. It strives to provide a comprehensive level of information so that students will develop a working knowledge of

ASL, reflected by their ability to recognize and use the major grammatical structures that make up the language. The central goal is for students to be able to use this communication system with depth and latitude.

The book's emphasis is practical rather than theoretical. It is distinguished from existing texts by two major factors. First, it uses the student's native language as a commonalty. Using English as a point of reference enhances the book's readability and provides an opportunity for students to respond to their habitual thinking patterns in learning a new communication code.

Second, the transition itself is unique and innovative. Utilizing a gradual, logical progression of topics and learning strategies, it carefully guides students along a strong communicative framework. The approach recognizes the multidimensional obstacles of moving to another language and another anatomical means of communicating.

The book uses postulated guidelines, rather than fixed rules, throughout. This instills an essential degree of flexibility that acknowledges American Sign Language's natural diversification and contextual nature of expression. It includes timely examples, illustrations, and applications. Each chapter is supplemented with a variety of exercises, drills, and other activities to enable students to apply the newly acquired information immediately. The workability of the text was developed through a decade of college use of the working draft.

Part 2 applies descriptive diagramming, a proven method for teaching English grammar as a unique strategy for teaching American Sign Language. Diagramming sentences represents a new approach to describing the construction of ASL sentence patterns, and is particularly appropriate because of the inherently high level of variability in ASL. The use of diagramming does not imply that ASL has fixed or rigid sign order, but it does illustrate that sign order within an ASL sentence possesses some degree of predictability. The diagrams outline graphically how each grammatical unit is treated and illustrate the various relationships that can occur within a sentence construction. An ASL compound is expressed graphically by a curved line. However, in this book compounds will be expressed by double diagonal lines (//) between its root signs.

ASL, with its own grammar and syntax, represents one end of a continuum in manual communications (Friedman, 1975). At the other extreme is Signed English, a signed reproduction of spoken–English syntax. Between these end points lies a variety of different codes and pidgin derivatives that blend English structure with ASL signs to varying degrees. *The Linguistics of American Sign Language* approaches manual language as a communication phenomenon and American Sign Language as an understandable language.

Outline of a Course on This Topic

Part 1: Understanding ASL as a means of communication

Chapter 1. "ASL Phonology" introduces the sign as the basic semantic element of manual communication. It investigates sign articulation emphasizing that each sign is composed of a series of physical parameters that define a sign phonetically.

Chapter 2. "Communication Styles" compares an array of communicative characteristics, highlighting the differences between English and ASL. Viewing words and signs as the vehicles for carrying semantic meaning, this chapter explores the role of auditory versus visual association.

Chapter 3. "Economization" explores a distinguishing principle of manual language, the concise, economized quality of its communicative style. The chapter carefully outlines the strategies and methods ASL uses to conserve both time and energy.

Chapter 4. "Compounds" probes the various incorporating methods ASL uses to create new lexical units. The discussion focuses on the morphological mechanisms that combine parameters, signs, and concepts to create new lexical units. Next, various characteristics are presented that enable the signer to distinguish a compound from a phrase. The chapter concludes with a discussion of the evolution of the compound and its practical applications.

Chapter 5. "Perceptual Communications" broadens the discussion of communication by addressing the cognitive process involved in receiving information. The chapter compares receiving input from the auditory versus visual sensory pathways. It also explores the advantages, benefits, and current role of iconicity in visual perception.

Part 2: Understanding ASL's linguistic structure

Chapter 6. "The Basic Structure" introduces the basic grammatical components of ASL: subject, verb and object. It then discusses how these components interact in a variety of ASL sentence patterns. Four distinct ASL sentence patterns are identified.

Chapter 7. "Topicalizing a Sentence" discusses ASL as a "topic-prone" language, which arranges information in a sentence according to its relative importance. The chapter presents and discusses several topicalized sentence patterns that deviate from the basic SVO order.

The Linguistics of ASL

Chapter 8. "Spatial Indexing" discusses ASL strategies for conveying pronominal references. It explores the practical and innovative advantages of using space to refer to persons, objects, or locations. It also presents the relationship between fixed verbs and indexing as well as the language's means for establishing the location of particular referents within the neutral sign space.

Chapter 9. "Multidirectional Verbs" discusses those verbs that make up the majority of ASL verbs. This class of verbs use movement and orientation to convey pronominal references indirectly. The signer can use these verbs to unambiguously indicate the subject and object of a sentence without using overt nominal signs.

Chapter 10. "Asking a Question" identifies the three methods used in ASL to create an inquiry. The yes/no question, interrogative question, and rhetorical question are presented along with each pattern's distinguishing nonmanual signals.

Chapter 11. "Modifying a Sentence" describes a variety of strategies, markers, and signs used to describe, limit, or qualify other signs in ASL. Such mechanisms as adjective modifiers, pluralizing, and auxiliary verbs highlight this discussion.

Chapter 12. "Expressing Time" discusses the collection of linguistic and spatial mechanisms used by the signer to convey relative time. The chapter covers such concepts as conversational time reference, specific and general time markers, and explicit temporal modifiers. The spatial contribution of a time line is introduced and explained.

Chapter 13. "Negating a Sentence" focuses on the ways ASL negates a message. Although ASL negation is dominated by nonmanual signaling, both nonmanual negation and negation signs are discussed.

Chapter 14. "Stressing a Sentence" is accomplished in ASL primarily by nonmanual behavior. This chapter discusses sign delivery as a means to influence the relative emphasis of a message and gives practical applications.

Chapter 15. "The Complex Sentence" addresses effects of interrelated clauses in ASL. Topics discussed include introductory phrases, compound sentences, complex sentences, and conditional sentences. The chapter identifies different strategies used to arrange sentences in order to create more meaningful communication patterns.

Part 1
Understanding ASL as a
Means of Communication

American Sign Language (ASL), like any language, first functions as a means of communication. ASL exists as a symbolic code that enables signers to translate their mental ideas (a sensory image of something or someone being thought about), feelings, or intentions into a physical form that others can understand. The prelude to understanding ASL as a technical language with its own grammar and syntax is to understand ASL as a means of exchanging information that has its own philosophy and communicating style.

Part 1 investigates American Sign Language from different perspectives, each relating to the dynamics of interpersonal communications. The following chapters address such issues as why an ASL sentence economizes its form, how explicit is its semantic content, whether it is an iconic language, and whether it can communicate abstract concepts. Many of the topics presented in this part have never before been addressed in a sign language book. In addition, many of the learning strategies found in this part are an innovative approach to teaching American Sign Language.

Other areas that will be explored include a variety of morphological mechanisms, each centering on the process involved in attaching meaning to a sign. The discussion of the phonological characteristics of a sign leads the way for the subsequent chapters to expand on the principles of interpersonal communication as it applies to manual language. Part 1 concludes with a discussion of the receptive and perceptual dimensions that complete the communication cycle.

Throughout Part 1, the adjustments necessary to communicate in manual language are addressed according to the process involved when a hearing person shifts simultaneously from a familiar modality (speech/hearing) to an unfamiliar modality (manual/visual) and from a native language to a foreign second language. The outcome is a working knowledge and understanding of the many dimensions that make American Sign Language a means of communication.

1. ASL Phonology

The English word and the American Sign Language (ASL) sign have much in common. Both lexical items share the same alphabet in written form. There is minimal convincing evidence to differentiate the written form of these semantic devices, so a sign and a word can appear essentially the same. For instance, the graphic representation of a word like "slow," and the sign SLOW are hardly distinguishable. Separating the two lexicons by lowercase versus capital letters is a purely arbitrary and practical division, not necessarily an inherent characteristic nor a linguistic division.

This equivalent inscription encourages the perception of interchangeability between a word and a sign, but this perception is incorrect. A typical misconception of many novice observers and beginning students is that signs and words with equivalent inscriptions apparently mean the same thing. This misconception leads some people to believe erroneously that English and ASL are two expressions of the same language. The use of signs to perform English sentences as in Signed English tends to reinforce this belief.

But learning to express yourself in manual English is not the same as learning manual language. Learning manual English is not much different from learning Morse code, but no one thinks Morse code represents a second language. Using signs to pictorialize English has little or nothing to do with expressing yourself through American Sign Language. Manual communication in English is one way to express yourself. Manual communication in ASL is a completely different way to express yourself. But ASL involves a variety of linguistic components and strategies that distinguish it as a separate language entity. Thus, though the sign and the word may share a written representation, they do not necessarily share grammatical identity or utilization.

What is involved in the articulation of speech? How do lip movements, tongue movements, mouth movements, and the use of the nasal cavity enter into the way that speech sounds are produced? How do vocal organs and vocal cords contribute? You need only reflect on the massive coordination task, the intrinsic selection process, and the sequential arrangement of the sound system that make up the word to realize that spoken communication is a physical phenomenon. A native English speaker who wishes to acquire a second language in ASL must begin by understanding the structure of a word. This understanding is a prerequisite for understanding the principles that make up a sign. Thus, to understand the sign as a linguistic unit of ASL, we begin with a review of the spoken word.

The "word" can be defined as a sequential series of speech sounds that when articulated is capable of symbolizing and communicating meaning. When you analyze all of the fine motor coordinations involved in such a detailed activity, you will note that there is little room for production errors. A spoken miscue, a slippage in articulating a key word or phrase can turn a well-meaning compliment into an insult or turn praise into gibberish.

As the smallest meaningful linguistic unit, the word is composed of a series of specific speech sounds referred to as "phonemes," the distinguishing units of speech. Individual phonemes are usually not capable of conveying meaning independently, although there are a few exceptions (e.g., the word "I"). Phonemes divide the word into a voluntary succession of sounds emitted by the speech mechanism as it performs a series of definite physical actions.

Phonemes can also be viewed as bundles of harmonious articulation properties, called "distinctive features." The phonemes' distinctive features give it individual character. Such features reflect whether the sound is voiced or unvoiced (the presence or absence of vocal-cord vibration as in the voiced |d| versus the unvoiced |t|); whether it is plosive (referring to a sudden release of compressed air to make an explosive sound such as |b| or |p|; or whether the sound is nasal (air passes through the nose as in |m| or |n|). A phoneme is a family of distinctive features that together distinguish its sound from all other sounds of the language.

Each phoneme requires the speech organs to be placed in certain definite positions and to move in well-defined ways. Phoneme production is not accidental or random. The speaker must make a definite effort, and produce the particular sound features intentionally. In order to form an intelligible word, the phonemes must be arranged in an appropriate sequence (e.g. |t|–|e|–|n|).

It is also possible to represent a word graphically with symbols, most commonly a series of letters of the alphabet. Using a descriptive set of graphic symbols to represent the spoken word is a written form of communication. The spoken (phonemic) word is one channel, and the written word is another channel, and these channels do not necessarily intermix. If you write down the actual sounds of a word, you will find that these phonemic sounds often represent a word differently than its alphabetic letters. Similarly, if you try to produce each sound represented by the alphabetic letters, you will not always be able to accurately produce the actual sounds of the word. This incongruence between symbolic letters and actual phonemes is well illustrated by an ordinary word like "question." The sound production of "question" involves the sequential set of phonemes: |kwestʃˆn|. Sounding out its alphabetic letters, "Q–U–E–S–T–I–O–N," results in something sounding like "u–es–te–on." There is no existing phoneme, for instance, that represents the letter "Q." Such an alphabetic letter is regarded as a "silent" letter. A similar attempt to sound out the letters of a more exotic word like "xerophyte" (a plant suited for day climates) will help you appreciate better how far apart these inscribed channels can actually be.

Another factor that influences production characteristics is language change. New modern words evolve, and outdated words fade from ordinary usage. Can you recall ever using the word "thou" in casual conversation? And how long has the word "Jacuzzi" been part of your vocabulary?

All major dictionaries provide the written form (alphabetic) and the spoken form (pronunciation) of English words side-by-side as separate entities. This practice has become necessary to maintain an accurate representation of the English vocabulary. Uttering a word is one matter, but spelling it is another. And as the English language continues to grow and change, the differences between production and alphabetic representation can be expected to move farther and farther apart.

The production of a spoken word depends not on its written form, but rather on producing an accurate physical matrix. In other words, it is physical characteristics that distinguish an individual word. Because phonemes describe the "sound system" of spoken language, you must use phonemic transcription to distinguish one word of a language from all other words within the language.

Further, the phoneme itself and not the actual sound produced serves as the major determinant of what word is expressed. A change of even a single phoneme is capable of changing one word to another word with a completely different meaning. When the phoneme |n| for instance, as in |not| (pronounced "note") is exchanged with the phoneme |b|, the newly created word becomes |bot| (pronounced "boat"). The exchange of a single phoneme thus alters the idea from "a short informally written message" to the idea of "a small vessel that floats in water." In contrast, two different sounds can belong to the same phoneme, to the same fundamental means of physical production. The vowels in a word like "creek" for illustration, can be pronounced either as |krēk| or |krik|. But in either case, the word expresses the same idea. Sound variations may cause a person to speak with an accent, but they seldom change the word or make it completely unintelligible.

Historically, sign production has been described by various means. Signs have been described through such media as hand drawings, photos, and narration. Some writers have devised elaborate sets of codes either to describe a sign or to accompany sketches and better qualify its various elements. Ink drawings, which offer a fine display of the visual image of signs, can be an effective way to learn how to produce its basic formation.

A useful method of describing the visual properties of a sign is to represent it visually through a series of drawings. But although this is a most satisfactory way to learn how to produce a sign in isolation, it does not teach the signer how to use a series of signs in discourse or what rules govern its constraints. Studying phonology provides students with a structure that will enable them to recognize violations within a sign's production and to distinguish such misarticulations from normal and acceptable dialectic variations. Just as poor speech habits can result from an inadequate understanding of word articulation, poor sign production can result from a too generalized or limited understanding of sign articulation. Phonology also provides sufficient standardization for an instructor to fairly and objectively assess a student's knowledge, to correct errors in the student's articulation, and to monitor the student's progress. Time spent on the phonology of signs can thus enrich the student's appreciation of ASL and help develop a higher level of mastery regarding sign production.

Because the phoneme (oral or manual) represents the smallest unit in the productive framework of a language, it will serve as the basis for understanding the structure of the ASL sign system. A phoneme comprises a specific set of parameters. These parameters are physical properties that determine the characteristic production of a given lexicon unit (word or sign). In English for instance, the phoneme |i| comprises a set of physical parameters that distinguish it from all other phonemes. When expressed in its long form it is alphabetically denoted by the letter "e" as in "eat," "treat," and "see." The physical parameters that describe its formation include (1) the tongue is in a near closed position, (2) the tongue is placed in a front-central location within the oral cavity, (3) the lip position is vertical, (4) the range of mouth opening is narrow to medium, (5) the sound source is created by producing a considerable amount of muscular tension, and (6) the movement consists of the tip of the tongue touching the lower teeth. The essence of such physical parameters make up the English phonemic system.

The first real insight into the phonemic framework of an ASL sign occurred in 1960, when William Stokoe published a monograph that analyzed the structure of a sign in linguistic terms. To describe manual parameters, Stokoe coined such terms as "tabula," "designator," and "signation." Later, Stokoe and his colleagues published the first ASL dictionary constructed in accordance with linguistic structure (1965). Other new terms emerged including "cheremes," which is derived from the Greek word *cheir* meaning "hand" to refer the sign parameters, and the term "cherology" to refer to the study of ASL phonology.

Stokoe's analysis established the groundwork for the study of manual phonemes. It allows us to analyze a sign in various dimensions. For instance, we can define a sign by the number of parameters that are incorporated in it, or by the rules that govern an intelligible sign formation from unintelligible nonsense. Each ASL sign consists of a set of physical properties that determines its characteristic shape as a visual form. Both manual and spoken language share a similar rule structure that governs both the number of possible physical properties and the possible combinations of these parameters into lexical units.

Certain modifications of the physical features that make up the ASL phonology have emerged since Stokoe's first monograph, but ASL analysis has retained both its basic premise and its rationale (Battison, Markowicz, and Woodward, 1975; Stokoe, 1972; and Friedman, 1975, 1977). One such modification has been the identification of a fourth parameter (palm direction [orientation]) as an integral part of the phonological system.

In Stokoe's system, the term "phonology" describes the articulation properties, regardless if the physical production is performed verbally or manually (Battison, 1974; Woodward, Erting, and Oliver, 1976; Friedman, 1977). The organization of the sign is described according to the fundamental composition of four basic parameters: hand configuration, palm direction, hand position or place of articulation, and hand movement (Woodward, 1974; Klima and Bellugi, 1979). Stokoe (1960, 1965, 1972) and Siple (1978) present a unique notation system intended for written communications and research.

The Sign Frame

One particular physical aspect of manual language is treated relatively more stringently in ASL than in English: the maintenance of direct visual contact between participants during a communication event. The minimum separating distance for an ordinary ASL conversation is two feet between the signer and reader. Maximum communicating distance is the farthest distance from which both participants can see each other's manual expression.

A restricted area of space located directly in front of the signer's body defines the general visible borders in which most signs are confined. This area, referred to as the "neutral" sign space, is loosely shaped in a rectangular area (see fig. 1) with the basic outline limited to:

Top border: the uppermost line is approximately 6 to 8 inches above the signer's head

Side borders: the lateralmost lines are parallel to the sides of the signer's body with the elbows close to the body

Bottom border: the lowermost line is parallel to the signer's waist (Klima and
                 Bellugi, 1979)

Figure 1. The neutral sign space

The majority of ASL signs involve physical parameters confined to this
space, but there are exceptions. Certain signs are routinely formed outside
of this neutral sign space. The signs for SUN and EXERCISE, for example,
extend above the head, and the sign for TROUSERS drops below the waistline. But such exceptions are definitely limited in number.

The outermost distance of the sign frame, how far the hands move forward toward the reader, is a modest extension. It can be described as a comfortable distance that the arms extend with bent elbows.

Conformity to the neutral sign space is an important constraint in the
articulation of signs. Regulating the relative degree of movement is similar
to regulating the loudness of one's voice in using spoken language.

Four dominant articulatory parameters formulate a sign's composition (Stokoe, 1965; Friedman, 1975). These basic physical parameters distinguish one sign in a language from all other signs in that language. Similar
to words being created by sequential patterns of sounds produced from the
vocal organs (tongue, lips, teeth, palate, etc.), a sign is created by a simultaneous pattern of static and moving elements produced from the manual
organs (hands, wrists, body, etc.). The sign parameters involve a set of
hand motions, hand placements, and hand configurations. Signing utilizes

various hand shapes and hand cues in relation to the body. Like the phonemes of a sound system, the parameters of a manual system are physical.
Knowledge of these parameters and of their physically oriented characteristics serve as the "phonological" framework. The task is to learn how to
produce these parameters, to learn how to interchange them, and to learn
the result of that exchange.

Each sign is defined according to its four fundamental parameters,
representing the essence of the physical matrix for a particular sign. The
essential parameters are: (1) the *hand form,* the particular configuration or
hand shape that the hand(s) assumes; (2) the *palm direction,* the orientation
in which the palm(s) aligns itself; (3) the *hand position,* the orientation of
the hand(s) relative to the body; and (4) the *hand movement,* the active
and/or passive movement involved as the hand(s) executes a specified pattern.

The combined outcome of these four basic parameters constitutes the
linguistic construction of the manual sign and are governed by the grammatical constraints of American Sign Language. Deviations occur periodi-
cally and certain deviations represent natural, acceptable variations, while
others are regarded as articulation errors that result in unintelligible communications.

Sign Production

Hand Formation

The initial hand parameter, hand form or hand configuration is viewed
as the "form" of the articulators (Friedman, 1975). Approximately forty
distinct hand shapes exist. When a sign uses both hands, the hand formation for each hand may either be the same or different, and each formation
will be designated. Most signs, singular or two-handed, generally use only
one hand form per hand. When a sign uses only one hand, the hand used
is usually the signer's dominate hand. When a sign is designated by the use
of both hands, identification of each hand is made by such terms as "primary" (dominate) and "secondary" (nondominate) hands. The following
list provides a functional description of some of the more commonly used
hand forms:

Open hand:	the hand is in a natural open position with the thumb and fingers extended and touching
5 hand:	similar to the open hand, but the fingers and thumb are separated
Touch hand:	similar to the 5 hand, but the middle finger is bent inward toward the palm

Bent hand:	similar to the open hand, but all fingers are bent at a 90° angle toward the palm
Modified O hand:	similar to the bent hand, but the thumb is squeezed firmly against the fingers
Index hand:	the index finger is extended and all other fingers and thumb form a modified fist
Letter hand:	the hand forms such letters as, "L, A, S, Y, U, W, H, X," etc. using standard fingerspelling descriptions.

The different hand forms can be further subdivided, according to their relative state of transformation. "Fixed" hand forms retain the initial hand shape throughout the production of the sign. Examples of signs with fixed hand forms include DENTIST, TOGETHER, and LIGHTNING. In contrast, a "variable" hand form occurs when a sign initially takes one shape but during its production changes to a different shape. This transformation usually occurs during the actual production or articulation of the sign and can include one or both hands. Examples of signs with variable hand forms include LEARN, TAKE, and TEACH. Although there is an exception to every rule, there are virtually no common signs in ASL that use more than two different hand forms in any single hand. Certain compound signs, by an accumulative process, may involve an additional hand change but multiple hand forms are rare. ASL uses only a limited number of distinct hand shapes.

Palm Direction

The orientation of the articulators (the hands), is determined by the direction of the palms. The orientation of the hand(s) in relation to the body provides an important distinctive feature and serves as an effective means of redefining each sign more specifically. There are six basic palm directions:

1. Forward: the hand palm faces forward, toward the reader
2. Inward: the hand palm is reversed to face inward, toward the speaker
3. Up: the hand palm turns up to face the ceiling
4. Down: the hand palm turns down to face the floor
5. Facing: the palms of both hands face each other
6. Toward side: when the left palm is involved, it faces toward the right; when the right palm is involved, it faces toward the left.

Hand Position

The neutral sign space represents the visual framework that encapsules nearly all signs. While minor variations exist, this imaginary field is an anatomical reference that provides a workable boundary to establish the place of articulation. The hand position is loosely similar to tongue position within the oral cavity, used to produce different sounds. The hand position represents the place of articulation and refers to either an area on the signer's body, or an area within the neutral sign space in which the articulation is performed. The position feature is defined according to the particular location on and around the body within the spatial field. To date, over eighteen distinct positions have been associated to this parameter.

Figure 2. The neutral space consisting of the focal and peripheral tracts

The neutral sign space can be further subdivided into a "focal" tract and a "peripheral" tract (see fig. 2). Something like a vortex that draws everything from its outer limits into its center, the sign field centralizes the reader's focus.

When an optical system converges on a limited focal space, any image located within its central core can be seen particularly distinctly and clearly. The focal tract is the centermost region, the area that the reader visually attends to. It is loosely defined by the forehead, shoulders, and upper-chest area. Here, visual discrimination is at its highest level, and signs tend to incorporate more precise, detailed parameters. Signs made in the focal tract display relatively more subtle distinctions in hand form and position than signs formed in the outer, peripheral region. A single parameter such as an initial hand form may be all that distinguishes an entire group of signs. Readability of these minor variations is made possible by the natural enhancement created by facial landmarks. The majority of focal-tract signs typically use only one hand, for example, THINK, UNDERSTAND, IDEA, and KNOW.

The peripheral tract is the region represented by the outermost limits of the sign field: the waistline, near-extended arms, and above the forehead. Because visual focus is less defined near the periphery or outer bounds of the sign space, signs made here require comparatively more supplementary information than signs closer to the focal tract. Reading signs performed near the peripheral borders is similar to trying to read a book held to either side so that one must use only peripheral vision: clarity is relatively subdued. Thus, signs produced within the periphery of the sign field use relatively larger movements and contain more redundant components. Consequently, the actual parameters typically exceed normal dimensions, for example, as in LIGHTNING, NEVER, CLOUDS, and SUN. These signs are characterized by superfluous movement, tend to be more repetitious, and more frequently involve both hands. Constraints based on visual acuity influence the perceptibility of meaningful interpretation (Hoemann, 1978).

A related matter is the precise location of hand position within the neutral sign space. Like a vortex, the closer the hand position is to the face, the center of the sign space, the more specific the hand position. Such signs as GOOD, DENTIST, and EAT are specifically positioned at the mouth. Signs outside the center region tend to be more generalized. FINE, for example, is signed at the chest level, but the signer has a certain amount of freedom in determining its actual location. Many signs designate the handposition parameter as an "approximate reference."

There are at least four approximate references typically associated with hand positions. Two of these references are located within the focal tract. The first is the "chest level," a position assumed by placing the hands in front of the signer. It represents the lower half of the focal tract (e.g., HELP). The second approximate reference is the "face level." Located above the chest area, it occupies the upper half of the focal tract as in WORRY.

The remaining two locations are part of the peripheral tract. The first is the "head" reference and calls for the hand or hands to assume a comfortable position just above the forehead, or level with the top of the head. The head reference occupies the upper periphery region. The final location is the "waistline" reference, the position below the chest level. It occupies the lower peripheral boundaries.

Another positional dimension is whether a sign involves a "free-style" or a "contact" component. A free-style sign denotes the absence of contact by the hand(s) with either the body or the other hand. The sign WORRY or FOLLOW are free-style signs. In contrast, a contact sign includes physical touching in some manner. The four basic contact regions are: (1) the hands, most typically represented by two-handed signs (e.g., SAME);

(2) the arm, such as touching, tapping, and sliding motions (e.g., TIME); (3) the body, a common reference source throughout the sign field (e.g., HAPPY); and (4) the head/face region, which provides an array of reference positions (e.g., HOME).

When a sign involves both hands, its hand-position parameter can be distinguished according to whether it functions as a "symmetrical" or "asymmetrical" sign. A two-handed sign is symmetrical when its positioning is essentially identical for each hand. When a sign, for example, designates "both A hands, side-by-side, and palms facing" (WITH), a symmetrical position is formed. The hands are also considered symmetrical when aligned next to each other, regardless of whether they touch. If the hands do make physical contact, it is usually in the same or corresponding position relative to the body. Hand movement is symmetrical when each hand follows the same, corresponding, opposite, or alternative routes (e.g., WAIT, ALLOW, and OPPOSITE).

An asymmetrical hand position occurs when each hand performs a separate, distinct function (e.g., YEAR). Since each hand performs a separate function the signer must designate the role of each hand. To describe this, we will use the terms "active" and "stationary." An active hand is the primary hand, responsible for conveying the dominant movement within the sign production. A stationary hand is represented by the secondary hand. It performs either only a limited movement or remains immobile. A stationary hand position often serves as a "base" component, usually designated to assume a specified hand form (e.g., HARD).

Hand Movement

Hand movement is probably the most important and least categorized parameter of the articulation of a sign. "Hand movement" is the action of the articulator(s) as the hand or hands move from one point to another within the neutral sign space. Stokoe (1965) identified twenty-four distinct movement parameters. Movement in a sign always occurs in relation to specific points of location within the neutral sign space. This locational feature is defined by the hand position in its initial and final placement relative to the body. Locational or directional movement will be discussed in depth as part of our multidirectional verb discussion (see chapter 9).

Hand movement involves a relatively natural degree of motion. It becomes a question of how much is enough movement and how much is too much involvement? There are parallels in spoken language. Imagine the voice of an excited young child who wishes to let her mom know that an ice cream truck is coming down the street. She has so much difficulty holding in all of her extra energy that she nearly shouts in anticipation, and mom usually interjects something like, "Now, now, slow down and tell me what's so important." The child momentarily stops, takes a deep breath, and restates her request at a reasonable level. On the other hand, have you ever noticed how people typically lower their voices when entering a church or similar establishment? Even when such a place is empty and the lights are off, there is a natural tendency to talk just above a whisper. Just walk into a large library some time and notice the voice change.

Like regulating one's voice, regulating degree of movement in manual speech is a subjective, personal decision. There is a natural tendency to monitor yourself and then to automatically adjust the intensity to a suitable level. When speaking manually, observe your own movements to find a reasonably natural degree of hand movement that will most compliment your personality.

Hand movement also involves decisions over speed of delivery. An important consideration is the intelligibility of the sign. A good communicator knows how to regulate speed. A clear, smooth, manageable rate of production enhances articulatory delivery. Refined articulation rather than strict speed is the hallmark of a talented manual communicator. Talented manual communicators learn how to control speed, to use it to create the kind of delivery and image that they want to convey.

The articulation of an intelligible word or sign is the result of putting together the right elements in the right order and delivering these components effectively. Articulation depends on precision and careful attention to detail. It relates to the ability to re-create a given lexicon according to its established parameters.

Individual signers all have different size hands and varying degrees of manual dexterity. There is individuality in arm strength, in physical flexibility, and in muscle tone. Each signer has certain natural skills and coordination. Such individual peculiarities are a source for many subtle deviations in manual expression. The magician, pianist, and professional card player are examples of how far level of hand dexterity can be developed. Hand movement is a tool that is developed and enhanced to improve the quality of manual communication.

The Composition of a Sign

To respect the different hand preferences, the traditional use of left and right hand designations will be replaced with more general terms. "Primary" will denote the signer's dominant hand and "secondary" will refer to the signer's nondominant hand. A right-handed person's primary hand and side is the right, and the secondary hand and side is the left. A left-handed person's primary hand and side is the left, and the secondary hand and side is the right. So when a description calls for the hands to "move crossway from secondary to primary," lefties move their hands from the right (secondary) toward the left (primary). Responding to the same description, right-handed persons move their hands from the left (secondary) toward the right (primary).

There is an inherent articulatory difference that separates a sign from a word. A word consists of a series of sound patterns organized sequentially. No two sounds are ever produced simultaneously. In contrast, an ASL sign consists of a series of spatial parameters that occur simultaneously. Rather than a sequential pattern, an ASL sign is a formation of simultaneously occurring components representing several spatial dimensions (Klima and Bellugi, 1979). Observing the multidimensional action of two hands completing a symmetrical movement demonstrates the simultaneous nature of ASL sign. A sign uses one or two hands. It performs a particular formation while moving in a defined manner. At the same time, it maintains a constant respect to positioning and location within the neutral sign space. A sign depends on visual perception to accurately interpret the manual shapes moving systematically in space.

The description of a sign is based on its neutral form, its form as it appears in isolation as a representative of the basic vocabulary. The description of a sign's composition does not reflect changes that many occur in discourse or when the sign appears as part of a sentence. The format we use here to describe each sign will consist of the four major sign parameters in the following order: hand form (HF), palm direction (PD), hand position (HP), and hand movement (HM). Following these designations come comments on the particular sign, including variations, peculiarities, and help hints.

The Composition of a Sign

Base Meaning: (related meanings)	HF	(hand form): specifies the hand or hands and their shape(s)
	PD	(palm direction): describes the orientation of the palm(s)
	HP	(hand position): provides a referential position oriented to the body
	HM	(hand movement): describes any action, change, and contact involved
		(Comments on variations, peculiarities, and other helpful information)

The composition of a sign is represented by its initial formation or parameter matrix, but the majority of signs include some movement. Since movement is represented by one of the basic parameters, it is common in studying signs to concentrate on the initial static parameter matrix, its inceptive configuration. Completing the particular composition is then a matter of following through. A few introductory signs are presented to illustrate the above method of describing a sign in terms of its fundamental parameters.

SIGN	HF:	both index hands
	PD:	facing
	HP:	chest level
	HM:	alternately circle the hands out, down, in, and up again

LANGUAGE	HF:	both L hands
	PD:	down
	HP:	waist level, side-by-side
	HM:	separate hands in a wavy motion

(Variation: position palms forward, touch thumbs, and exhibit a rocking motion from side to side)

FINGERSPELLING	HF:	primary 5 hand, with fingers bent
	PD:	forward
	HP:	chest level
	HM:	move hand crossway from secondary to primary side while "wiggling" fingers

(Variation: substitute 4 hand for 5 hand)

ASL (AMESLAN)	HF:	both A hands
	PD:	facing
	HP:	chest level
	HM:	alternately circle hands (as in SIGN); then change the hands from A to L hands; turn palms down, separate hands in a wavy motion

(Comments: this is a "compound" sign, which will be discussed in detail later. It incorporates the basis of the units SIGN and LANGUAGE into its composition.)

ENGLISH (ENGLAND)	HF:	both relaxed open hands
	PD:	down
	HP:	waist level
	HM:	grasp the outer, upper edge of the secondary wrist with the primary hand

YES	HF:	primary S hand
	PD:	down
	HP:	waist level; arm remains stationary
	HM:	nod the hand downward

(Variation: substitute either the A or Y hand for the S hand)

NO	HF:	primary U hand, thumb extended
	PD:	forward
	HP:	chest level
	HM:	snap index and middle finger against the thumb

The Phonology of Signs

Battison (1974) defines "phonology" as the level of systematic-formational structure that deals with sign production, the submorphemic units that combine to form each unit, and the restrictions and alterations among these combinations. No intentional relation exists, direct or indirect, between the phonology of signs and the phonology of words.

Not every possible combination of the basic phonological parameters of signs will result in a legitimate sign. General constraints limit the possibility of parameters coming directly from the articulatory dynamics of the body (Battison, 1974). Such physical considerations serve as the basis for supporting both the composition of signs and the nature of phonological change. The phonetic articulation of signs is determined at the lexical level.

Phonologically, there are three classes of two-handed signs: (1) both active and identical hands; (2) one active/one passive nonidentical hands; and (3) one active/one passive identical hands. Two-handed signs have a natural symmetrical potential. When a two-handed sign involves a symmetrical hand formation, it is unmarked except for the reference "both hands." Descriptions of asymmetric signs mark each hand's role.

Battison (1974) contends that if both hands are active in a two-handed sign, the hand formation and movement parameters must be identical. He calls this the "symmetry principle." Further, palm direction must be either identical or directly opposite, and hand position must be either symmetrical or polar opposite (see fig. 3). In terms of hand position "polar opposites"

Figure 3. The sign OPPOSITE

refers to the hands making identical physical contact with the same part of the body, on one or the other side. The symmetry condition provides the basis for the first type of two-handed signs: both active and identical (e.g., TRY, TRANSLATE, LIVE, WONDERFUL).

A second principle governs two-handed signs that involve nonidentical parameters. The "dominance condition" (Battison, 1974) relates to signs that involve one active hand (usually the dominant hand) and one stationary or passive hand. The active hand executes the movement while the static hand serves in a supportive role. The stationary hand is defined by seven different hand forms: (1) the A hand, (2) the open hand, (3) the G hand, (4) the modified O hand, (5) the C hand, (6) the 5 hand, and (7) the index hand (e.g., THAT, BOTHER, WEEK, RULE). Two-handed signs involving different hand formations for each hand are limited to only one active hand per sign.

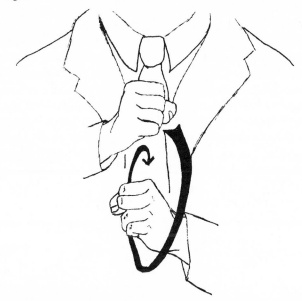

Figure 4. An asymmetrical sign, YEAR

A third principle applies to signs that mix the symmetry and dominance conditions. In such signs, each hand is defined by the same handformation parameter (symmetrical principle), but only one hand is active (dominance condition). Only the active hand performs the movement parameter (e.g., PAPER, YEAR, HOUR).

The wide use of symmetry in sign formation is like the use of redundancy in spoken language. The linguistic advantage of symmetry helps to improve the perceptual focus of the sign reader. Symmetry strengthens the visual perceptual properties of signs performed in areas of low visual acuity, especially within the peripheral focal area.

Readability is further enhanced by controlling the relative degree of production complexity. If a two-handed sign involves individually separate hand parameters that perform isolated movements, then the complexity of the sign is high, and it will be difficult both to perform and to read. Moving both hands in a coordinated way to produce a symmetrical or near symmetrical sign helps mitigate this articulatory constraint. Similarly, if the two-handed sign calls for nonidentical activity, sign complexity can be constrained by assigning only one hand to be active while the other remains immobile.

The sign complexity of two-handed signs involving nonidentical hands is also mitigated by limiting the hand formation possibilities of the stationary hand. Asymmetrical signs that involve a static hand typically assign the immobile hand to form only one of seven different hand shapes. These seven hand formations represent some of the most basic, uncomplicated hand shapes of the sign system. To maintain a reasonable control over the relative complexity of sign articulation, the ASL system constrains such variables as two active hands versus one active hand, varying hand formation versus identical hand formation, and asymmetrical versus symmetrical movements.

A phonological approach to sign description illustrates the naturalness of signs and helps us understand some of the linguistic constraints imposed by American Sign Language. The following ASL signs are described in this linguistic format.

NAME		
	HF:	both H hands
	PD:	facing
	HP:	fingers facing forward; hands crisscrossed in front of chest; primary hand above secondary hand
	HM:	tap the middle finger of the primary H hand on top of the index finger of the secondary H hand

GOOD (THANK)		
	HF:	primary open hand
	PD:	inward
	HP:	touch the chin
	HM:	move hand from chin forward a slight distance in a downward arc

(Variation: THANK, complete the same sign parameters with both open hands)

BAD		
	HF:	primary open hand
	PD	inward
	HP:	front of mouth, fingers facing secondary side
	HM:	slide fingers across the mouth while moving

them toward the primary side, and then sharply fling the hand down so the hand finishes with fingers facing down

PRACTICE

HF: primary A hand; secondary index hand
PD: primary down; secondary nearly inward
HP: stationary secondary index faces near forward and toward primary side; hand near waist level
HM: rub the top of the secondary index finger with primary A hand using a back-and-forth motion

AGAIN
(REPEAT)

HF: primary modified O hand; secondary open hand
PD: facing
HP: stationary secondary fingers face foward; both hands near chest level
HM: move fingertips of primary hand in a semi-circular arc motion toward the secondary palm and finish with fingertips touching the secondary palm

EASY

HF: both bent hands
PD: primary facing secondary side; secondary facing upward
HP: stationary secondary hand is above waist level
HM: move primary hand to make contact with the back of the secondary hand; brush the fingers over the back of the secondary fingers as it passes by in an upward direction

IMPROVE

HF: both open hands
PD: primary nearly inward; secondary down
HP: stationary secondary hand is held across and in front of the waist
HM: use little-finger edge of primary hand to tap secondary wrist then tap arm, and finish tapping close to elbow while moving in a "jumping" manner

WANT

HF: both bent hands
PD: upward
HP: hands are side by side just above waist level
HM: move hands simultaneously inward a short distance
(Variation: substitute 5 hands for bent hands)

SLOW

HF: both open hands
PD: down
HP: hands crisscrossed; primary above secondary near waist level
HM: touch the back of the secondary hand with a

		primary finger and then slowly move them backward over the secondary hand, wrist, and then arm

FAST   HF: modified T hand
(QUICK)   PD: facing secondary side
(RAPID)   HP: near waist level; knuckles forward
       HM: snap thumb out of hand
(Comment: conveys the image of "shooting a marble")
(Variation: both L hands, palms facing; hands move inward while closing into S hands)

TRY   HF: both S hands
(ATTEMPT)   PD: facing
       HP: hands are side-by-side at chest level
       HM: move hands in a pushing abrupt manner forward a short distance
(Comment: mimics the idea of EFFORT)
(Variation: substitute either A hands or T hands for S hands; substitute palms inward for facing palms, and a forward up-down movement while turning palms forward)

HELP   HF: primary S hand; secondary open hand
       PD: primary upward; secondary inward
       HP: primary above secondary at waist level
       HM: place primary hand on top of secondary palm and then lift hands slightly

MUST   HF: X hand
(OUGHT)   PD: downward
(NECESSARY)   HP: near side of waist
       HM: drop hand slightly

WAIT   HF: both relaxed 5 hands
       PD: upward
       HP: hold primary hand in an outward position away from the waist; hold secondary hand relatively close to waist; face fingers of both hands toward a secondary side
       HM: wiggle the fingers of both hands
(Variation: substitute bent hands for 5 hands; switch palms to a facing position; move fingers up and down simultaneously)

LET   HF: both open hands
(ALLOW)   PD: facing
(PERMIT)   HP: hands are side-by-side, fingers facing forward
       HM: move hands forward in a semicircular motion that arcs down and back up again a short distance
(Variation: substitute both L hands for open hands; switch palms to inward while index fingers are facing; then rotate hands forward until the palms are facing and index fingers face forward)

ALWAYS
(EVER)

HF: index hand
PD: upward
HP: near chest level; index finger facing forward
HM: rotate the hand in a small circular motion
(Comment: lefties tend to use counterclockwise
motion; right-handed people tend to use clockwise
motion)

MAKE

HF: both S hands
PD: facing
HP: primary hand is on top of secondary hand
        near waist level
HM: rotate the hands outward so that the hands
        finish with the palms facing inward and con-
        tinue touching
(Variation: following the rotation, tap hands together
twice)

HERE

HF: both open hands
PD: upward
HP: hands are side-by-side at waist level
HM: move hands in small, flat circular motions,
        each hand moving outward, inward, and
        back again
(Comment: left hand moves counterclockwise and
right moves clockwise)

FRIEND

HF: both X hands
PD: primary inward; secondary down
HP: near waist level
HM: firmly interlock momentarily the hook of the
        primary index on top of the secondary index
(Variation: repeat in reversed positions)

Training Exercises

A. Practice fingerspelling each question, then repeat adding ASL signs. If a partner is available, alternately and randomly ask each other the questions and give a complete response.

   1. What kind of work do you want to do?
   2. Would you rather work indoors or outside?
   3. Do you think I would enjoy working with other people? Why?
   4. Would you prefer to work alone?
   5. Are you willing to relocate? How far away?
   6. Do you like to travel?
   7. Do you enjoy stable, routine work?
   8. Do you like to work regular hours?
   9. Do you have any special interests or skills?
  10. What kind of work experience do you have?

B. Several phrases and combinations can help train the hands to move smoothly from one sign to another. In this exercise, a few words are intermixed that must be fingerspelled. Begin very slowly and practice until you obtain and maintain a natural speed and flow. Attend to the use of appropriate pauses between each phrase.

be it	your dress is pretty	they just left	you yourself
I am	we need your help	it is difficult	that is mine
we are	we-two are careful	please help me	we-two were
he was	watch your driving	it is necessary	Kim told her
they are	the sign language	spell your name	we all know
yes, you	you have your work	I teach English	it was true
is it	they were not prepared	wash the dishes	was myself
she was	we-two will be late	sign language	no English
the sign	Joe was very sick	speak English	be yourself
there is	my wife is happy	your language	no, you are
be there	I learned to drive	you will know	Ameslan is
yes I was	we-two will leave	I suppose so	no, not now
they were	they won the race	your English	I am sorry
your mine	English language	visit me soon	there you go
they sign	it might be true	spell America	Jan called
there was	they themselves	help yourself	you know
your wrong	it is hard to do	stand here now	you are it
look at me	she wrote to me	you never have	the end

C. Sign the following sentences, supplying pronouns and then interchanging the pronouns in every available way.

1. (_____) selected (_____) new shoes.
2. The instructor suggested that everyone read (_____).
3. (_____) and (_____) need to complete this homework.
4. (_____) friend expressed (_____) desire to have dinner with (_____).
5. (_____) should pay (_____) entry fee.
6. It was (_____) who answered the phone.
7. (_____) lawyer advised (_____) to settle the case.
8. Randy and (_____) were pleased with (_____).
9. If (_____) happen(s) to remember, give (_____) a call.
10. Both my cousin and (_____) were there last night.
11. If (_____) wants a raise, OK.
12. (_____) is the only one who is on time.
13. Who forgot (_____) keys?
14. Everyone knows (_____) phone number.
15. My friend(s) is(are) selling (_____) house.
16. If (_____) call(s), tell them (_____) will be late.
17. Do(es) (_____) want (_____) dessert now?
18. It looks like (_____) won't be here.
19. Where did (_____) hang (_____) coat?
20. Where did (_____) go?

2. Communication Styles

So much can go wrong in communication. A helpful suggestion can be mistaken for a blatant criticism. A useful comment can go entirely unnoticed. An earnest question can be interpreted as an invasion of privacy, and a seemingly harmless, good-natured joke can be mistaken for an unforgivable insult. We all have known of incidents where a seemingly gracious comment unexpectedly transformed into a sudden "slap in the face" or turned an event into a blushing embarrassment.

The purpose of human communication is to allow us to transfer our thoughts, ideas, and emotions to another person. Since mental activity has no physical form, it can not be sent to another person directly. The only conceivable way to make such information transferable is to insert it into some physical, deliverable form. Such a physical form, referred to as a "communication signal," may consist of a series of sound patterns or hand gestures — anything that can be received by another person.

Senders strive to choose the words or signs that will best represent the information they wish to send. But, unfortunately, communication signals are never exact replicas of mental information. Rather, they are series of coded instructions that lead receivers to reconstruct their own understanding of the perceived message.

A related matter concerns the amount of information each individual unit of the communication signal or its lexical items can send. The degree of information receivers can derive from a lexical item depends on how well the receivers can interpret its meaning without special instructions. The amount of information in a symbol is directly related to the number of symbols from which one has to choose (Sanders, 1971). Thus, the significance of an individual symbol as a vehicle for carrying information depends both on its associated meaning and, to some extent, on the other lexical items that surround it.

The selection process used to choose which individual signals represent a given message is not completely random. The language used by the participants places constraints on the selection, manner of arrangement, and delivery of the signals. Each constraint influences the degree to which a person who understands a given language will be able to interpret a particular message.

The constraints of spoken English, for instance, are different from the constraints of American Sign Language. These fundamental differences are due in part to the dissimilarity of the communication media, one based on acoustic, one on visual associations. The use of vocalized sound pattern to represent semantic units has developed into a vast vocabulary, reducing the relative number of constraints imposed on the speaker's selection of words. In contrast, ASL, a system based on visual concepts, places more constraints on the signer's selection of signs to construct the message. ASL, like all visual-concept languages, maintains a strong association to the immediate experience of actual things and events. It tends to be specific, sensory oriented, and succinct.

To illustrate the fundamental difference between acoustic and visual associations, imagine you are in classroom when the instructor raises a question. The instructor looks over the class pondering whom to pick for a response. In scanning the instructor has complete freedom to pick anyone they wish. The only constraint is that the respondent must be present in the classroom at that particular moment. This open-ended selection process is similar to an acoustic-based communication system. In such a system, any member of an entire class of elements is available for selection.

But imagine that the instructor decides to call on a female student of medium build, five to six feet tall, blue eyed, wearing glasses, blonde, and who currently has her hand raised. Such requirements restrict the selection to only a few students. These selection requirements also create a vivid mental image of the student to be called on to respond to the question. This sensory, description-oriented process is similar to a visually based language.

A system based on visual imagery is more sensory oriented than a system based on acoustic association. In ASL, a visually based system, signs are chosen and used based on their effectiveness in communicating semantic meaning through perceptual imagery.

The choice and use of vocabulary and the timing of its delivery are part of what determines a person's "communication style." Communication style tells how people express themselves and how well they do it. Communication style also relates to how communicators adapt their expressive style to match the purpose, the topic, and the nature of the audience. But communication style is also constrained linguistically by constraints on arranging lexical units as governed by the rules of a particular language. Such constraints can influence the way one thinks about the world.

Therefore, it is important to understand some of the characteristics that differentiate communication in American Sign Language from communication in English.

Symbolic Units of Communication

Each lexical unit that makes up a communication signal represents a semantic symbol that is potentially capable of carrying information. Just how much information and what kind it conveys depends on many factors including how well its receiver can derive meaning from its symbolism, and on what level it is interpreted. Lexical items can often be interpreted on different levels of meaning beyond their literal representations. When a symbolic unit of communication has different layers of meaning associated with it, it is said that the lexical unit has both "connotative" and "denotative" interpretations.

The denotative meaning of a word (or sign) is its literal meaning as described in a dictionary. It is a rather straightforward semantic interpretation that is based on its historically agreed-upon definition. A denotative meaning for a word like "home," for instance, is its dictionary-defined meaning, "a place where one lives." Concrete words like "table," "window," "glass," "word," etc. are usually restricted to their denotative meanings. A concrete lexical item names something that can be perceived by one of the five senses. Its tangible and perceptual qualities limit the range of interpretative meanings and, as a result, provide a precise semantic unit of information.

A connotative interpretation is the emotional or judgmental meaning associated with a lexical item, especially with a word. Connotation involves the psychological impact that a word conveys, reflecting its different shades of meanings. While the literal meaning of the word "home" is "a place to live," this same symbolic item also brings to mind "a safe haven; a man's castle; a place of comfort, privacy, and intimacy." These suggested associations are the connotations of the word "home." Connotative meanings represent a word's alternative layers of understanding. The context in which a word is used determines whether the literal or implied meaning will be received. For instance, the words "taxi," "limousine," "all-terrain vehicle," "motorcycle," and "station wagon" all denote or literally mean "transportational vehicle." All of these words basically mean the same thing. But depending on one's frame of view and the particular context, each word can be interpreted in different ways; each lexical item can elicit different implied meanings. "Taxi" may imply or connote the idea of city traffic, urban life, or a particular kind of conveyance. It also implies being chauffeured — as does "limousine." But "limousine" is distinguished by its implied image of wealth, elegance, and success. "Station wagon" may also imply chauffeured services, but unlike "taxi" or "limousine," it brings to mind such ideas as family, mother, and a carload of kids. Thus, though each of these words means a form of transportation, each word carries a variety of implied associations.

Another example of the influence of connotative versus denotative interpretation is illustrated by the description of a person as "slender." Such a word can be literally interpreted as "slim," but "slender" also implies that this person regulates and maintains his or her weight well. On the other hand, "thin," though also describing a "slim" physical state, implies an acceptable weight that is not being controlled very well. And "skinny" carries the strong implication that the person is underweight from a lack of adequate control. While all three words mean "slim" (dictionary meaning), the actual interpretation attached by the listener depends more on the word chosen, how it is used, and the context that surrounds it. The same message can often be expressed in a variety of different ways, each with its own shade of meaning.

When words with multiple connotative meanings are used, a listener (or reader) may be uncertain how to interpret the utterance. Consider an expression like, "It is a gay event." Does the speaker mean that the event was attended by homosexuals, or that it was a lively, joyous occasion? Such words can convey more to others than one intends. The potential for misunderstandings and uncertainty often leads to such remarks as "That's not what I said" or "You didn't hear me right" or "Let me say that again differently."

But when communicators choose words (or signs) that carry strictly denotative meanings, the message will be more readily understood. This is because the receiver is confronted with fewer possible interpretations. When lexical units are restricted to their defined meanings, there are fewer ways a message can be understood and less likelihood of semantic misunderstanding.

The existence of denotative and connotative interpretations represents a fundamental difference between spoken English and manual American Sign Language. While spoken English contains a vast vocabulary and is rich in connotations, ASL is relatively more constrained, and its smaller vocabulary relies more heavily on direct literal interpretation. On a semantic level, at least in terms of overt signs, ASL is more limited in its use of connotative layers. Because the communication style of ASL is based on a straightforward use of semantic symbols and denoted, literal meanings, semantic misunderstanding in ASL is relatively low.

Multisense Words

English words can often be defined in multiple ways. In other words, the same word will express different meanings when used in different contexts. The majority of the English vocabulary consists of multisense or "equivocal" words, each having more than one designated meaning.

Consider a word like "run," for example. It literally means "to go faster than a walk." But this same word has many other meanings that are acceptable in different contexts. In a phrase like "*run* a horse" it means to gallop. In a phrase like "*run* for office" it means to enter an election. A "*run* in your stocking" means a lengthwise unravelling. "The color may *run*" means to spread or dissolve. "To *run* things" means to administer. And "the engine *runs* well" means the engine is operating satisfactorily. The variety of alternative meanings is extensive.

A multisense word is identified by a number of denotative meanings, each described in a general-purpose dictionary as a legitimate definition. The word "run" has so many meanings that in different contexts it can also be used to mean "hurry," "become," "function," "hunt," "drive," "creek," "trip," and "tendency."

Multisense words promote ambiguity. Since these words can be understood in so many ways, the listener may not be sure which specific meaning is being expressed at a given time. Multisense interpretation is a major factor accounting for the high incidence of misunderstood communication that occurs in English.

We have said that a fundamental difference between ASL and English is the relative size of their respective vocabularies. A related difference is the relative number of defined meanings they assign to each lexical item. Multiplicity of meanings in signs occurs less frequently and is more limited than in English. Though ASL signs may have more than one meaning, the alternative meanings are usually related. The exceptions are infrequent. The ASL sign RUN for instance, is not used to mean "to unravel," "to administer," or "to function" as in English. Nor is it used to mean "to hunt" or "to drive." In ASL, it means "to move quickly by foot." The sign for RUN represents its basic concept and incorporates all of the shaded subtleties associated with the core definition. Thus RUN conveys such ideas as "dash," "scamper," "scurry," and "scoot."

Similarly, the ASL sign MUST when used in a phrase such as YOU MUST... means "urgency; an imperative requirement." If it incorporates all of its related subtleties it would be used to convey such terms as, "you have to," "you need to," "you should," "you ought to," etc.

English uses multisense words; ASL uses conceptual signs. While there are exceptions, the conceptual imagery generally maintains its core meaning along with its shading references. As a result, the limited possibilities for interpretation associated with signs encourages specificity of expression.

Another feature differentiating the two languages is their use of indirect communication. "Indirect communication" refers to words or phrases that mean something other than what is explicitly represented either by its designated definition or by the sum of its combined words (or signs). In English, a communication is often not a matter of what we say but what we mean when we say it.

Two common forms of indirect communication are idioms and the creation of new lexical items by combining verbs with prepositions. Idiomatic expressions, such as "back burner," "she turned me around," "hold your horses," "all tied up," "break a leg," or "hang in there" are all interpreted in ways other than the straightforward interpretation of the combined meanings of their individual words. The expression "he is a pain in the neck" for instance, is not intended to be understood by a word-for-word interpretation.

The combination of verbs and prepositions in English is another way of forming idiomatic expressions, although more subtle. An example of this type of expression is the phrase "passed out," which means something quite different than the combined meanings of its individual words.

A preposition used in such a phrase is called a "particle." Particles can be created from prepositions, conjunctions, and certain adverbs, and they serve in a limited relationship to the verb to which they are attached. The participle "up" alone essentially means "rising to a higher level." But when it is combined with various verbs or nouns, the combined expression creates a totally new concept. As a part of everyday conversation, such expressions are at the very heart of the English language. To illustrate just how common this strategy is, we present, "Something's Up."

Something's Up

To illustrate just how ambiguous English phraseology can be, I have rounded up a few examples. So try not to get mixed up, tangled up, or tripped up as you look up a few ways to use "up." I won't make up any, so ease up and lighten up before you get fed up. I will come up with a strong line up before my time's up so I won't play catch up. I promise not to clam up until I've conjured up enough to count 'em up.

Wait up for me and I'll drag up a couple more. Since you've shown up, try to shut up, or I'll talk up so that you can listen up. Let's hurry up and rake up some more. I'm all booked up. Who's up?

Skip up here and hand that up. Let's stay up all night and keep up the fun. I've had it up to here with you shooting up. I heard you got your knee banged up when you tried to carry up too much. When you straighten up and maybe grow up, then you can act up like a grown-up.

I smashed up my watch trying to climb up a tree, so don't try to shimmy up that one. Yesterday somebody snatched up my patched-up bike. The guy just strolled up and hopped up. If I meet up with whoever seized it up, I'll make 'em own up and 'fess up and maybe I'll string 'em up. Otherwise, I'll chalk it up to experience so I don't get broken up about it.

My sinuses are all blocked up and I'm all stuffed up. My clothes are all wrinkled up because I forgot to snap up my coat. Now I've got the hiccups. Last night I tried to read up for the test, but my brother sprang up and grabbed up my notes. So I bound up the little bandit and left him bottled up in the closet. I had to divide up the remaining notes. Maybe I can touch up a few and then tally up my losses. I let my dog lap up my soda pop.

What's up, doc? The doctor will scrub up, so step up for your checkup. You're up next, and then you're next up. Wad up that paper. Cough up some money and let's rack up a game of pool. He's barking up the wrong tree, and he seems to ham it up a bit too. He's busy wiring up the TV and can't be freed up right now. You better size up the situation. I'll sharpen up your knife and seal up the box if you'll cart it uptown. Scoot up while I scoop up some ice cream but don't scuff up my new shoes. Who soaped up my window? Stop roughing up the dog, and don't beat up my furniture.

Since I haven't warmed up or heated up anything to eat up, let's wash up, and I'll call up a restaurant. If he doesn't hang up, we can order up something for him to deliver up. If I get tied up when he shows up, please stand up and open up the door. I need to brush up on how to chop up turnips that need to be fried up. I'll soften up some dough to bake up something. You should stir up the stew before you serve up the food. While I soak up some rays, set up the table and dish up the dessert. I'll leave it up to you to boil up the potatoes, slice up the carrots, grind up the cheese, mince up the onions before putting the ground-up meat into the greased-up pan. I'll rustle up some grub if you can scrape up the cash. Who clogged up and stopped up the drain? Measure up one teaspoon to fatten up the pig. Once you lift up the broiler, build up the fire. Be careful it doesn't smoke up or burn up or it'll stink up the place, and it will need to be freshened up. Is that water bubbling up? Let's freeze up some ice cubes. We'll probably wind up cooking up more food.

I moved up our date so we can run up to a bar before sunup. A couple drinks, straight up, will help you loosen up, so bottoms up! Dont' get shook up. You must chew up your gum and drink up your 7-Up without throwing up. If I buy up any more drinks, I might go belly up. If you get dressed up, we'll play up the evening. I'll even double up your drinks as long as you can hold up. If you can't sneak up to my place, I have a backup who I call my runner-up who just split up with her friend. Now don't force it up or you might end up spitting up. You need to smarten up and learn to live it up.

Go ahead and tee up. Surf's up! Without screwing up, stick up a sign and tape up another one to the post stating we need change-up pitchers to sign up so we can trade up for more talent. The day's up. We'll pair up saying you were good at doing lay-ups. Dont' get your hopes up, you don't have it sown up yet.

Jack up my car. Somebody gummed up the motor, which needs a tune-up but not a fill-up. I had my engine hooked up because it won't fire up, and it starts up, I plan to step up its power and rev it up. So buckle up if I speed up. My boat is still fouled up. It would race up then slow up as something popped up. So the boat was covered up and tied up and will be laid up.

I hesitate to bring it up, but you need to shape up and firm up. Push-ups and sit-ups might help tighten up your muscles. Face up to it, you should strike up a conversation with your stuck-up friends. Boy, is she ever dolled up! Wait up so we can walk up together. You're such a cut-up, it's hard to get up the energy to keep up. Don't butter me up. If my blood pressure goes up a bit higher you'll have to drive up. Please lean up so I can move up there. Wake up! It's time to get up, so jump up and get going. I'll be right up. If you shack up, you may find it's a set-up.

I'll bet you even up that if you saddle up, your horse will "giddy-up" as we ride up together. I get fed up when my glasses fog up as I kneel to wax up my car. Before class is up, I'll pull up in my banged-up pick-up so we can fly up to Cleveland. It seems to cloud up whenever I park up a hill.

Cheer up! We can drum up more phrases and dream up more uses to help us wise up as long as we type 'em up. They must also be sent up to be printed up so they can be stored up for follow-up. Put up the pin-ups and fold up the rest while you nail up the new one. Flip up the window when you lock up. Before you curl up with that book, wipe up the mess, sweep up the dirt, and mop up the floor. Will you be first up tomorrow? Don't coast up but turn up your radio as you work up to the house. The wind fluffed up your hair. Who did your hair up? It needs to be trimmed up. Don't back up or you might cause a jam-up.

I had to board up my house because weeds are springing up everywhere. I plan to spruce up the place before anyone gets steamed up about the bike being chained up. Which side is up? I was going to open up my store but I forgot to clean up the showroom. So I closed up and lit up my home instead. Now I must rest up before I roll up the rug and rid up the living room. My laundry has piled up, my cake has dried up, and there's not time to nuzzle up by the fireplace. Button up your overcoat and hang up your hat. I'll gather up this mess, take it upstairs and we'll pack up. Step up so she can ring up the items at the marked-up price since the sale's up, and then she'll package it up too. Keep your chin up when you rise up to suit up. If you can't zip up, then just slide it up. When you load up the car, don't pump up the tires or they may blow up. Were you home when you got knocked up? Keep your head up and let up on yourself, so we can team up until things clear up.

This might be the last up because everything is used up and nobody is speaking up, so why bother to stack up more without anyone to tack them up?

If you think up or dig up more, don't call me up. I'm going up the wall with "up," and I don't want to get locked up, so I give up. But, on your way up here, add up or figure up the number of ups because I don't want to be passed up or be shown up now that I have finished up. So let's settle up.

If I repeated the exact "up" twice, I'm sorry but it might be because I'm cracking up . . . "Beam me up, Scotty."

Manual language does not use particles to create new expressions with new meanings. Rather than using implied meanings, ASL prefers designated semantic representation. To express a phrase like "fed up," for instance, the sign might be TIRED or SICK. To express "turn out," the sign might be MEET or CONVENE. ASL encourages the use of specific, concrete lexical items over vague, multisense expression. To understand the difference between implied and actual representation, consider several common English phrases along with an equivalent sign (in parentheses): "figure out" (SOLVE), "figure in" (ADD), "face off" or "face up to" (CONFRONT), "fill in" (SUBSTITUTE), "get up" (RISE), "let in" (WELCOME), "push on" (CONTINUE), "put together" (MAKE), "put up" (BUILD), "call off" (CANCEL), "a lot" (MUCH or MANY), "go over"

(REVIEW), "draw up" (MAKE), "do over" (REPEAT), "get rid of" (RE-MOVE), "turn up" (DISCOVER) and "turn aside" (PREVENT).

Generic Communications

Another characteristic that differentiates ASL and spoken English is the relative frequency of general and specific terms. A "general" word (or sign) covers more semantic territory than is necessary. A general lexical item represents such a wide range of information, that it is all-encompassing. Its defined meaning is so broad that it applies to the whole; it represents every member of a class or group. English words having universal meanings such as "people," "individuals," "they," "anyone," etc. all communicate an idea that is void of any specific information or reference. Such generic words invite such open-ended interpretation that the message is hazy, and only generalities can be made regarding its content. When a communicator chooses words whose individual definitions cover a class of meanings rather than specific meanings, the result is "generic communication": "As I walked down the street, I could hear them whispering something about me. I am sure the people did not know that someone was nearby. None of these persons expected anyone to be walking by at that hour. It was a strange experience to be in such an awkward situation."

This generic passage illustrates how open-ended a message can be when the communicator uses an overabundance of general words. The absence of specific terms prevents identification of the participants, location, or situation. The passage leaves the listener guessing who is doing what to whom. Common general pronouns include:

it	as in	When it was presented.
this	as in	How could this have happened?
that	as in	That money belongs here.
such	as in	He told me such and such.
one	as in	One can notice many things.

General or universal words lack any referential index. They lack any particular reference to a specific person, time, or event. One purpose for using a general vocabulary is to relate to a wide audience. Good examples of applied generic communication are a horoscope in a daily newspaper or a message in a fortune cookie. A statement like "Your energy level may be too high, learn to relax more" is so vague that it can apply to virtually anyone.

A difference between English and ASL is the relative absence of general signs in ASL. Signers tend to avoid general pronouns, preferring instead to supply the specific reference, either directly or indirectly.

A "specific" sign (or word) is limited by definition to certain objects, persons, or qualities. Such specific vocabulary tends to be relatively free from ambiguity. A specific communication style promotes explicit utterances. The high content and specific vocabulary of ASL results from the visual nature and time restraints associated with manual language. ASL thrives on semantic precision. ASL signs are chosen and used according to how effectively they will communicate a precise vivid message.

ASL is based on content, and content favors specific information. Although it may not always be feasible during a conversation to search for the most specific sign, it is useful to strive to establish the habit of specificity. It is helpful to get in the habit of using a specific rather than a general vocabulary. If language is viewed as a means to shape, clarify, and express one's thoughts to others, then ASL strives to meet this objective as specifically as possible.

We have said that general words are wide open in meaning. In contrast, specific words are precise, definite, and limited in scope. Here are a few examples:

General	Specific	More Specific
they	my family	my parents
people	acquaintances	my guests
one	an individual	Tim
certain times	evenings	evenings when I work
someone	a man	a tall man with a beard

Differentiating the ASL Noun from the ASL Verb

Most nouns and predicates are unrelated lexical items. And since nouns and verbs ordinarily have no perceivable relationship to one another, there is no need to define their distinctive properties directly. But when a noun-predicate pair shares the same articulation parameters, we must define their semantic distinctions if we are to interpret them accurately. A noun-predicate pair in ASL is defined as two grammatical units that share the same physical parameters: hand formation, palm direction, hand position, and hand movement.

One reason nouns and verbs in these pairs need to be differentiated is that there exists the potential for ambiguity and interpretative confusion. Another reason is that these lexical items tend to exist by associated meaning. The predicate often expresses the activity performed with or on the object represented by the noun (Supalla and Newport, 1978). An example of an exact dual representative noun-verb pair is seen in English word pairs like "brush/brush," "paint/paint," "show/show," etc. In such pairs, the hearer relies essentially on context to identify the intended form. More frequently however, related noun-verb pairs are not exact duplications, but rather are closely related items.

Spoken English often differentiates nouns from verbs acoustically by adding semiproductive suffixes. Such suffixes may consist of an extra letter or set of letters, and they make it possible to distinguish a noun from its related verb in such pairs as: "idol/idolize," "like/likeness," "laugh/laughter," "bat/batting," "plan/planning," "wash/washer," etc.

ASL does not use such suffixes. Rather, nouns are differentiated from verbs by the specific manner of movement associated with each sign.

A noun-predicate sign pair share the same base parameters. But to differentiate the verb from the noun, the signer performs the noun with a relatively smaller range of movement. But though a noun's movement is restrained, it is also usually repeated. In a verb-noun pair such as DRIVE and CAR, for instance, each sign is composed of the same base parameters. But the sign for the noun CAR, unlike the sign for the verb DRIVE, is restrained and repeated. The sign for DRIVE is articulated with relatively larger unrestrained movement and without repetition.

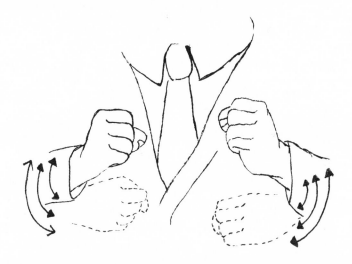

Figure 1. CAR

Nouns are executed with relatively smaller defined movements than verbs. The noun movement tends to be restricted, and the hand(s) rebounds to its original position. This "boxed-in" pattern of restrained movement is repeated. In contrast, verbs use a continuous motion pattern (the hand or hands move without any interruption) and do not repeat. Thus concrete nouns and action verbs in sign pairs share the same base parameters but are differentiated from one another by the manner and

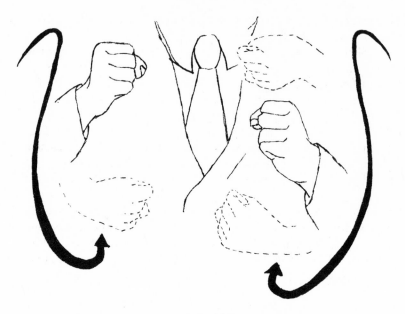

Figure 2. DRIVE

frequency of movement. This systematic difference enables ASL to create new noun signs from existing verbs by restricting and repeating the movement of the sign (Supalla and Newport, 1978).

Sign	*Noun form*	*Verb form*
CAR/DRIVE	Move both S hands up and down in a restricted repeated movement (as if the steering wheel were stuck)	Move both S hands in a large up-and-down movement (as if a driver were steering a car wildly down the street)

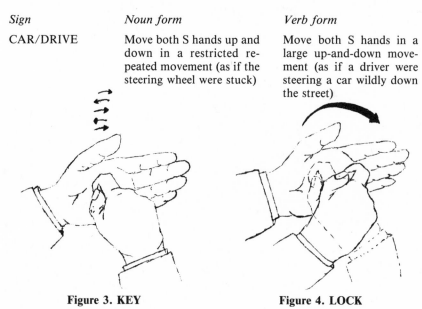

Figure 3. KEY   **Figure 4. LOCK**

KEY/LOCK UP   Move modified A hand back and forth in a restricted range and jiggle the hand (as if the key were stuck in the lock and you were trying to jiggle it free)   Move modified A hand freely back and forth (as if trying to start a car)

Figure 5. FOOD   **Figure 6. EAT**

FOOD/EAT   Move compressed O hand to and from the mouth in a restricted (short distance) manner several times.   Swing compressed O hand up and down from the mouth in a free style. Repeat.

Figure 7. AIRPLANE   **Figure 8. FLY**

AIRPLANE/FLY   Move LY hand forward in a jerking back-and-forth manner   Swing LY hand forward and up in a single sweeping motion

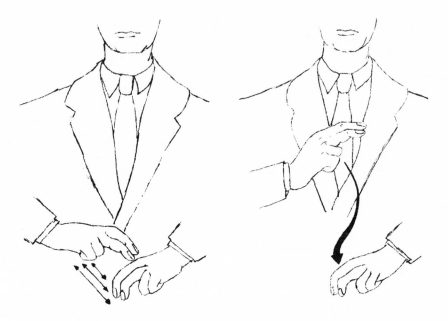

Figure 9. CHAIR   **Figure 10. SIT**

CHAIR/SIT	Tap active bent U hand on the passive bent U hand several times	Swing active bent U hand forward and down to touch the top of the passive bent U hand in a single motion.

Nominalization

Under ordinary circumstances, when speakers describe an action or an occurrence, they include supplemental information about the things or persons that the verb describes. Consider the sentence: "I feel satisfied after I finish my work." The verb "satisfy" expresses a relationship between "what I feel" and "why I feel it." A basic function of a verb then is to describe a relationship. But in a sentence like "Satisfaction follows a job well done," the verb assumes a noun construction. The strategy of using a verb as if it were a noun is known as "nominalization."

When a verb is used as a nominal object, a deletion of references usually results. Sentences using nominalizations customarily lack any reference, stated or implied. In other words, they lack the "what" and "who" specifications. The above example does not specify who is feeling satisfied and only vaguely implies what about. "Satisfy" is a verbal representation of a mode of being (feeling) but "satisfaction" implies a persistent object.

In ordinary conversation, a nominalization can sound very meaningful but actually be quite vague. Unless the references are supplied in some manner, the possibility of ambiguity is high. Nominalization enables a single sentence to communicate a multitude of different interpretations. Such sentences, because they lack references, can relate to virtually anyone or anything. A message that involves a nominalization, particularly as the subject, is so vague that it is difficult to know who or what the message is communicating.

Nominalization	*Verb*
The *satisfaction* of a good job was felt.	I feel *satisfied with my job.*
An awareness of an approaching storm was felt.	I am *aware* of the storm.
The utter *comfort* of an over-stuffed chair was felt.	I feel *comfortable* in this over-stuffed chair.
The *decision* to quit was finally made.	I finally *decided* to quit.
The *frustration* was quite evident.	She looked *frustrated.*
It was a good *decision* to wait.	I *decided* to wait.
It was a wonderful *sensation.*	I *sensed* a feeling of welcome.
I could see your *happiness.*	You looked *happy.*

Manual language rarely, if ever, uses the linguistic strategy of nominalization. A nominalization is a derivative expression of a basic concept. Nominalization turns an action into an object by adding or subtracting certain suffixes to a base word. Such words as "laugh*ter*" (nominalization of "laugh"), "ang*er*" (nominalization of "angry"), "refus*al*" (nominalization of "refuse"), "depart*ure*" (nominalization of "depart/leave") and "beli*ef*" (nominalization of "believe") illustrate how these alterations enable verbs to change into nouns. Since ASL does not use the affixes (suffix or prefix), it has no means of creating nominalizations.

English	*ASL*
My satisfaction was high.	ME TRUE SATISFY PAST
The awareness of her presence was apparent.	ME KNOW SHE NEAR
The comfort of the chair is what I like.	MY CHAIR COMFORT
The decision was postponed.	ME DECIDE LATER
The experience was a good one.	WE-TWO HAVE GOOD TIME
Your happiness is apparent.	HAPPY YOU
Continuation of the meeting was announced.	MEET ANNOUNCE WILL CONTINUE
Your endurance at work is appreciated.	YOUR CONTINUE WORK, ME PLEASE

The Homograph

"Is that your new gold watch carefully what I am about to do."

These two overlapped but well-formed sentences demonstrates a peculiar source of English ambiguity. The unusual overlapping of two independent sentences is possible because one of the words in the above sentence is a homograph. A "homograph" is a pair of words that are spelled and usually pronounced alike but have different definitions. The first sentence, "Is that your new gold watch?" is a question in which "watch" serves as a noun homograph. In the second sentence, "Watch carefully what I am about to do," "watch" is a verb homograph that describes a particular action. "Watch" is a lexical unit that can function either as a verb or as a noun without changing its alphabetic or articulate properties. Other sentential pairs involving a homograph (italicized word) include: "I can't find my *brush* your teeth after every meal"; Is there anyone here who can *help* is something that we all can use at times"; "There goes my last *hope* you can visit us soon"; and "I wrote down the *question* deserves an answer." The occurrence of one word representing both a noun and a verb is a cause for potential misinterpretation and subsequent misunderstanding.

Homographs do not exist in ASL. ASL differentiates objects from actions through manner of production or by the sign that represents its semantic meaning. The idea of the English noun "watch," for instance, is represented in ASL by the sign TIME. Likewise, the English verb "watch" is conveyed by the ASL sign LOOK (at).

Voice

In English, verbal "voice" indicates whether the subject of a sentence is performing the action of a verb (active voice) or whether the action of the verb is being directed upon the subject (passive voice). In passive-voice sentences, the subject receives the action of the verb, and the object of the verb is placed in the initial position of the sentence. Thus, the word order becomes object-verb-subject. The sequence of the passive-voice sentence is illustrated by a sentence like "The butter was made by Mary." Reversing the expected word order, the passive voice is based on the third person.

Another variation of the passive sentence occurs in a sentence like "Examination of the book proved to have merit." This variation uses a nominalization to place the action of the verb (e.g., "examination") in the position of the main topic. In doing so, the sentence omits certain references (for example, "Who" examined "what" book?) and converts the verb to a noun. As a communication style, the passive voice places greater focus on the receiver of the action than on the agent of that action. The subject performs no action but instead has something done to it.

The verb phrase of a passive sentence always includes: (1) some form of the verb "be" (or occasionally "get") in an auxiliary-verb capacity, and (2) a past participle (verb ending in –d or –ed for regular verbs). The subject of a passive-voice sentence usually assumes the position of object of the preposition. The passive voice is often regarded as a formal style, but it tends to be more wordy and more obscure than the active voice.

The active voice involves the word order of subject-verb-object, as in "Mary makes butter." In an active-voice sentence the subject performs the action of the verb. In a sentence like "Tracy hired Lucy," the subject "Tracy" is performing the action of hiring. The active voice is a less formal, more direct sentence type, and it often creates a more emphatic statement.

The option of voice enables the English speaker to arrange the basic word order in two fundamentally different ways, each expressing a similar semantic message but in different communication styles. Reversing voice allows the speaker to use word order to weigh major sentential components differently. In an active-voice sentence like, "Gina is selling her home," the person "Gina" is the subject and the focal point. But in the passive form, "The home is being sold by Gina," the object "home" assumes the position of principle attention. The option of reversing voice allows the speakers to modify the focus of the sentence by placing either the subject, the object, or even the verb in the head position. Switching the head word subtly changes the emphasis of the information in the sentence. In the active-voice sentence, attention is directed on what Gina is doing. But in the passive-voice sentence, attention is on what was happening to the home. The passive voice emphasizes the receiver of the action over the doer.

ASL verbs do not have voice. But ASL structure can be viewed as an economical, active style of communicating. First-person pronouns and action verbs highlight its construction. Its use of the active style as opposed to the passive means it effectively avoids smothering verbs, camouflaging topics, or hiding things in the shrubbery of meaningless modifiers. ASL's active style conveys meaning directly and with more semantic distinction.

Like the English active voice, ASL emphasizes action verbs and succinct, direct communication. But ASL also shares characteristics with the passive voice. For example, ASL employs various sentence patterns that place different grammatical parts in initial position. In addition, sentence reversibility is common.

The following sentences illustrate the different communication styles formed by the voice of a verb.

Active: I understand you bought a car.
Passive: It is my understanding that a car was purchased by you.

Active: I read your letter.
Passive: Your letter has been placed on my desk for my attention.

Active: You passed the test.
Passive: It has been determined that the test was passed by you.

Active: The students were separated.
Passive: Separation of the students was accomplished.

ASL Style

American Sign Language is an active, denotative communication system. In ASL, information and feelings are exchanged on the basis of actual, direct experience rather than on the basis of indirect, associative interpretation. ASL's literal orientation removes some of the need to "read" meaning into its sentences.

But the communication style of ASL is also distinguishable from English by other important features. First, unlike in English sentences, the strongest emphasis in ASL sentences occurs first within the sentence structure (Baker and Cokely, 1980). This principle of placing the strongest emphasis at the beginning of a sentence is called "topicalization" (see chapter 8 for a detailed discussion). Briefly, this strategy involves placing the topic or theme in the beginning of a sentence as a means of drawing attention to it. In the process of topicalizing the focal point, however, pronoun references tend to assume a secondary position. In other words, a person pronoun such as "I" as in "I know the answer" is not necessarily placed at the beginning of an ASL sentence as it would be in an English sentence. Rather, ASL may use a strategy that places the object into the first position of the sentence. The subject and action would then follow to complete the sentence as in: ANSWER, ME KNOW.

A second syntactic difference between ASL and English is that ASL adheres closely to the principle of economization. "Economization" is a principle whereby an ASL sign will be included in a sentence only if it is contributive and informational alone or by an association with signs bordering it. Economization (chapter 3) is a linguistic constraint that considers the relative amount of information a sign contributes to a sentence. As a result of economization, ASL, unlike English, does not include any signs in its sentences that serve purely a functional role. Thus, there are no ASL signs that represent the English articles ("a," "an," or "the"). Each sign included in a manual sentence must carry directly meaningful information.

Spatial Expression

A hallmark of ASL is its use of the spatial aspects of manual motion. Space serves as a conceptual framework that influences nearly all of ASL's grammatical processes, including the basic formation of signs. Spatial variations that are superimposed on the movement patterns of most if not all ASL signs convey a good deal of information.

The ASL signer makes use of the concept of spatial referencing. In "spatial referencing," a communication event is viewed as an imaginary stage empty of props or back drops. The actor (signer) stands alone communicating to an audience (the reader). An imaginary line joins the signer to the reader. This sign line is an understood communicative association that extends directly outward from the signer and is reserved for first- and second-person references. The location of the signer's body represents the location of the neutral sign space (Friedman, 1975).

Through a variety of methods, a signer can use spatial referencing to convey more than sign formations. Spatial referencing gives a signer an unambiguous means of referring to persons, objects, or locations that may or may not be actually present. Once a referent is established on the stage, a signer can then use other ASL strategies to move toward and/or between the imaginary referents, thereby expressing anaphoric references. An "anaphoric reference" is a grammatical substitute that refers back to a preceding reference (Klima and Bellugi, 1979). Such referencing strategies are a significant feature of ASL.

There are more contrasts than similarities between the strategies used to reference pronouns in English and ASL. English refers to persons through pronouns, designating one pronoun specifically for each major referent: One is for the speaker, one for the listener, and three for all other persons. Except when a message is stated in direct quotation, English pronouns are not interchangeable. A third-person pronoun, for example, can not be substituted for a first-person pronoun and mean the same thing. English will not allow, for instance, the third person to be referred to as "I" to convey the meaning of "she," regardless of the circumstances of time and/or spatial considerations.

ASL, on the other hand, allows a signer to establish a frame of reference in the sign space, specify the referent, and then refer back to that point at any time during a discourse. Within the neutral space in front of the signer's body, the signer can set various points of reference to signify different persons, objects, or locations. And once these reference points are in place, the signer has access then as if each reference were metaphorically present.

Training Exercises

    A. To appreciate the number of multisense words in English, use a general-purpose dictionary to look up the definitions of the words: "high," "cut," "drop," "draw," "hold," "set," "strike," "stand," and "shoot."

B. Substitute one carefully chosen sign that can more precisely express the meaning of the idiomatic phrases below.

Example: hash over _____discuss_____

1. done in	_____	16. let in	_____
2. come around	_____	17. lay aside	_____
3. call off	_____	18. keep up	_____
4. set off	_____	19. horn in	_____
5. tire out	_____	20. hold in	_____
6. toss about	_____	21. hear of	_____
7. wait on	_____	22. hang around	_____
8. walk out	_____	23. do up	_____
9. rip off	_____	24. do for	_____
10. roll out	_____	25. close out	_____
11. run after	_____	26. turn in	_____
12. play up	_____	27. act up	_____
13. mark up	_____	28. bear out	_____
14. make up	_____	29. attend to	_____
15. look into	_____	30. all in	_____

C. Find an ASL sign or phrase that can express the idiomatic meaning associated with the following phrases.

Example: cook up   ASL sign: INVENT

1. back burner
2. she turned me around
3. hold your horses
4. all tied up
5. break a leg
6. hang in there
7. hold out for more
8. she gets under my skin
9. get off my back
10. puppy love

D. The ability to overlap sentences reflects potential ambiguity in a language. It illustrates how certain words share the same sound pattern but have completely different meanings. See how many of the following homographs you can use to create well-formed Enlgish sentences that overlap. Example: Put the picture in a wood *frame* this photo before it gets bent.

hand	mix	spring	play	glue	file	pick
patient	frame	watch	walk	swing	move	conduct
push	duck	joke	jump	race	spread	spell

E. Convert the following passive voice sentences into the active voice.

   1. The work must be approved by Ed.
   2. The winner will be announced by Tim.
   3. The office was locked by the security guard.
   4. Your examination will be conducted by the physician's assistant.
   5. The game was delayed by rain.
   6. The yard work was maintained by professionals.
   7. The problem was eventually solved by two scientists.
   8. Satisfaction was gradually felt by the relieved mother.
   9. The sale was suddenly stopped by the manager.
  10. The water leak was finally plugged by the experienced plumber.

3. Economization

Among the various elements that make up an ordinary English sentence are the grammatical parts of speech. The remaining elements serve different functions and vary in the amount of information they impart. Martin (1972) contends that the linguistic structure incorporates such concepts as rhythm, intonation, and syntax. All these are properties peculiar to the fundamental motor system and affect the form or manner in which information is expressed to another person.

There is evidence that speech production and the perception of speech are related to its fundamental mode of communication: the vocal-auditory modality. The rhythm of speech, for instance, can be described by straightforward rules that specify the relative placement of sound sequences in time. Speakers characteristically use different rhythms to denote different, predictable types of messages. As a result, a listener can use speech rhythm to anticipate what will be said instead of listening to it word for word. This potential for forecasting what will be said makes the perceptual system more efficient. The hearer picks up messages both through undivided attention and focused listening, thus enhancing the level of comprehension (Wilentz, 1968).

Verbal English has a natural sequence, a natural flowing quality, and it seems reasonable that this enhances auditory perception. In addition to word order, pacing of information in time is a substantive aspect of the synchrony between the speaker and the listener, forming a linguistic bond.

When a person listens to English, part of what allows him or her to understand each idea as it is presented is the functional elements that act as transitions to build a relationship among the different grammatical parts of a sentence. Examples of these kind of words are "and," "the," "a," "so," "thus," "as," and "while." The shift from one idea to another occurs in time, and the natural transition from one sound pattern to another allows the listener time to move from one idea to another without disruption or confusion. Thus, transitions between sentence elements, which reflect the underlying linear-sequencing of English, are part of the basic structure of the language.

Language serves two inherent functions: to exchange information and to communicate emotion. When you consider how an English sentence works to accomplish its task, you will notice that not all of the words involved in a sentence are included to supply content. Instead, some words serve to provide context, surrounding the content words in order to throw light on their meaning. Thus, some of the features of English are intended more as special rhythmic components than as conveyors of content. Such transitional components serve a valuable role in enhancing the attention and perception of the listener during the communication event.

Thus, the various words that form a discourse can be divided into two basic groups. The first group consists of the words that supply the listener with substance and meaning. These are the actual information-carrying components. The second group consists of those words that serve as linguistic vehicles permitting understanding. This second group consists of "functional" words that allow the speaker to create a smooth-flowing utterance by providing natural transitions. A sentence like "The man is saying that there is someone here," for instance, contains a nearly equal number of content and function words. In this example, the content words "man," "saying," "someone," "here" provide the semantic substance, as reflected by the fact that these words alone are sufficient to express the intended idea. The function words "the," "is," "that," "there" express scarcely any substance or meaning but do serve as a means of auditory "lubrication." These words are the transitional mechanicsm that helps to create a rhythmic flow of ideas. Function words serve as bridges between parts of a sentence. They enable several ideas to be expressed with enough transition that the listener can follow along. Outside of improving the mechanics of the sequential format, function words serve little purpose.

Perceiving visual information and perceiving auditory information are very different processes. Signing is a physical event. Perception of the rhythm of hands is quite different from perception of the rhythm of speech. Yet linguistic terms that specify manner of expression can describe either. Speech production and its perception are related to its vocal-auditory modality; manual production and its perception are linked to its own avenue: the manual/visual modality.

If you compare the time it takes to produce oral words and manual signs, you might expect a big difference in the speed of transmission of more complicated messages. In ordinary conversation, a person typically speaks at a rate of approximately five syllables per second or roughly three simple words. In the time span of one minute, an average speaker may utter as many as 180 words, all spoken intelligibly. It takes roughly double the amount of time to produce a single ASL sign as it does a single English word. Yet, although the rate of articulation of a word and a sign are substantially different, according to Friedman (1976), the rate of transmission per minute is the same or equivalent for an ASL sentence as for a similar sentence spoken in English.

To understand how this linguistic paradox occurs, we must focus on the dynamics of sign production. Signs are produced more slowly than spoken words because the boundaries of the manual articulation space are considerably larger than the boundaries of the space used to voice a word. As a result, covering the physical distance involved in a sign's production takes considerably more time. In addition, a sign uses one or both hands, which may work jointly or separately. The hands may move relatively large distances, and may incorporate multiple body references while simultaneously performing an intricate set of coordinated movements. All of these production elements influence the length of time it takes to execute a sign.

But although isolated sign production is a comparatively time-consuming process, an ASL sentence makes up for this time in efficiency. For one thing, ASL avoids grammatical functionalities (Friedman, 1976). Reducing a sentence to the elements that contain actual content saves significant production time. ASL sentences eliminate the functional elements necessary in oral English, and the result is a more economized sentence. Thus, the succinct ASL sentence is more time efficient than the wordy English one. ASL strategies allow the signer to use fewer ASL signs to communicate a sentence than he or she would need words in English.

The linguistic structure of American Sign Language is built upon the principles of succinct communication. An ASL utterance can be articulated at a rate that will keep pace with English discourse. An ASL sentence like MAN HERE WANT GO-TO FISH contains no function signs. But since each sign supplies meaningful content, it is a relatively straightforward process to translate the sentence into English; one simply adds the appropriate function words to create a smooth verbal transition: "There is a man here who wants to go fishing." Thus, a major difference between English and ASL is the presence or absence of function words.

Economizing Communication

English communication is often overly wordy. In the following phone conversation a caller turns a simple request into a rambling, endless speech.

> Hello. Is this the High Hat Restaurant? Well, I just want you to know that my husband and I have really enjoyed your fine cooking, friendly hospitality, and the divine cozy atmosphere of your fine restaurant so much that we have talked it over and decided to phone you and hope that you might be so kind to check your books and see if you can give us a reservation for dinner this Friday night, say, sometime around 10:00. We prefer the later dinner hour because, you see, my husband likes to take a warm shower before going out, and he never seems able to get home from work until late,

at least during the winter months because of the roads and traffic, and I really don't know with the snow, and all if we could even get to your restaurant much before then unless, maybe, if I ask my husband to ask his boss if it is ok with him if he left a little early and of course, that would mean his work had better be done before . . .

The caller consumed over 160 words to ask the simple question "Is there an opening for dinner this Friday at 10:00?"

"Wordiness" is a communication pattern that uses too many words to convey a thought. Although wordiness in casual conversation is often easy to identify, it can interfere with a conversation's focus.

"Wordiness" is virtually nonexistent in American Sign Language. Rather, ASL's sentences adhere to a process referred to as economization. "Economization" is a communication strategy that promotes brevity of expression by eliminating all unnecessary or superfluous elements from discourse. An economized expression deletes any lexical units that exist merely as padding or for mechanical construction. One of the main objectives of economization is to eliminate wordiness while maintaining a comprehensibility. Economization is a linguistic way of saying "Leave out anything you don't absolutely need" (Friedman, 1976). In ASL, signs that do not contribute to content are dropped. Thus, ASL effectively discards all traces of waste or time-expensive verbiage.

The natural difference in articulation time between a word and a sign is counterbalanced by reduction of execution time that results from economization in ASL. ASL avoids syntactic redundancy by deleting all function-only grammatical elements. Using such grammatical elements to maintain a smooth transition within a sentence is a characteristic of English, but is not necessary in the manual/visual mode. Instead ASL incorporates a great deal of information into each sign used within a sentence. The signer chooses all signs and phrases according to their semantic contribution. Since functional lexical items do not convey meaning, he does not choose them. Learning to eliminate wordiness is one of the most critical objectives of moving from English to ASL. A signer must learn to be economical and direct in selecting signs. When every effort is made to achieve a more concise, understandable discourse, the signer saves precious articulation time. If an element does not convey semantic content, ASL has no use for it.

The effect of economization is well illustrated by a sentence like "There is a lady here who wants to speak with you." In English, the spoken sentence contains eleven words. But translated into ASL, the equivalent content is conveyed in only five signs: LADY WANT SPEAK WITH YOU. Furthermore, if even the sign WITH is dropped, the sentence retains its essence (LADY WANT SPEAK YOU). Without losing any substantial information, the ASL sentence conveys the communication. This is an important facet of economization: the sentence must be reduced to its semantic essence without losing any of its semantic content.

As a hearing, native-English speaker, you have learned to think in English. You have learned to use function words habitually in virtually every utterance. Because of this, you may find it unusual at first to regard certain words as purely mechanical. English function words do create smooth transitions within an utterance, and they seem so right, so familiar, that it seems difficult to communicate without them. It is function words that makes a sentence "sound right."

It takes time and practice to become comfortable with sentences formed strictly from content items. A useful analogy is the practice of conserving energy. Everyone is encouraged to turn off unnecessary lights to save our valuable energy resource. But often we innocently leave on a few lights that are not really necessary. Function words are those extra unnecessary lights. If you are in the habit of using them, you must constantly keep in mind that they are not part of ASL sentences.

Economization is the strategy of removing unnecessary elements while retaining the essential semantic content. It must be accomplished without losing, altering, or distorting the intended essence of meaning. "Essence of meaning" is the kernel of a communication, a sentence that is understood according to its expressed substance alone, without "reading into it."

The most basic method of economization is to eliminate certain major function groups including articles, interjections, conjunctions, linking verbs and expletives.

Economization Strategies

Eliminating Articles

Articles in English signal that a noun follows. An article can introduce a commodity, a proper name, or the best of something. An article also can imply the singularity of something or someone. Since articles do not supply semantic information in and of themselves, ASL omits all use of the articles.

English	*ASL*
The boy is the star.	BOY FAMOUS
A happy day.	HAPPY DAY
It is an animal.	ANIMAL
The man is the tallest.	MAN MOST TALL

Eliminating Interjections

Interjections function as intensifiers. English interjections are used to emphasize (e.g., *"Gosh,* I'm sorry."); to call attention (e.g., *"There,* I'm done."); to introduce a remark (e.g., *"Well,* what did she say?"); and to express surprise (e.g., *"Wow,* you look sensational!"). Since interjections generally lack meaningful content, ASL omits those that serve in a surplus capacity. Thus, interjections such as "well," "wow," "gosh," "gee," "oh," and "there" are discarded.

But ASL does not omit all interjections. When an interjection is used for an informative purpose such as to ratify or emphasize a particular point (e.g. *True,* I said that.) ASL will retain it.

English	*ASL*
Wow, it's a boy!	IT BOY
There, I am finished!	I AM FINISHED
Sure, you can go.	TRUE, YOU CAN GO-TO
Gee, you're beautiful!	BEAUTIFUL, YOU

Eliminating Expletives

Expletives are words or phrases that introduce or are inserted in an English sentence to fill a vacancy. Expletives are used frequently in English. When the expletive occupies the position of the subject, it anticipates a subsequent word or phrase that will supply the actual content. "There" for example, serves as an expletive in a sentence like "There we were waiting."

Expletives, like linking verbs, are functional parts of speech that add nothing semantically to a sentence, and, predictably, ASL does not use expletives. To translate the English sentence "There is a road ahead" into ASL, begin by dropping the expletive, article, and linking verb, and then locate the subject and comment — ROAD AHEAD. THERE is used in ASL, but not as an expletive.

"It" often serves in English as a subject that denotes the verb action of an unspecified agent, for example, "it" in "It is raining." Such phrases as "it is important to ...," "it is easy to ...," "it is time to ...," etc. are additional examples of expletives. The words "this" and "those" are other expletives. The following sentences illustrate the use of the expletive (italicized) in English and ASL equivalent.

English	*ASL*
There is nobody home.	HOME PERSON NONE
It may snow tonight.	NOW NIGHT SNOW MAYBE
This is my first trip.	NOW TRIP FIRST
There are more people expected.	EXPECT MORE PEOPLE
It feels better now.	FEEL BETTER NOW

Those books are Dan's.	BOOK-BOOK BELONG DAN
That is my exit.	MY EXIT

Eliminating Conjunctions

An English conjunction is a function word that is used as a connector. It serves to connect words, phrases, or clauses. Many words can serve as such connectors, including "and," "however," "but," "or," "nor," "for," "after," "while," "when," "where," "because," "if," "since," "till," "as," "either," "neither," "so," "yet," and others. Conjunctions are divided into two classes: coordinating conjunctions and subordinating conjunctions. "Coordinating conjunctions" (e.g., "and," "but," "or") join words or phrases that are logically equivalent in rank. Subordinating conjunctions (e.g., "because," "though," "it," "so," "as," "after," "since," "until," etc.) are used to join dependent (or subordinate) clauses with main clauses.

ASL uses conjunction signs infrequently. Those conjunctions that are used in ASL usually do more than correct, they also supply additional content. A few examples include: BUT (an association by exception or exclusion), BECAUSE (an association by reason or account of), and FINISH (an association by temporal reference). But ASL omits most conjunctions.

English	*ASL*
I bought some apples and Coke.	ME BUY APPLE COKE
The truck roared down the street and pulled to a stop.	TRUCK MOVE THERE STREET. STOP
Fill the tank and check the oil.	FILL TANK LOOK-AT OIL LEVEL
I left because I had an appointment.	ME LEAVE BECAUSE APPOINTMENT

Eliminating Linking Verbs

English linking verbs function strictly to connect the relation between the subject and the subject complement (a word or phrase that completes the relationship with the subject). The most common linking verb is any form of the verb "be." In a sentence like "Judy is smart" the verb "is" provides a grammatical transition. But when this sentence is translated into ASL, the verb is dropped: JUDY SMART. An ASL sign must supply content; it cannot serve simply as a transition. Thus, ASL omits linking verbs.

English	*ASL*
Derek is worried.	DEREK WORRY
The ice is melting.	ICE MELT
The tire is flat.	TIRE FLAT
The old man is driving.	OLD MAN DRIVE
She was right.	SHE CORRECT

Condensing

Articles, interjections, expletives, conjunctions, and linking verbs are all parts of speech that virtually do not exist in American Sign Language. But such formal grammatical components represent only a small fraction of the function elements used in spoken English. To transform a spoken English sentence into a succinct manual form, an ASL signer must delete unnecessary words and must either keep or change the content items into more exact, more specific terms. Thus, ASL uses fewer semantic elements to communicate more.

In casual conversation, there are many everyday phrases, clichés, and other expressions that sound meaningful, but supply little content. When such expressions are dropped, no substantial information is lost. This type of verbiage includes various social expressions, which make up much of what is commonly referred to as "idle chatter." In the following examples, a person tells a companion that s/he is "a nice person." But in each case, the content statement ("you are a nice person") is preceded by a friendly but frivolous introductory remark. This type of remark is eliminated from ASL communication.

May I just say that ... (you are a nice person.)
Not to change the subject, but ... (you are a nice person.)
I just want to say that ... (you are a nice person.)
I don't want to be personal, but ... (you are a nice person.)
I would like to say that ... (you are a nice person.)
Please don't take this wrong, but ... (you are a nice person.)
Needless to say ... (you are a nice person.)
Let me make it perfectly clear that ... (you are a nice person.)
Have I mentioned that ... (you are a nice person.)
Not meaning to second guess, but ... (you are a nice person.)
I don't want to interrupt, but ... (you are a nice person.)
To make a long story short ... (you are a nice person.)

The ASL equivalent of any of these is NICE PERSON, YOU. The following is a list of phrases that fail to supply meaningful semantic content. Omitting such phrases will often improve sentence comprehension.

The point is this	on and on	apart from
in the event that	as well as	according to
on account of	as long as	instead of
the fact of the matter is	in regard to	as to
in regard to	in spite of	in case
inasmuch as	in order to	contrary to
be as it may	in place of	as for
it is well known that	in relation to	purpose of
before you know it	on behalf of	found that
in a very real sense	in contrast to	

Another type of meaningless jargon is found on the word level. Various English words serve strictly technically. ASL omits such function words. Here are a few examples.

Word	Part of Speech	Example
also	adverb	He can *also* go.
as	adverb	*As* much *as* I know
	conjunction	It fell *as* she moved.
	pronoun	in the same class *as* my sister
	preposition	works *as* a clerk
besides	adverb	*besides,* who else can?
	adjective	who *besides* me?
	preposition	*besides* you, no one
either	adverb	not in debt *either*
	adjective	use *either* car
	pronoun	*either* one of us
	conjunction	*either* stay or leave
else	adverb	Where *else* were you?
	adjective	What *else* did you say?
ever	adverb	Do you *ever* work?
neither	adverb	*neither* did she
	adjective	*neither* class
	pronoun	*neither* one of us
	conjunction	*neither* did we
so	adverb	I think *so*.
	adjective	That was not *so*.
	pronoun	Do *so* soon.
	conjunction	Be quiet *so* she can study.
such	adverb	*such* nice people
	adjective	never heard of *such* a thing
	pronoun	*such* was the case
though	adverb	I knew it *though*.
thus	adverb	*Thus,* the answer was revealed.
too	adverb	*too* much work; you did *too*

Ordinary spoken conversation contains many messages, comments, and words that supply meaningful content. Unfortunately, this content is often surrounded by meaningless filler. When content is buried in useless verbiage, removal can improve clarity. Tailoring sentences by selectively discarding irrelevant, needless, or redundant units creates more effective, explicit communication. One strategy for achieving this is reduction. "Reduction" is a method of condensing a sentence into its essence by deleting meaningless elements, but retaining meaningful content. The following phrases have been reduced. The semantic substance is retained (in capital letters) while the function words (in parentheses) are deleted.

English	ASL
REPEAT (again)	REPEAT
(over) THERE	THERE
FINISH (up)	FINISH
HURRY (up)	HURRY
(absolutely) FREE	FREE
MEET (with)	CONVENE
QUIET (down)	QUIET
(The) EARLY (part of) NEXT...	NEXT EARLY
PLEASE (do not hesitate to)	PLEASE
(have you seen) WHERE TOM (has gone?)	TOM WHERE?
(do you have the) TIME)?	TIME?
(how) OLD (are) YOU?	OLD YOU?
(at a) LATER (time)	LATER
DURING (the time of); (all) DURING (the)	DURING
(I wish to) THANK	THANK
(on a) DAILY (basis)	DAILY

Substituting

When translating spoken English into signs, it is a common practice to substitute more specific lexical items for general lexical items. This strategy often involves shifting connotative words into denotative signs, promoting specificity of meaning. Many English expressions that require phrases can be expressed manually with one or two well-chosen signs. To illustrate how well substitution functions, we supply a list of common, everyday expressions in English along with an equivalent ASL sign.

English	ASL
through the use of	WITH
by means of	
it is doubtful that	MAYBE
may or may not	
it is probable that	
whether or not	
if it should	
in many cases	OFTEN
it is often the case that	
at the present moment	NOW
at this point	
at this time	
as I speak	
it makes no difference	NO MATTER
it really doesn't matter	
the reason is that	BECAUSE
owing to the fact that	
on the grounds that	
in view of the fact	

it may, however, be found that you may have a point but	BUT
as a matter of fact to be quite certain absolutely sure unquestionably certain	TRUE
over with done with	FINISH
a number of	MANY
a considerable amount of	MUCH
in a position to	CAN
in terms of	ABOUT

ASL also frequently substitutes more specific signs for general English words. The following list of words illustrates this strategy. The sign chosen would depend on the context.

English (meaning)	*Possible ASL Sign(s)*
Even (level; steady; fair)	EQUAL, FAIR
It was an even deal.	FAIR DEAL
an even dollar	DOLLAR
Just (exactly; very recently; reasonable; righteous; deserved)	FAIR, HONEST, ONLY
He is a just man.	HE HONEST MAN
I received just a note.	I RECEIVE ONLY NOTE
Wait just a minute.	WAIT
It just might happen.	MAYBE HAPPEN
Need/Necessary (an urgency of obligation or want)	MUST, REQUIRE, WANT
It is necessary to write.	I MUST WRITE
I need your notes.	I WANT YOUR NOTE
Shall (future)	WILL
We shall see.	WE WILL SEE
It shall be necessary.	WILL REQUIRE
Then (that time)	NOW, PAST
the then-president	PAST PRESIDENT
He lost but then he knew it.	HE LOSE BUT NOW HE KNOW
While (a period of time)	DURING, UNTIL, TIME
while you study	DURING STUDY
Remain while I look.	STAY UNTIL I LOOK
worth your while	WORTH YOUR TIME
Yet (exception; a specific time)	BUT, STILL
may yet find it	MAYBE FIND IT STILL
He will stay, yet he knows better.	HE STAY BUT KNOW BET- TER

Other ASL Strategies

The remaining material in this chapter also illustrates that ASL has its own, discrete linguistic structure, targeting selected parts of speech. The areas to be discussed are demonstrative pronouns, prepositions, auxiliary verbs, tense markers, and proper names.

Demonstrative Pronouns

The English demonstrative pronoun is a universal pronoun. Demonstrative pronouns function to point out something or someone that has been mentioned shortly before. The four pronouns "this," "that," "these," and "those," are sufficiently vague that each one can represent a person, thing, or idea. In terms of abstract references such as "*this* time," "*those* choices," "*these* feelings," etc. the demonstrative pronoun provides a transition. ASL omits most demonstrative pronouns, but uses the sign THAT to convey the idea "to point out an object or person." Typically, the demonstrative sign THAT points out concrete elements, as in THAT HOUSE.

English	ASL
This coat is mine.	THAT COAT MINE
to wait this long	WAIT LONG TIME
That is what she said to me.	(SHE) TELL (ME)
This is for you.	INDEX (ACTUAL ITEM) YOU
This feeling I have is good.	ME FEEL GOOD
These ideas are mine.	IDEA MINE

Prepositions

The part of speech in English that expresses specific relationships is the preposition. A preposition is a connective word that indicates a relationship between two words while implying a sense of time, location, or direction. Such prepositions as "across," "after," "as," "at," "before," "between," "by," "for," "from," "in," "like," "of," "on," "over," "to," "until," "up," "upon," etc. are a function-oriented part of speech. Prepositions are commonly connected with an object (and any modifiers) to form a "prepositional phrase," as in "for that matter."

Because most of the prepositions commonly used in English are in essence functional elements, they are not used in ASL. Examples of such prepositions include "as," "of," and "to." The prepositions "at," "by," "for," "in," "on," "to," and "upon" are expressed in ASL only occasionally. The following prepositions (in parentheses) would be omitted.

(with) great effort	(to) rent	(in) common
once (upon) a time	(to) be there	(in) the morning

(with) great force	(to) do	(in) the area
(by) yourself	(to) the door	(in) the sky
(through) it all	(to) walk	(in) this way
(for) that matter	(from) now (on)	type (of) move
(for) your sake	(at) this time	(of) course
happy (for) ever	(on) your way	(of) liberty

But there are cases when a preposition supplies information; the idea it expresses cannot be determined by context alone. In such cases, ASL uses an appropriate sign to supply the information. Most content prepositions express a locational relationship between two or more objects or persons. If, however the idea represented by the preposition can be understood by the context, ASL will delete the preposition. Experience is often the best indicator of when a preposition should be retained or deleted.

English	*ASL*
Everyone sit around the table.	SIT THERE TABLE
Let's meet at my house.	WE CONVENE FUTURE MY HOUSE
He is standing by the fence.	HE STAND NEAR FENCE
The dog is lying under the tree.	DOG LIE UNDER TREE
Put the umbrella under the seat.	PUT UMBRELLA UNDER SEAT
The boy's head is above the water.	BOY HEAD ABOVE WATER

Auxiliary Verbs

Auxiliary or helping verbs are verbs that connect to a main verb to form a verb phrase. English commonly uses auxiliary verbs to provide transitions. Such verbs are strictly functional and are deleted in ASL. Such functional verbs include the various forms of "be" such as "am," "is," "are," "was," "were," and "been." Other functional helping verbs include "do," "shall," "may," "could," "might," "have to," "going to," "used to," "is about to," "ought to," etc. In ASL, transitional auxiliary verbs are deleted. The main verb is sufficient to supply the action of the sentence.

Another use of the English auxiliary verb is to convey action in progress. Auxiliary verbs can be attached to main verbs to create a progressive verb phrase, as in "am seeing," "was leaving," "will have been waiting," etc. The progressive verb form consists of some form of the verb "be" along with an suffix attached to the main verb. Progressive verb forms are one way of expressing the present tense in English. Instead of using the progressive, ASL relies on the main verb alone to represent all expressions of the present tense.

Another use of the auxiliary verb is to construct a verbal infinitive. In English, the infinitive is mostly used as a noun or occasionally as an adjective or adverb. The infinitive is typically formed by combining the word "to" with a verb. To convert an infinitive into ASL, the signer reduces the sentence to its essence. If the infinitive fails to contribute content, it is deleted, as in the sentence "I wanted to have a cup of coffee." When this same thought is expressed in ASL, the infinitive "to have" is deleted to produce: COFFEE, ME WANT PAST.

Sometimes more precise signs are substituted for strictly functional infinitive phrases, such as "to be," "to do," "to have," etc. substituted for a more precise sign.

But ASL does use some auxiliary verbs, particularly when a helping verb is combined with a main verb to create a new semantic expression. Typically, a secondary or auxiliary verb is used when the supplemental information it adds cannot be derived through the context. Such helping verbs might supply such content as "person, number, possibility, capability, etc.

English	*ASL*
I have to think about it.	ME MUST THINK SELF
She must have been tired.	SHE TIRED
You ought to help pack.	HELP PACK
Terry was going to call Marsha.	TERRY PHONE MARSHA
I was about to write the letter.	LETTER, ME WRITE NOW
I used to read a lot.	ME READ MUCH PAST
You shall not talk.	TALK NONE

Tense Markers

Tense markers in English express the time of the sentence's action. Tense markers include such suffixes as "–ing," "–s," "–en," "–ed," etc., which are attached to verbs. Tense markers change the verb form to tell the listener when the action took place. They let the listener know whether the time frame of the action as past, present or future.

ASL does not mark verbs for tense. There are no suffixes to change the verb form or to indicate the time frame. Such markers as "–ing," and "–en" that are found in certain modern sign codes or pidgin derivatives do not exist in ASL.

In most ASL communications, time is anchored to the moment of the communication event. But ASL has also developed a unique use of spatial dimensions to shade the time frame. It is sufficient at this point to realize tha the use of tense markers in English has no equivalent in ASL. In terms of economizing your sentences, eliminate suffixes.

English	*ASL*
Present	*Present*
I am feeling better.	ME FEEL BETTER
He does know.	HE KNOW
The teacher allows no talking.	TEACHER ALLOW TALK NONE

Past	*Past*
She was smiling.	SHE SMILE PAST
Amy broke her leg.	AMY BREAK PAST HER LEG
If I had known	MAYBE ME KNOW PAST
I knew him.	ME KNOW HIM
He worked all night.	PAST NIGHT HE WORK
My friends were about to leave.	MY FRIEND(S) NOW READY LEAVE

Future	*Future*
I will see you later.	ME SEE FUTURE YOU LATER
Tom is to know that.	TOM KNOW FUTURE
Tina is going to call.	TINA CALL FUTURE
My friends will be leaving soon.	MY FRIEND(S) LEAVE SOON

Economizing and the Proper Name

Sign language is a visual phenomenon. Because at least two persons must be physically present and in actual sight of each other to communicate in ASL, there is much less need for proper name referencing when conversing. Signers typically do not include proper names in ASL communication. The lack of personal name references during an ASL conversation contrasts sharply with the customs of verbal conversation. But repeated use of personal names during a conversation is time-consuming and semantically nonproductive. If each participant knows the other and is actively in conversation the use of proper names is unnecessary. Omitting them economizes movement and saves valuable execution time. So, when you use ASL, outside of introductions, drop the use of proper names.

In addition, ASL vocabulary contains no formal signs designated as proper person names. Proper names are either fingerspelled or expressed by way of a sign name. "Sign names" are informal personal signs created exclusively for an individual. Such individualized sign names are a source of personal identification, loosely analogous to nicknames used by hearing persons. But an ASL sign name is more important than a nickname; it is the familiar recognition for that person. Sign names are used for introductions and certain references, but in active conversation, direct references to the persons present are usually accomplished by indexing or gesturing. Sign names are used only in introductions.

The use of titles such as "Mr.," "Mrs.," "Dr.," "Rev.," etc. are typically fingerspelled in their abbreviated form. Such titles are usually included only when a person is introduced. If a title is used to provide a certain occupational or professional reference, as in DOCTOR HERE NOW (meaning "The doctor is in now."), the reference DOCTOR serves not as a title but to identify a particular person and the topic of the conversation. The reference DOCTOR is usually sufficient and will be followed by the proper name only if the reader is uncertain who specifically is being discussed.

ASL is a pragmatic, precise communication system. Even in its treatment of abstracts, ASL tends to convey more explicit meaning and information with fewer individual units than English. The underlying principle of economization is best stated in this reminder: Make every sign count. Delete whatever adds nothing to content.

Training Exercises

A. Underline each word or marker that should be omitted under the economization principle. Then circle all altered word forms and write the base form.

Example: I saw the sun set in the west.

1. A moment like that should last forever.
2. The rose has been wilting.
3. A man seeing an accident should stay on the scene.
4. Riding a horse or a bicycle takes skill.
5. The elevator is malfunctioning again.
6. The tourists soon became homesick.
7. The boy wrote the note for Bill.
8. Karen graciously invited the reporters to lunch.
9. I don't know where he came from.
10. I have been trying to ready this book.
11. They are all eager to work hard for you.
12. Perhaps we had priced our vegetables too high.
13. She had laid the book aside.
14. She seemed to forget I was there.
15. The pup had been set in the box.
16. The coat was still lying there.
17. I have heard no more rumors.
18. I received word that my application had been accepted.
19. When the speaker entered, the audience rose.
20. The toy soldier has been rusting in the yard.

B. Revise these sentences, focusing on being clear, complete, and concise, while retaining clear, structured sentences.

1. The ball game has been tied for the last three innings.
2. I will need to please change my appointment.
3. If you don't make your plane reservation soon, you may not get the particular flight that your plans call for.
4. Silence is golden when used at the right time and by the right person.
5. I want to take this opportunity to tell you just how pleased I am that you moved into our neighborhood.
6. As per your letter, we are enclosing herewith the applications for membership.
7. Your car was apparently damaged by the last storm that passed through here.

8. Your training in manual language can soon affect your personal opportunities in the future.
9. Let me know of your vacation plans as soon as possible.
10. Please find my enclosure where a check has been attached in the amount of $100.00.
11. I want you to know that it is our off season and if you want a quiet place to stay, now is the best time.
12. You will learn how important it is to please your customers and to try not to have too many mistakes.
13. If you aren't able to get a place to stay where you want, you will probably be unhappy because your vacation will be in the wrong place.
14. Trusting you will respond to my letter as soon as possible, we remain patiently waiting.
15. The leaves with their fall colors are a delight.
16. I am sending you a carbon copy of the very same.
17. I would appreciate your sending me the title of the book.
18. You can rest assured that you will be notified of our decision as soon as the decision has been made.
19. You are probably the most thoughtful person I have ever known to bring me such a fine gift.
20. Please don't even hesitate to get in touch with me any time if I can be of any service to you either now or later since I am available to assist you in any way that I may be able.

C. Cross out all necessary words. Write in any needed substitutions above each sentence.

1. Who is doing the driving here?
2. I have to get something for me to drink.
3. We really would be pleased to treat you to a delicious ice cream cone.
4. A haircut is needed by him and yourself.
5. The two of us, referring to Terry and myself, will stay right where we are.
6. Since it is your ball, I guess you can do whatever you want with it.
7. If you agree with this letter in regard to this important matter, then sign the papers.
8. The keys that I need to use are in your coat.
9. We have all had a happy experience that we could only vaguely remember.
10. We are still waiting here for word as to who is right.
11. He told me that he wants to ride with anyone who may be going to the game.
12. Let's find out who owns it before we give it away.
13. There is always someone around who would like to own a new car for free.
14. How long has it been since you played any tennis?
15. Whom shall I say is calling?
16. Each person, regardless of gender, will be given only a few minutes to make their selection.

17. There is no real reason I can think of as to why you will have to wait more than an hour.
18. Many an hour has passed since I first heard the report.
19. Once you rewrite your draft, it will probably become a best seller.
20. Paul is the only teenager who seems to always eat a balanced meal.

D. Revise the following questions into more economic and direct form.
    1. With whom am I speaking right now?
    2. When was the last time you washed somebody else's car?
    3. When was the last time you tried to stick to a diet?
    4. Are you one who really enjoys eating a fattening dessert after a big meal?
    5. How many pizzas have you ever eaten just in one day?
    6. Could you advise someone else on how to dress appropriately for an interview?
    7. Have you ever fallen while skating in an ice rink?
    8. If you were going to learn to play a musical instrument, which one would you want to try?
    9. Have you ever experienced a visit to any Pacific islands?
    10. When you first hear a phone ring, how many times does it usually ring before you are able to answer it?

E. Edit this rather ordinary, but cluttered example of a story. Eliminate wordiness, but retain content.

I saw Julie the other day—you know who I am talking about, the blonde-haired girl or was it red hair? Anyway, she used to come around and sell chocolate candy bars for some project at school. She always came in second, although I think she tied once for first. Well, Julie went to one of those new sun-tanning places where you put on your bathing suit and lie in some kind of light room or something like that and after 15 minutes you go and take a shower. As I hear it, she wasn't having much success, so she moved into a new apartment that has its own swimming pool and it even has one of those saunas. Julie is such a lovely girl, and she always has such lovely hair. Well, I saw her the other day at the grocery—or was it at the beauty shop—and you should see how tan she is becoming ever since she moved and stopped seeing what's-his-name. You know, I was wondering if we might invite her over for dinner one of these days and of course, it really doesn't matter what time we eat, just as long as we eat before my TV programs come on, so why don't you call her, and would you mind if I asked a few friends too?

4. Compounds

Where do new signs come from? Are they made up or coined from slang? Are there means of building signs (or words) to reflect new meanings? Such questions are the focus of "morphology," the study of the internal structure of lexical items (words or signs).

Recent evidence shows clearly that American Sign Language has morphological processes that allow a signer to combine individual units of meaning (morphemes) to form new signs (Bellugi, 1980). Thus, American Sign Language is a fully expressive language, containing its own strategies for modifying its internal signs. Not only is ASL vocabulary richer than many people assumed; vocabulary growth in ASL is an active on-going phenomenon.

Included in the various morphological strategies for modifying the words or signs of a language is its inherent ability to form different items from the same lexical base (Klima and Bellugi, 1979). A predominant example of this type of modification is affixation in English. Affixation is the derivational process of attaching one or more sounds or letters to the beginning or end of a base word. It can produce either a derivation of that word or an entirely new word. When a prefix is added to the beginning of a word, a word like "mark" becomes the basis for the formation of the word "remark." The new word means something quite different than the base word. Similarly, the use of a suffix such as "-ment" added to a base word like "judge" builds the new word "judgment," which has its own distinctive semantic meaning. The adjective "real" serves as the basis for the formation of such words as "reality," "realization," "realize," "really" and "realtor."

One reason affixation is such a common and widespread morphological device in English is because it fits so well into the phonological structure of English. Affixation is based on the simple concept of adding or subtracting sounds or letters from a base unit to modify its meaning. This sequential process fits precisely with the fundamental formation of an English "word," a series of sounds arranged in a linear sequence that has meaning.

For the same reason that affixation applies so well to English, it is, in effect, rejected by American Sign Language. The formation of a sign is not linear; it is simultaneous. A sign's multiple physical parameters are performed at the same moment in time, and an attempt to add an extra parameter to this spontaneous temporal event would add complexity, not meaning. Thus, there is natural and strong resistance to sequential segmentation in ASL (Bellugi, 1979). Adding letters to a sign is simply not regarded as a viable communicative option. Affixation, therefore, does not exist in ASL. Instead, most signs are modified through spatial and temporal deviations.

Initializing a Sign

A form of sign creation that loosely resembles a variation of affixation is the process of initializing signs. "Initialization" is a linguistic strategy that allows a signer to create new signs by changing the hand formation of an existing base sign to the first letter of an English word that closely resembles it in meaning. Initialization does not attach additional letters to a sign. Instead, the specific hand shape of a sign is replaced by a letter, which produces either a derivation of that sign or an entirely new sign. Substituting a letter for an existing hand shape converts, for instance, a sign like CLASS to the sign FAMILY. In many initialized signs the first letter of the English word is formed on the primary hand as the sign is executed (Hoemann, 1978).

EAT for instance, is a base sign that involves a modified O hand moving up and inward so that the fingertips touch the mouth. When the same parameters are performed but a D hand substitutes for the modified O hand, the sign becomes DENTIST (the D hand moves up and inward to touch the mouth). Thus, the base sign EAT becomes the foundation of the sign DENTIST. Other initialized signs include RIGHT (derived from the base sign KEEP), REASON (derived from the base sign THINK), REHABILITATION (derived from the base sign HELP), VALENTINE (derived from the base sign HEART).

Initialization involves a form of bilingual association. On one hand, the newly formed sign represents an associated meaning that is derived from its base sign. But on the other hand, the hand formation of this newly created sign refers to an existing English word.

The use of initialization implies that a signer who is competent in English might have an advantage over someone who is not bilingual. But such knowledge of English words is not critical because a sign with an initialized hand form can be learned as easily as one without such a hand shape. The execution of the sign does not depend on the signer realizing the association of the sign with English. Many signers use initialized signs without knowing that the hand form is associated with an English word, even as they use other signs without overtly knowing their origins or early iconic associations. Knowledge of sign origin is not critical for competence in American Sign Language.

The strategy of using letters of the alphabet to create new semantic signs is a widespread practice in modern code systems. Initialization is a common strategy in manual versions of English like Seeing Essential English (Anthony, 1974) and Signing Exact English (Gustason, Pfetzirg and Zawolkow, 1972). The specialized manual dictionaries currently being created rely heavily on the influence of English as a source language for sign-vocabulary expansion (Hoemann, 1976).

When ASL employs initialization, it limits the practice to one hand shape and the initial position. In contrast, some modern manual systems expand the strategy to allow initializing of both hand shapes and in either the initial or the final position. In the modern sign WOULD, for example, the W hand moves forward from the face while changing into the D hand. Such a modernization of signs reflects a heavy influence of English, but also demonstrates the nearly limitless number of possibilities initialization provides.

The modern use of initialization tends to breach some of the principles of ASL phonology. First, when a two-handed ASL sign involves two active hands, both hands usually form the same hand shape. Second, when the hands in a two-handed ASL sign are shaped differently, only the dominant or primary hand transmits meaningful information; the secondary or passive hand plays a base or locational role.

American Sign Language uses initialization only sparingly and not always in association with English. Furthermore, initialization is only one of several possible modifications of the different ASL hand formations. Another modification, which has no affiliation with English, occurs in certain compounds when the initial hand formation is changed naturally to anticipate the approaching second sign. In a single-double–handed compound sign such as REMEMBER, for example, the initial hand shape of KNOW is changed eventually from an open hand to an A hand. This form of "initializing" is motivated not by English words but by the need to create a smoother transition of movement.

One of the various morphological processes that exist in language is a productive modification mechanism called compounding. "Compounding" is a method of creating a new lexical unit (word or sign) from two or more existing units. A compound joins two equal lexical items together to form a new lexical unit that functions as a separate semantic item in the language.

When the word "head" for instance, is combined with such words as "ache," "board," "first," "light," "long," "master," "phone," "quarters," or "way," it creates such new compound words as: "headache," "headboard," "headfirst," "headlight," "headlong," "headmaster," "headphone," "headquarters," and "headway." Each newly formed word is regarded as a separate entry in a general-purpose dictionary. Compound words tend to be either nouns (e.g., "fanfare," "cheesecloth," "bandwagon") or adjectives (e.g., "homemade," "old-fashioned," "harebrained"). Compounding is a highly effective strategy for enriching a language's vocabulary.

An important distinguishing characteristic between a compound and a word phrase is that a compound is a single semantic entity. A phrase, on the other hand, is a sequential combination of several semantic entities. A "word phrase" may be defined as a group of two or more related words in close proximity. But though the words of a word phrase are close together, they remain unattached. Thus the meaning of a word phrase is obtained by assessing the meanings of the individual words sequentially and relating them to the context of the sentence. In English, when two words are separate, distinct sequential semantic units we derive their meanings individually, as in "chocolate cake," "marble cake," and "upside-down cake."

Another way to identify a word phrase is that it is substitutable. Any word within a word phrase can be replaced with another (within certain constraints) to create a different phrase and a different meaning. A compound cannot undergo substitution. Although a compound is created from the linguistic bonding of two root words, compounding results in a new meaning that is often drastically different than the individual meanings of its root words. This newly formed meaning may be so different that it cannot be understood from assessing the meanings of its root words individually. Consider the word "fanfare," for instance. As a compound, "fanfare" means "a showy outward display." But its root words, "fan," which means "a device for moving air," and "fare," which means "to travel" or "dine," provide little insight into the semantic representation of the resulting compound. Thus, an attempt to substitute words within a compound will destroy the new meaning.

The ASL Compound

Compounding is used by American Sign Language as an effective morphological process for creating new signs and expanding vocabulary. A compound sign acquires its own defined meaning and its own specific parameters, which are distinguishable from the root signs that are joined to create it. Thus, an ASL compound is distinctively separate from its root signs and their meanings, and it is entered as a separate lexical sign in a manual dictionary. An ASL compound is expressed graphically by a curved line, herein double diagonal lines (//), between its root signs, e.g., THINK // SAME is the sign for the compound AGREE.

There are at least three strategies that can be used to determine whether a pair of signs are functioning as a single compounded ASL sign or as different corresponding parts of a sign phrase. The first strategy assesses whether you can insert modifiers between the root signs. If modifiers can be inserted, the signs are serving as part of a sign phrase. In an English phrase like "a color TV," additional qualifying words can be inserted into the middle of the phrase to create various modifications in its meaning. Thus, "a color TV" can be expanded to create such phrases as "a color RCA TV," or "a color, dented, 1982 TV." A similar type of strategy can be applied to manual ASL phrases. In a sign phrase like, THINK SAME (meaning "think in the same way" or "think alive"), various qualifying signs like ALMOST or ALWAYS can be added to create different phrases such as THINK ALMOST SAME (meaning "think in similar ways"). Another example is the sign phrase WHITE FACE. This phrase can be expanded to create such phrases as WHITE PAPER FACE ("a face created out of white paper") or WHITE // RED FACE (a "pink face") etc. When two or more signs can accept signs between them, they are operating as a sign phrase, not a compound.

But when two signs create a compound, the newly formed sign functions as a single lexical item. When the signs THINK and SAME are fused together, the result is the compound AGREE (THINK // SAME). The movement parameters of a compound effectively eliminate the opportunity for modifying signs to be inserted between the root elements. Thus, the fused compound WHITE // FACE (meaning "pale" or "dull") for instance, will not accept such signs as PAPER or RED between them. Because a compound represents a separate lexical entity, the two root signs that form the compound cannot be separated by intermediate signs. As another example, the compound WAITRESS, formed by the root signs GIRL and SERVE cannot accept intermediate modifiers. If this particular sign pair were a phrase, a signer could insert modifiers between the root signs. Thus, the phrase GIRL SERVE ("the girl is serving") can be expanded to qualify the girl's service manner, as in GIRL GREAT SERVE ("the girl is serving very well"). But the compound GIRL // SERVE cannot accept such insertions. The root signs are no longer treated as separate signs, but rather as a continuous series of parameters that together form a single sign.

A second strategy for distinguishing between a compound sign and a sign phrase is to assess whether the newly created compound can perform the same grammatical operations as a single sign. One such operation is reduplication. Reduplication (repeating the sign's parameters) alters the fundamental meaning of a sign by such semantic shadings as "a series of," "the same old thing over and over again," and "regularly" (Klima and Bellugi, 1979). The grammatical inflection that accomplishes this shading involves a slow repetition of the movement parameters of the sign. It is possible in ASL to reduplicate a compound, but it is not possible to reduplicate a sign phrase.

This second strategy for distinguishing between compounds and sign phrases works because an ASL compound has acquired its own individual meaning, which is often completely separate from the combined meanings of its original root signs. Sometimes, of course the meanings are related. In a direct compound, for example, such as SWIM // CLOTHES, the newly formed item BATHING SUIT continues to hold a semantic association with its root signs. Similarly, there is a straightforward semantic association between the root signs of the compound LIVE // ROOM which bonds to form LIVING ROOM. In an indirect compound, however, the semantic association is more obscure. The compound STRANGER for instance is derived from the root signs FACE and NEW. But the phrase FACE NEW which means "a facial" holds no appreciable association with the semantic identity of these same signs formed as a compound.

A third strategy is to assess whether the sign pair in question can be used to modify another sentence component. In a sentence like PAINT WHITE FACE, a request is being made for someone to "paint a white face." Since the signs WHITE and FACE can serve in a supportive capacity, the sign pair must be a phrase. If the pair were a compound, no alterations that might affect either individual component within the compound would be permitted. The sentence PAINT WHITE // FACE (compound) means either "paint (it) pale" or "pale paint." Thus bonding two signs into one is not only semantic; it is also structural. And such bonding occurs both on the grammatical and the physical levels.

Articulating the Compound

When two or three ASL signs are arranged as a sign phrase, each sign within that phrase continues to be treated as an individual item. The signer performs each sign's distinctive articulation characteristics unaltered. The fact that the sign is part of a phrase does not substantially influence its production parameters. In addition sufficiently perceivable transitional boundaries (end points) are maintained between the signs. A sign as an isolated item, a sign as part of a sentence (e.g. subject), or a sign as part of a sign phrase is treated the same in terms of its manual articulation.

A similar consistency of articulation is maintained in English. A word like "maximum" is pronounced the same if it is a single noun or if part of a word phrase such as "maximum overdrive." Even words in multiword phrases are uttered separately with their own starts and their own finishes as in a phrase like "the little brown jug." The distinctive articulation indicates that the relationship between the words is semantic, not structural.

English compounds are distinguished to a large part by different intonation. The articulation and delivery of a compound is different from that of a word phrase. Notice the different intonation that occurs in the phrase "black board" and the compound "blackboard." The same difference in inflection separates a phase like "second hand" from the compound "secondhand" or the phrase "green house" from the compound "greenhouse."

In an English word phrase the intonation stress is usually on the second word, as in "kick back" or "kick off." The first word is unstressed, followed by the stressed second word. But in an English compound, the opposite inflection sequence usually occurs. In an English compound, the stress is placed on the first word, as in "kickback" and "kickoff." Notice the difference between the compound "blackball" and the phrase "black ball." A similar difference can be heard between "sidearm" (a compound) and "side arm" (a phrase). Such examples illustrate that while the phonological shape (sound pattern) of the components of an English compound remain essentially intact, the specific inflection of the sound pattern can undergo certain phonemic changes as a result of compounding.

Duration of the Compound

American Sign Language approaches articulation differently from English. In part, this is because manual language does not use intonation. American Sign Language does, however, distinguish between compounds and phrases, but, reflecting the visual dimension of signs it does so by the use of rhythm.

The articulation of an ASL compound is accomplished by three main processes. First, the initial component sign is condensed, usually to a brief contact. Second, any repetition within the movement parameter of the sign is dropped. Third, the base hand of the second component sign assumes its position earlier than usual. Thus, both the transitional time element between the two signs and their individual movement parameters are drastically reduced (Klima and Bellugi, 1979). These three basic articulatory characteristics bond the compound and serve to distinguish compound signs from other types of signs or phrases.

In condensing the transitional movement that normally exists between two signs, compounding omits the individual characteristics of the initial root sign's end points. A similar loss of articulatory boundaries is observed in English compounds. Rather than saying each word in sequence, as in "black board," English speakers articulate the compound "blackboard" as if it were a multisyllabic word. Such articulation is also illustrated by such examples as "playback," "rowboat," "schoolroom," and "textbook."

Within the ASL compound, the first sign's parameters are nearly always condensed relative to the form of the second sign – often drastically. In other words, the initial sign's movement parameter is shortened to the briefest form it can maintain without losing its semantic identity. This shortening occurs only in the initial sign.

In undergoing shortening, the initial sign loses its original individual stress and repetition of movement. Any movement parameter that includes an alternating or corresponding motion is reduced in length and in duration. One-handed signs are usually economized into a brief contact or a stop motion that represents merely the onset of the sign; often the succeeding movement pattern is lost. Signs that normally have a circular movement are typically condensed so drastically that the movement is transformed into a brief point in space that suggests the onset of the sign. The ASL compound also discards any repetitious movement associated with the second composite sign, but it retains its average duration of movement.

As a result of such alterations within the movement parameter of a forming compound, the duration of a two-sign compound is typically shorter than the duration of a phrase that contains the same two signs. This shortened time element of motion moves the compound closer to the temporal size of a single sign.

Just as a compound English word can be regarded as a multisyllabic word rather than as a group of words, a compound sign can be regarded as a multiparameter sign and not as a group of signs. The external evidence that a compound sign is a separate semantic entity is that it assumes a new meaning. The internal evidence for compounding is the condensation of its movement parameters to form a new sign articulation.

Transition

The presence or absence of a transition between two signs is a major distinguishing feature between sign phrases and compound signs. The absence of transition clearly identifies a multiparameter sign as a compound. The single-double–handed sign serves well to illustrate the influence of transition on the structure of this particular linguistic arrangement.

In a single-double–handed sign only one hand performs the initial sign, but both hands execute the second sign. An example of a single-double–handed sign phrase is the sequential arrangement of the signs FACE and STRONG. FACE uses only one hand in its formation, but STRONG uses both hands. When these signs are arranged in close proximity to each other, they form the phrase FACE STRONG, which means "a distinguished appearance." The first sign FACE uses only one active hand; the other hand remains in a rest position. (Whenever an initial one-handed sign does not require an active second hand, it either remains at rest or it serves in a supplemental capacity as a locational base for the active hand.) The inactive hand remains at rest until the beginning of the second sign.

But according to Klima and Bellugi (1979), a different pattern occurs when two signs form a compound sign. Within a single-double-handed compound sign, the initial free hand will anticipate its role in the articulation of the second sign, and during the formation of the initial sign it will begin to assume the proper hand formation and palm direction for the second component. This anticipatory maneuver makes the sign appear as if both root components require two hands. Thus, in a single-double-handed compound sign the resting hand moves into place as the base reference earlier than it would in a sign phrase. The effect is a smoothing of the transition into an uninterrupted flowing motion.

This effect is somewhat like the anticipatory action that occurs in spoken English in the process of elision. An example of the single-double-handed compound sign is RESEMBLE, which is derived semantically from the root signs FACE and STRONG. While the active index hand performs a condensed version of the parameters for FACE, the free hand actively anticipates the second sign STRONG by simultaneously forming the initial hand formation of STRONG. This anticipatory action occurs so early that it appears that both signs are using a second hand.

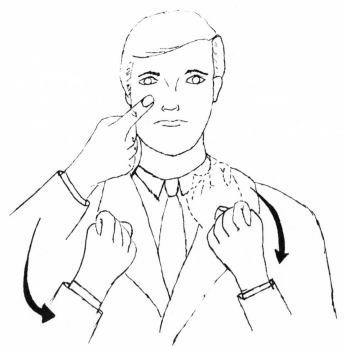

Figure 1. FACE // STRONG, creating the compound RESEMBLE

The final phase of modifying the transition between the root signs is accomplished by physically bonding the two sign components into one uninterrupted pattern by condensing the spatial and temporal movements. The signer reduces the spatial movement in a compound by bringing the two signs physically closer together within the sign field. In other words, the hands are placed closer together than would occur in a sign phrase. Thus the boundaries that define the neutral sign space of a compound sign is more restricted than the neutral sign space of a sign phrase (Klima and Bellugi, 1979).

The example THINK // TOUCH (meaning "keep thinking about") represents a single-double–handed compound sign. If it were a phrase, a single hand would first perform THINK and would then drop down to approximately waist level while changing to the appropriate hand formation for TOUCH. But when these signs are bonded together to form a compound, the base hand used for TOUCH is assumed earlier than in the phrase and is held in place at a relatively higher level than in the phrase, thus noticeably reducing the relative distance the index hand moves from the forehead to the base hand. This proximity strategy allows the initial active hand to begin its articulation and proceed unhindered to the conclusion of the second sign matrix. The combined effect of reducing the spatial distance and maintaining a smooth, continuous transition enhances the bonding of two signs into one. It incorporates certain aspects of both signs into a newly formed movement parameter and establishes its identify as a multiparameter sign.

In another example, ADEQUATE (derived from GOOD // ENOUGH), while the active hand performs the initial one-handed sign, the free hand simultaneously forms the base for the second component. At the same time, the base hand is held relatively close to the body during the articulation of the initial sign component. As the active (open) hand moves down from the mouth, it drops only slightly and finishes by brushing across the base hand. Within a single movement, the hand moves from the mouth, down and across the secondary S hand. This continuous flowing movement conveys further internal evidence of two components forming a singular sign.

Thus, two characteristic traits play major roles in fusing the two root signs into a compounded single sign. First, the movement parameters of the two sign components are integrated into one smooth, continuous parameter. Second, by changing the relative position of the signs the space between the signs and/or hands is reduced. This temporal and spatial compression of selected parameters retains the basic identifiability of each source sign in creating a new compound sign. The following supply further examples of this compounding procedure.

Figure 2. GOOD // ENOUGH, creating the compound ADEQUATE

ASL Compound	Initial Neutral Movement Parameter of Initial Sign	Initial Neutral Movement Parameter in a Compound
TIME // SAME (meaning "simultaneous")	Tap the index hand on the secondary wrist.	Briefly make contact between the single index hand and the secondary wrist and then swing the index around to meet the other index hand (palms down).
TOMORROW // MORNING (meaning "the next morning")	Arc a single A hand in an up-forward-down motion from the side of the face.	Touch cheek with the single A hand and then swing it in a single opening-while-turning motion as it articulates the motion in MORNING along with its base hand.
FACE // STRONG (meaning "resemble")	Use the index hand to describe a large circular motion around the face.	Point the index hand to the face and then move it down while changing to an S hand so that both S hands sign STRONG.

ALL // IN (meaning "everything included")	Swing the open hand forward, across, down and up again around a base hand, eventually making contact with the palm of the base hand.	Swing the open hand forward, across, down and up again while changing it to a compressed O hand. Finish by touching the inner space created by the C base hand.
TALK // NAME (meaning "mention")	Move the W hand (palm sideways) back and forth in front of the mouth.	Begin the W hand in front of the mouth. Move it forward and down while changing to the H hand. Tap the secondary H hand to complete the sign NAME.
THINK // SAME (meaning "agree")	Tap the index hand on the forehead.	Make brief contact between the index hand and the forehead. Then swing it down to meet the other index hand (palms down).

Compounding is a rule-governed process that expands the vocabulary of a language. The newly associated meaning of a compound is distinctive from its source signs, and in many instances is far removed from the literal meaning of its root components. A compound sign that retains an association with its root signs is called a "direct" compound; one that does not is called an "indirect" compound. A direct compound represents a new sign that reflects the essential meaning of its two source signs. An indirect compound creates a new meaning unrelated to the individual meanings of its root components. In other words, the relationship between a direct compound and its root components is transparent; that of an indirect compound is opaque.

The Direct Compound

A direct compound has an immediate association with its source signs. It is a straightforward relationship in which the linear arrangement of the source signs provides substantial insight into the semantic identity of the compound sign. The meanings associated with the signs PAST and NIGHT for instance, provide insight into what the compound means by its linear sequence: PAST // NIGHT meaning "last night." The semantic concept formed in a direct compound is usually directly predictable from the linear arrangement of its original root concepts. Examples of compounds that reflect this direct semantic relationship include COURT // ROOM (meaning "courtroom"), MOTHER // LAW (meaning "mother-in-law") and WATER // MELON (meaning "watermelon"). A direct compound is a rather straightforward lexical item that is relatively easy to interpret once you know the root signs and the sequence. The meaning of the compound is compatible with the literal meaning of the elements combined to form it.

Direct compounds are typically arranged in a logical and semantically accurate sequence. The specific sequence of the root components directly influences the newly formed compound. Combining the signs LIVE and ROOM into the compound LIVE // ROOM (meaning "living room") reflects this sequencing process. In a direct compound, the literal meaning of each root word appears in the same sequence as its meaning is retained in the newly formed compound.

English vocabulary is filled with similar examples of direct compounds such as "guidebook" (a book of information for travelers), "hard-handed" (hands made hard by work), "keyboard" (a board of keys), "meadowland" (land used for a meadow), "ropewalker" (a person who walks on rope high in the air), etc.

Some direct compounds can be translated directly between English and ASL. These include WEEK // END ("weekend"), BLUE // BERRY ("blueberry"), HALL // WAY ("hallway"), MOTOR // BIKE ("motorcycle"), "WASH // ROOM ("bathroom") and SLEEP // ROOM ("bedroom"). But this direct translation does not always work. A literal translation of the components of the English compound "highway" into ASL, for instance, would result in meaningless gibberish. Capturing the essential meaning of English compounds in ASL compounds usually requires paraphrasing.

The Indirect Compound

An indirect compound is a new semantic sign that can not be directly predicted from its source signs. Though it is created by combining two existing signs, it evolves into a completely new sign with a separate semantic meaning, distinctive and independent of its root sources.

The sign phrase WATER SOFT for example, means "soft water." But when these same components are fused together into WATER // SOFT the root concepts that separately mean "a type of liquid" (WATER) and "something that is agreeable to the senses" (SOFT) come to mean WET or MOISTURE. The following indirect compounds illustrate the distinction between the indirect compound sign and its root signs.

Source Signs *of Indirect Compound*	*Essential Compound*
AT // LAST	FINALLY
EAT // MORNING	BREAKFAST
FEMALE // MARRY	WIFE
WILL // WORRY	REGRET
SLEEP // DRESS	PAJAMAS or NIGHT CLOTHES
OFF // WORK	LAID OFF
MIND // FREEZE	SHOCK, STARTLE
BED // SOFT	PILLOW or MATTRESS
GET // UP	RISE
WRONG // HAPPEN	ACCIDENTIAL, INCIDENTAL, BY CHANCE
WHITE // FACE	PALE, DULL
EGG // MIX	SCRAMBLE (eggs)
FINE // WOMAN	LADY
SELL // REDUCE	SALE
MONEY // REDUCE	BARGAIN
COAT // PANTS	SUIT
THRILL // INFORM	ENTERTAINMENT
RED // BERRY	CHERRY
RED // SECRET	STRAWBERRY
LIGHTNING // THUNDER	STORM
GREEN // GROW	GRASS
FOOD // BUY	BUYING GROCERIES
COOK // ROOM	KITCHEN

ASL and English rarely use the same root elements to produce the semantic units expressed by indirect compounds. One language may choose to represent a particular meaning with a compound but the other language will not necessarily represent the same idea in a similar form. An important reason for this is the inherent difference between ASL and English in communicating on varying semantic levels. In an English compound such as "highway" and "blackboard," the meaning is derived by connotation. The English compound "highway" does not literally mean "a high level way." Although there is no mention of a road, "highway" means "a main direct road." Likewise, an English "blackboard" is usually neither black nor made out of sawed lumber.

In American Sign Language, on the other hand, many compounds are based on general concepts and visual perceptions. The indirect compound that represents BRUISE, for instance, is created from the root concepts BLUE and SPOT, BLUE // SPOT. Such a compound holds no linguistic parallel in English. The number code used for mailing purposes, for example, is expressed in English as "zip code." but in ASL, it is expressed by compounding the base signs LETTER and NUMBER (meaning ZIP CODE). The English compound "credit card" refers to a physical card that provides personal identification so that a customer can charge retail items, but in ASL it is expressed as the compound SIGNATURE // REC-TANGULAR. While both English and ASL use compounding, translating from one language into the other depends on paraphrasing so that the semantic essence is transferred.

Another example of ASL compounding occurs when a signer wishes to distinguish a noun or verb from a person, profession, or occupation. There are two basic strategies to convey the concept of a person or occupation. The first method is to use a conventional single sign whose meaning conveys a person, such as DOCTOR, DENTIST, POLICE, and NURSE. But only a few signs exist that represent specific persons or occupations.

The more common method of conveying the concept of a person or occupation is to combine a particular content sign with the PERSON MARKER to form a grammatical compound sign. The PERSON MARKER assumes the position of the second sign and supplies the idea of a person's function, skill, or profession.

PERSON MARKER: HF: both open hands with fingers facing forward
                   PD: facing
                   HP: place heel of the palms at the sides of the body at
                       the chest
                   HM: slide hands down to the waist

When this marker is added to a sign like LEARN or NEAR it creates the corresponding compounds STUDENT (LEARN // PERSON MARKER) and NEIGHBOR (NEAR // PERSON MARKER). All of the basic characteristics of compounding apply. When the initial root sign is a one-handed sign such as AIRPLANE, the second hand, which ordinarily is at rest, anticipates the second sign and assumes its position early. Further, the sign field is restricted to condense the degree of movement. In this case, the compounding produces PILOT (AIRPLANE // PERSON MARKER). The following table demonstrates several of the person compounds formed with the root sign PERSON MARKER.

Content Sign	*Compound Sign*
PSYCHOLOGY // PERSON MARKER	PSYCHOLOGIST
AUDIOLOGY // PERSON MARKER	AUDIOLOGIST
LAW // PERSON MARKER	LAWYER
PLAY // PERSON MARKER	PLAYER
SPEAK // PERSON MARKER	SPEAKER
FARM // PERSON MARKER	FARMER
YOUNG // PERSON MARKER	YOUNGSTER
AMERICA // PERSON MARKER	AMERICAN
SUPERVISE // PERSON MARKER	SUPERVISOR
ADVISE // PERSON MARKER	ADVISOR
JUDGE // PERSON MARKER	JUDGE

VOLUNTEER // PERSON MARKER   VOLUNTEER
SERVE // PERSON MARKER   WAITER/WAITRESS
ACT // PERSON MARKER   ACTOR/ACTRESS

The Evolution of the Compound

Many signers use compound signs every day and are unaware that such signs were once derived from two other root signs. This reflects just how well the compounding process economizes the multiple parts of a two-sign phrase into an single sign—a sign that now has the characteristics of a whole, undivided lexical entity.

A by-product of compounding is the loss of iconicity (see chapter 5). Basically, "iconicity" is the pictorial imagery that conveys a sign's meaning. Iconic signs display their meanings by their obvious visual composition.

A sign receiver needs no specialized knowledge to understand the meaning of an icon. An example of an iconic sign that is understood by virtually anyone is an open hand held outward to mean "stop." Similarly, it takes no special skill to recognize that an index finger held in front of the mouth means "shhh" or "be quiet." Thus the index finger held in front of the mouth is an iconic sign for "quiet."

As more and more compounds are created, the compounding process streamlines. Certain parameters are absorbed—particularly movement and position characteristics. Expressive articulatory traits are altered. Further, the transition between the previous source signs is condensed and then smoothed out to create additional transformation. The result is a fluidity of motion that characterizes the harmonized single sign, as reflected by its synchronized parameters. Thus through the economizing process of compounding, all traces of iconicity of the original signs are eliminated and a new arbitrary form materializes.

Compounding has been an active linguistic process for generations, and it continues today. Compounding is evident in the evolution of many English words. Historically, a compound word begins to emerge when words are first combined to form a two-word phrase (e.g., "drive at," "postal card," "photo finish," "under way"). Eventually the phrase reaches a level of such widespread recognition that it is included and defined in the language's general vocabulary. Over time, the spelling gradually moves from two separate words to hyphenation, regarded as the sign of an early compound (e.g. "drive-in," "post-free," "photo-offset," "under-the-counter"). Finally, the hyphen is dropped and the two words fuse into a single compound word with certain natural changes in intonation (e.g., "driveway," "postmark," "photocopy," "underway").

ASL compounding involves a gradual structural change that

slenderizes the composite of each root component and leads eventually to a single compound sign. According to Klima and Bellugi (1979) the sign IN-FORM illustrates this evolutionary process. In 1920 an ASL signer who wished to convey the idea of "inform" performed the two individual signs KNOW and OFFER sequentially. Gradually, these two signs closed together to become a sign phrase: KNOW OFFER. As the sign phrase became more common, the initial one-handed sign KNOW abbreviated its movement, and the inactive hand began to anticipate its role for the upcoming two-handed sign OFFER. The distinguishing parts of each sign gradually merged together into a harmonious pattern that blended the various parameters into a new single sign. The eventual emergence of the newly formed compound sign INFORM places one hand at the forehead with the other hand held directly below it in neutral space. A single opening motion is simultaneously carried out in which both hands open into the same final configuration reflecting the movement parameter of OFFER. The visual outcome no longer transparently reflects either original source sign.

Figure 3. KNOW // OFFER, creating the compound INFORM

Another example is the evolution of the compound REMEMBER. Historically, REMEMBER was an implied meaning created by executing the single signs KNOW and REMAIN. This combination was effective semantically, so it eventually became the sign phrase KNOW REMAIN. Through time, the movement parameter associated with the open hand of KNOW began to condense until it evolved to a brief contact with the forehead. Anticipating the subsequent sign REMAIN, the initial hand formation of KNOW also began to transform. It dropped the open hand and eventually substituted it with the A hand shape. As the economizing process continued, the A hand came to touch the forehead and then drop downward to tap the other A hand to finish the production of the sign REMAIN. As the two root components merged together into the new single sign, the

Figure 4. KNOW // REMAIN, creating the compound REMEMBER

overall amount of movement systematically decreased into the streamlined compound sign REMEMBER. Today, many students would be hard-pressed to identify the root components of this particular sign.

The articulatory changes that the two-part compound sign undergoes over time begin when two separate signs are gradually paired together into a sign phrase. This sign phrase bonds together to emerge eventually as a new semantic entity. In the case of signs, more than words, compounding prompts a streamlining process in which the original source signs gradually lose identifying characteristics as they transform into a new identity.

The process of compounding provides substantial evidence that ASL (and English, for that matter) is an active, living phenomenon that is constantly striving to create new lexical entities. Compounding has produced such recent signs as DIRTY // AIR (the compound POLLUTION), MACHINE // COPY (the compound XEROX) and PREVENT // CAVITY (the compound FLUORIDE) (Klima and Bellugi, 1979).

Examples of Compound Signs

CARELESS	HF:	primary V hand; fingers upward
	PD:	facing secondary side
	HP:	at primary eye level
	HM:	swing hand across at eye level moving toward the secondary side
		(Comment: swiping a thought away)
HOW // MUCH	HF:	both open C hands
	PD:	both upward
	HP:	chest level
	HM:	move hands downward a short distance while closing into S hands
TOO // MUCH	HF:	both bent hands
(excessive)	PD:	palms facing
(too many)	HP:	fingertips facing; primary fingers behind the secondary fingers, touching at chest level
	HM:	move primary hand up to eye level while keeping secondary hand stationary
LESS // THAN	HF:	both open hands
	PD:	downward
	HP:	place primary hand under the stationary secondary hand, touching at chest level
	HM:	move primary hand down while keeping secondary hand stationary
MORE // THAN	HF:	both open hands
	PD:	down
	HP:	primary hand is on top of stationary secondary hand, touching at chest level
	HM:	move primary hand upward off secondary hand using wrist motion
ALL // GONE	HF:	primary C hand; secondary relaxed open hand
(used up)	PD:	slant primary palm toward secondary side and inward; secondary palm is down
	HP:	chest level; rest primary hand on top of secondary wrist

HM: slide primary C hand forward over the back
of secondary hand while closing into S hand
(Comment: shares certain similar parameters with
the sign EARN)

ALL // RIGHT
(fine)

HF: both open hands
PD: primary facing secondary side; secondary facing upward
HP: stationary secondary hand at chest level
HM: touch secondary thumb with small edge of primary hand, then slide across the secondary palm moving toward the primary side. Finish by sliding upward a short distance.

NO // MATTER
(regardless)
(anyhow)

HF: both relaxed open hands
PD: up
HP: chest level; fingertips facing
HM: move hands alternately up and down while tapping together as they pass by

LET // US // SEE
(I see)
(we will see)

HF: primary V hand
PD: facing secondary side
HP: near primary eye
HM: swing hand forward, back, forward again

NEXT // TURN

HF: "L" hand
PD: palm up (index forward)
HP: waist level
HM: begin with primary hand near primary side and arc up and over toward the secondary side to finish palm down

Training Exercises

A. Match the source signs with the appropriate compound sign.

1. TALK // NAME
2. SLEEP // ROOM
3. LIVE // ROOM
4. KNOW // OFFER
5. ALL // IN
6. FACE // STRONG
7. EAT // NIGHT
8. THINK // SAME
9. EAT // MORNING
10. RED // BERRY
11. SELL // REDUCE
12. OFF // WORK
13. GREEN // GROW
14. FINE // MAN
15. WILL // WORRY

a. AGREE
b. LAID OFF
c. EVERYTHING INCLUDED
d. PAJAMAS
e. LIVING ROOM
f. DINNER
g. MENTION
h. GRASS
i. BEDROOM
j. RESEMBLE
k. BARGAIN
l. REMEMBER
m. REGRET
n. SALE
o. BREAKFAST

16. COAT // PANTS	p. CHERRY
17. MONEY // REDUCE	q. INFORM
18. BED // SOFT	r. MATTRESS
19. KNOW // REMAIN	s. GENTLEMAN
20. SLEEP // DRESS	t. SUIT

B. Determine the conceptual meaning being expressed by the compounded source signs in the following sentences.

1. ME BUY SWIM // CLOTHES
2. JERRY PLAN MEET YOU TIME // FOUR
3. HE PAINT OLD COOK // ROOM
4. YESTERDAY MY YOUNG BOY // SAME OLD // SEVEN
5. NOW // NIGHT WARM
6. YOU MEET MY MALE // MARRY?
7. LEARN YOU OFF // WORK
8. WANT RED // BERRY PIE?
9. ME MIND // FREEZE WHEN HEAR NEWS!
10. PATIENT ILL + WHITE // FACE
11. NANCY BECOME WATER // SOFT IN RAIN
12. LAW // PERSON MARKER LOOK // STRONG MY UNCLE
13. WE NEVER THINK // SAME
14. TERRY GIVE VOLUNTEER // PAPER TO YOUR SISTER
15. YOU KNOW // REMAIN MY NEAR // PERSON MARKER?
16. PAST // WEEK // END ME PAINT MY LIVE // ROOM
17. YOU LOOK STRONG FINE // WOMAN
18. MY NEW JOB ACT // PERSON MARKER
19. ME TALK // NAME YOU MY FRIEND
20. THINK // TOUCH PROBLEM MORE TIME

5. Perceptual Communication

Anytime a native speaker of one language tries to learn a second, foreign language, there is a natural potential for confusion or bilingual interference (Trevoort, 1978). This potential for linguistic confusion reflects the inherent influence of the native language on the acquisition of a second language. Although each language exerts an influence, the relatively stronger effect is usually the native language, which imposes upon the acquisition of the second language. Thus, native English speakers who wish to learn French will experience a strong influence from the linguistic patterns of their native English as they develop mastery of French. Interference is most prevalent when the two languages coexist in the same geographic area. The bilingual environment of Canada, in which both English and French are major languages, exemplifies this cross-over effect.

A native language is intrinsically learned rather than selectively acquired, but the same does not hold true for a second language. It is the conscious attempt at acquisition that promotes the conditions for mutual interference.

In learning ASL as a second language, native English speakers must cope with a predominantly acoustic system intermixing with a predominantly visual system. In addition, these are inherent differences between an orally expressive language that is based on a linear sequencing of sound patterns and a spatial, temporal-oriented language that is based on visual perception. But the most fundamental linguistic difference is the principle processing sense organ: the listening ear versus the seeing eye. A native English speaker who wishes to acquire manual ASL as a second language must consider the potential for bilingual interference.

The basic device that carries information in a language is the lexical unit. When translating from one language to another, the meaning must be translated to the second language. The fact that a particular meaning is coded in one language by means of a particular lexical item (word or sign) does not mean it will necessarily be coded with the same lexical item in the other language. In fact, even if the lexical item seems identical, it is unlikely

83

that both langauges will attach the same explicit meaning to the same linguistic element.

The relationship between signs and words is a major part of the potential environment for bilingual overlapping. A literal translation of the elements of one language into the other language frequently results in semantic nonsense. Content items create few translational problems. For instance, items like "table," "woman," and "rain" are easily translated between English and ASL. But functional or abstract concepts often create crossover difficulties. These arise because the lexical units (signs or words) function differently in the separate grammars of the two languages. In other words, understanding the different patterns of arranging the lexical units in a language is more difficult than understanding a series of lexical items produced in isolation. Because of this, grammatical functioning creates most of the interference and uncertainty in translation (Trevoort, 1978).

Some ASL signs are difficult to translate into English, and some English words do not have a counterpart in ASL signs. Many of the English words that are difficult to translate into ASL are mere idiosyncratic devices that provide only vague grammatical information, but are tailored to the needs of formal English grammar (e.g., the functional verb "be"). Such functional lexical items are more prevalent in oral languages that are based on linear organization, than in languages based on spatial dimension. Because functional words impart no meaning, they are not used in languages whose grammar does not require them.

A lexical item must have a reality-oriented naming role to be represented in ASL. Functional words express no reality-oriented meaning (including, for example, the English articles "a," "an," and "the") and do not exist in ASL. Thus, the inherent differences between the languages makes translation a matter of semantic paraphrasing.

Human Perception and Pattern Recognition

There is a well-accepted premise that language is not understood unit by unit. Comprehension is not accomplished by interpreting each word or sign as it is received. Rather, human perception and memory function through a selective constructive process (Buckout, 1974). Visualizing an object, for example, is accomplished by identifying a few selected characteristics associated with it rather than by compiling an exhaustive list of visual components (e.g., shape, texture, light, color, and depth). Neither sensory perception nor memory functions through direct copying. Instead, perception and memory involve decision making in which the observer as an active rather than a passive agent evaluates fragments of information and then reconstructs them to reach cognitive conclusions.

A house drawn on paper, for instance, is typically represented as a triangular shape resting atop a square with or without a rectangle sticking out of the triangle. Thus, a series of geometrical shapes is used to represent a concrete object, and an abstract design becomes the surrogate for a house. In a graphic metaphor, visual information representing the actual object provides a literal identity. Such visual details as shutters, shingles, bricks, and roof lines are overlooked or regarded as unnecessary for recognition.

The formal educational process used for hearing children is highly systematic. It is based on well-developed strategies for processing, storing, and recalling information. Within this system, perceptual learning develops in an orderly fashion as visual images that are represented in the child's world are gradually replaced with abstract arbitrary representations. The child is encouraged to rely less and less on visual content and to replace them with verbal/auditory associations. Imagination and visual impressions are progressively neglected as learning shifts toward sequential auditory associations. This focus reduces the opportunities for visual-sensory content to develop and grow.

By the time hearing children reach the age of six, they are able to articulate their feelings and wishes in intelligible English. This spoken channel is nurtured and practiced every day in school. But proportionately few hearing teachers rely heavily on drawings, blackboard writings, or other visual displays to communicate information, and relatively few occasions exist during the educational years that promote visual learning. Enmired in this system, hearing children gradually lose all motivation to continue to cultivate a visual-gestural means of communicating information (Hoemann, 1978).

Hearing children learn to express themselves in speech from their very earliest years. As time passes, they find that spoken English provides a practical medium for conveying internal ideas and experiences. Because speech is ordinarily learned earlier than reading (Mattingly, 1972), hearing children learn to communicate and receive information verbally and auditorily before developing the same competence visually. Through the years, the speech process shapes the "appearance" and establishes the preferred medium of communication. As the connection between appearance and linguistic representations grows, the range of perceptions and associated meanings grows also and becomes habitual.

Lexical units, regardless of how they are transmitted (orally, manually, or written), are basically codes that trigger selected primary sensory systems and in turn stimulate certain images or learned associations. But a word or sign that has never been previously encountered will have no meaning because the receiver has no earlier sensory experience to apply to it. As experience in hearing and speaking develops in hearing persons, it prepares them to respond more confidently to future vocalized communications, but also makes it more unlikely that they will be able to communicate effectively in a visual medium.

This pattern of separation between the visual and auditory modes is further reinforced by the writing/reading process. A hearing child who is learning to read intrinsically learns to transfer the learned auditory sounds of the language into visual symbols that represent the same auditory signals graphically (Mattingly, 1972). For hearing children, learning to read is not a new learning process, but an extension of the auditory association process already understood and practiced daily.

Hearing persons can and do develop visual perception. Studies conducted on the efficiency of learning processes have found hearing people will recall sentences with strong images more accurately than sentences composed of weak, obscure images. Ideas high in imagery (e.g., "desk," "sunset," "ocean") are remembered substantially longer than abstract ideas (e.g., "hope," "certainty," and "situation"). This type of visual perception is based on a relationship between relative "appearance" and its associated meaning. Visual imagery allows the perceiver to link appearance and meaning directly. Over time, this linking of sensory patterns can habituate into a spontaneous communicative pathway.

Forming a mental image of something or someone is not new to most people. It is the most widely used method of duplicating one form of an experience into another form, regardless of the person's hearing status. To recall a pleasant memory such as a vacation, you mentally recreate the event. Forming mental images is a type of imitation made possible through perception. To recall a past event you form an image that contains certain essential features of the earlier experience. But since this image is a perceptual re-creation, it takes on a somewhat different form. The mental image is only a partial duplication, but it leads to an internal representation of something or someone.

Communication is received and eventually understood through sensory perception. Processing lexical units (words or signs) is a three-stage process. First, you gather input by collecting information. Next, you examine the input and search for meaning. Finally you process the input through perceptual channels, which leads to interpretation and eventual understanding. The primary sensory channels represent the pathways of processing communication.

The sentences of a language can be viewed as descriptions of scenarios (Norman, 1972). Sentence comprehension is a matter of identifying the action, the various roles of the actors, the location, and the time of the action. Thus, the listener or reader of a sentence fits the various pieces of information together to form a mental image and comprehend the sentence.

Consider the following sentence: "Peering around the corner of the old red wood barn, I could see the brown and white puppy dog comfortably sleeping in the tall green grass." What image did you form to process the above sentence? Many persons mentally see themselves peering around the corner of a barn to view a brown and white dog lying down.

Now consider the sentence fragment, "The little girl with blonde hair bent down and kissed...." You may have been forming an image around a little girl, but the scenario was abruptly disrupted. The idea of "kissed" was defined by the context as an action. But as an action, it requires completion: someone or something must be kissed. As it stands, the sentence is incomplete. It lacks a necessary receiver of the action.

These two examples illustrate that processing language involves both receiving the input and re-creating the scenario by putting the bits of information together in a meaningful way. When a key element of information is missing, comprehension is disrupted because a complete image cannot form in the receiver's mind. It is only when the missing element is supplied that the complete meaning forms: "The little girl with blonde hair bent down and kissed her new teddy bear."

Most grammatical rules in a language serve as a mechanism to assist the receiver of the discourse in better understanding how each semantically meaningful part of the sentence contributes to form an appropriate scenario. Although every language represents the various sentential components differently, the communication process remains essentially the same. Communicators mentally formulate a series of ideas they wish to make known. They then translate these mental thoughts into symbols (words or signs) that others can understand. Next, they arrange these symbols and express them in a sequential series. Receivers in turn make sense of the symbols sent by reconstructing an internal image that is similar to the original image intended by the senders. If the mental images of sender and receiver match relatively well, communication has occurred.

There is a good deal of evidence that the meaning of a sentence will remain essentially the same whether it is conveyed visually or verbally. In other words, meaning is separate from the code system used to convey it.

Perceptual Preference

The dominant perceptual systems are vision, audition, and to a lesser degree, kinesthesis (body sensations). When a person forms a mental image, the type of image formed depends in part on whether the person is oriented predominately visually, auditorily, or kinesthetically. Some persons tend to interpret information mentally in visual images and thus are referred to as "visualizers." Others tend to interpret information by creating mental auditory images and hence are referred to as "auralizers." A few persons prefer to interpret incoming information by creating tactile images, relying on "gut" feelings. However, tactile imaging is rare. A sensory preference is the sensory channel that is habitually used to interpret experiences. How well you incorporate a new visual communication code into your existing verbal modality will depend to some degree on whether you are a visualizer or an auralizer.

Visualizers find making pictures in their mind naturally easy and they use this strategy routinely. Many hearing persons frequently use visual imagery, but the practice is not as common as it is among the hearing impaired. Visualizers have well-developed visual-imagery capabilities, and they tend to approach events spatially rather than in linear, step-by-step fashion. The visual images they create are rich in detail, texture, and symbolism and are often in color. As they read written material, for instance, they form various different mental pictures in their minds, triggered by the printed words. The visual image system is most responsive to processing tangible information that can be organized spatially. A good visualizer learns to recall details accurately. A visualizer can create a mental scene with vivid clarity. In fact, the visualizer tends to picture the entire scene and then read off the details. The absolute representation of a visualizer is a person with a "photographic memory."

In contrast, an auralizer prefers to form auditory images. As auralizers read written material, they tend to hear their own voice inside their heads saying the words as their eyes report the visual patterns formed by what is read. Auralizers can mentally hear previous conversations as if they were listening to a tape recording, and they can hear music played back in their minds. A good auralizer can replay conversations held months, if not years, earlier. But auralizers do not hear "other voices." Rather, they have a well-honed memory ability and can recall auditory experiences accurately and vividly. Auralizers are very good at processing information through verbal association. This process is best suited for abstract material that can be organized sequentially. Auralizers internally "say" each word (heard or read) to themselves for comprehension. This occurs as if the auralizer was relaying the message to a third person.

Auralizers tend to write letters by reading the words out loud as they write, or they repeat each word internally. Thus, the auralizer mentally translates the printed words into internally spoken words. This acoustical representation is also what enables an auralizer to read (Norman, 1972). Auralizers write letters in a conversational style, as opposed to visual thinkers, who tend to write in a more formal style.

A nonvisual imager tends to think in association. Weak visualizers are notoriously poor at recalling or describing faces. Lacking a mental picture, these persons tend to remember only generalized details such as gender, approximate height, weight, hair color, or outstanding features. Nonvisualizers seldom remember dreaming in pictures. Their communication style emphasizes words, generalities, and abstractions. In their thinking, they talk to themselves rather than creating or combining mental pictures.

There are studies that show that the degree of relative learning depends in part on the amount of sensory content and in what form it is presented. Learning is likely to occur faster and is remembered more easily when information is rich in sensory content. Furthermore, a person who can see the actual object to be remembered is more likely to remember it than a person who sees only a picture of an object. Likewise, a person who can see a picture of the object is more likely to remember it than someone who sees only the written name for the object. The least effective learning process is when the person sees only the written name of an abstract concept.

Whether a person is predominantly a visualizer or an auralizer is dictated by how that person routinely processes information. But few persons are exclusively visualizers or auralizers. Your auditory sense for instance, does not stop functioning while you are reading a book. While all of the human senses process information at any given point in time, the dominant perceptual system momentarily holds the highest signal value and gives the "prime attention" to a particular experience.

Preference of one sensory channel over the others is a fundamental characteristic of an individual's communication style. But when the communication pathway is represented exclusively by visual input, there is no auditory contribution. How well a hearing person will adapt to exclusively visual conditions depends in part on his or her ability to develop some of the characteristics of a visualizer.

When hearing persons learn American Sign Language, they must often change their dominant processing channels. When a person who has been an auralizer elects to concentrate on a strictly visual task, a dual processing phenomenon occurs that is referred to as synesthesia. "Synesthesia" occurs when incoming information triggers the processing sensations within two of the major senses with equivalent effect. An example of synesthesia is when you remember what it looks like to be on top of a mountain and can feel yourself skiing down it. The pattern is simultaneously visual and tactile. Another example of visual-tactile synesthesia is when you visually imagine some favorite food such as a juicy steak or spicy spare ribs being prepared and at the same time begin to develop a hearty appetite. When the image is truly vivid, you might even smack your lips in anticipation.

Synesthesia constitutes a substantial portion of the meaning-making process. When a hearing ASL student begins to visualize language after learning through a lifetime of experience to process such linguistic information auditorily, the combined overlapping of sensory information can lead to the development of auditory-visual synesthesia. Auditory-visual synesthesia might occur when you hear music while visually imagining a band playing, or listen to the sound of the ocean's surf and visualize being on a beach. Likewise, visual-auditory synesthesia occurs if you see a picture of a loved one and mentally recall the person speaking. Synesthesia is a dual-processing phenomenon in which one sense seems to trigger another sense so that both sensory channels actively process the input in their own individual manners.

When hearing ASL students communicate through a visual language, they may experience an inherent desire to vocalize internally what is seen. Such a dual means of processing information can serve as a helpful communication strategy. Internal vocalizing reflects the habitual nature of an auralizer. Dual processing makes understanding signs less difficult for auralizers because they are still using their dominant processing channel as part of the communicative operation.

Memory and Signing

Research has shown that the visual-gestural system that forms the structural basis of ASL exhibits the same two-level system of communication used in spoken languages. First, there is a "surface level," which refers to the specific way that signs are bound together to form sentences (the grammatical level). Second, there is a "psychological level," which refers to the cognitive processing of meaning derived from the symbolic patterning (the semantic level). While ASL shares certain underlying principles of organization with spoken English, manual and oral languages represent very different pathways along the modality of communication. In spoken language, verbal patterns make up words, which are composed of sequentially produced sounds, each representing a unit of meaning. In contrast, signs are composed of contrasting formational manual parameters in which the sign and its inflection occur simultaneously (Bellugi, 1980).

The parameters of hand formation, palm direction, hand position, and hand movement collectively represent the linguistic description or properties of a sign. Within these properties are found evidence of metaphoric, iconic, and arbitrary components. A sign's symbolic elements are combined through parameters in orderly and constrained ways, governed linguistically by the phonology of the language. But these same properties also serve to provide the semantic information necessary for understanding. On the psychological level, a reader processes the sign's symbolism in order to comprehend its meaning, but the symbolism is created by the formation and interpretation of the sign parameters. The morphological structure of the language makes possible a wide range of semantic interpretations.

In terms of comprehending an ASL sentence's information and in retaining it, are ASL sentences processed differently than spoken English sentences? In experimentation with English, researchers have found that hearing persons rely very little on grammatical structure for anything beyond basic comprehension. In other words, hearing persons tend to rely on grammatical words order to understand discourse, but not necessarily to retain the information. Apparently, sentence structure exerts little influence on how a hearing individual stores information in memory.

Hanson and Bellugi (1982) studied a group of deaf adults whose native language was American Sign Language to determine how signers retained information in long-term memory — according to its grammatical structure or by some other process. They found that signers relied on the grammatical structure for comprehension, but not as a vehicle to remember its content. Long-term memory was based instead on a cognitive process that was independent of both the sign order and the holistic sign formation. Although the meaning derived from a sentence was retained, it was not retained in the exact grammatical pattern that it was received.

Thus, similar to English hearing/speaking persons, deaf adults rely on grammatical order to understand a message, but not to retain its information. The primary function of a grammatical sentence is communication of its semantic interpretation. And after information is understood and extracted from a sentence, the sentence no longer serves any purpose. A person will remember the essential meaning with little regard for the original sentence's morphological or syntactical composition. Both hearing and deaf persons seem to use a similar independent process for remembering information. Although cognitive operations may take place along different sensory perceptual pathways, hearing and deaf persons exhibit many similarities in the manner that they use to process information.

Iconic Language

Since sign language is a visual phenomenon, there is natural tendency to raise some questions about the role of iconicity. "Iconicity" is a relationship that compares some aspect(s) of a sign and some aspect(s) of its referent so that it can be recognized and interpreted (Battison, 1974). An iconic sign mimics what it represents so well that a receiver can readily understand what it means without possessing any special training or knowledge. An iconic sign draws a recognizable parallel between the sign and the real world. This relationship is so straightforward that if all signs were purely iconic in origin and design, they could not function in the capacity of a natural language. This is why the issue of iconicity in ASL is so important.

An icon is an image that establishes a pictorial relation to a subject, object, or event. A statue of Abraham Lincoln, for instance, is an icon of the late president. An encircled "P" with a slanted line through it has become an icon for "No parking" and a blinking red light is an icon for "Warning, danger."

As it applies to sign formation, iconicity implies that each sign represents something by pictorial description. An iconic sign consists of a set of parameters that together form a visual display of the associated concept. The parameters of an iconic sign are specifically arranged to reproduce the object visually. The outcome of such real-world visual representation is that any casual observer or nonsigner should be able to interpret signs.

The issue of whether American Sign Language is an iconic communication system is rooted in the fact that ASL is visual and pictorial by nature. Since hand formation and hand movement is the dominant means of expression, ASL is susceptible to claims of pure iconicity. It is true that some ASL signs are iconic. The sign DRINK, for instance, is based on the action of drinking. Another reason that some consider ASL an iconic system is the common practice of introducing new signs to students by relating a story of those signs might have originated. The sign GIRL, for example, has been explained by many stories pertaining to its origin. One story is that GIRL originated as the visual representation of the strings of a bonnet. Another story suggests that the visual traits of GIRL represent the smooth skin of the female gender. In a similar search for origins, the sign BOY has been explained as a visual representation of the visor of a cap. It is not important whether such explanations hold any truth or are just the result of someone's perceptual imagination. The important point is that such a practice tends to encourage the viewpoint that ASL might be an iconic code system. Though this viewpoint will probably continue, it is equally plausible to argue that these descriptions of the origins of signs have little to do with iconicity. Rather, they serve simply as a memory-enhancing strategy, a visual "cue" to help students to remember particular signs.

If ASL is in fact an icon system, then signs must be reasonably transparent. "Transparency" of a sign relates to how easily a sign is recognized and understood by an untrained observer. In other words, the meaning of a sign must be readily apparent to an observer who has no formal or informal background in sign interpretation. Just as someone can recognize a statue as representing Abraham Lincoln or a raised index finger held in front of the mouth to mean "quiet," an iconic sign must be equally easily recognized and interpreted. If a sign is truly iconic, it ought to be sufficiently transparent that a nonsigner who sees the sign for the first time can adequately and with reasonable accuracy understand its meaning.

While American Sign Language does take advantage of its inherent ability to depict recognizable associations visually, there is no convincing research to support the contention that an untrained observer can interpret the signs of an ASL sentence reasonably accurately. Iconicity in ASL appears to be confined to a limited number of signs, each typically expressed in isolation. Thus, though some iconic elements serve well as a part of the visual nature of ASL, they do so in an overall environment of abstract symbolism.

Even iconic ASL signs must be considered visual analogues that are governed linguistically by the language (Page, 1985). An icon cannot, for instance, alter or disrupt the syntactic or morphological content of an ASL sentence without destroying its intelligibility (Klima and Bellugi, 1979). Similarly, iconicity cannot so influence a sign's articulation that it violates the phonological matrix of allowable sign characteristics. Though a signer will modify the size of the hands, for example, to visually depict a TALL GLASS versus a SHORT GLASS, these iconic elements are constrained linguistically and spatially.

Another convincing argument that ASL signs are not pure icons is that ASL communicates in sentences. A language made up of purely iconic signs would produce each sign as an isolated entity. Sentence construction would not be possible.

But within the sentential environment of ASL, the sign experiences changes that reflect its relation to other lexical units as they are arranged in sequential patterns. Signs in sentences are distinguishable from the same signs produced individually. Such distinctions are a result of the changes required to create smooth transitions between signs, deletions and insertions, and the inherent need for simplification of manual-visual signals in a rapid and flowing context.

Furthermore, while such signs as PIE, EAR, EYE, and EAT each have some iconic characteristics, certain English words also bear iconic auditory resemblances to their associated concepts. Such onomatopoeic words as "roar," "hoot," "squeak," "slurp," "swish," "crack," and "crash" all exemplify an iconic auditory association.

When a person has no prior knowledge of ASL, a sign typically has little if any transparency. Transparency seems to be more often a post-understood phenomenon (Hoemann, 1978). After ASL students learn what a sign means they can sometimes pick out some aspect of its fundamental reference and make a visual association. But for most signs, it is virtually impossible to predict in advance which aspect (if any) of a referent will serve to represent that concept in the sign's composition. American Sign Language relies on a variety of different aspects to represent meaning, and this natural variation is sufficiently arbitrary that most ASL signs are completely opaque to the novice observer. A sign's visual resemblance can range from an entire object being visually represented (e.g., AIRPLANE) to only a partial representation of the whole (e.g., CAR) or no resemblance at all (e.g., WHAT).

Iconicity versus Metaphor

An icon is a pictorial image that represents a concept in a relatively direct way. To communicate an idea iconically, a person must use obvious pictures that illustrate the idea in a graphically vivid way. The essence of such a pictorial representation is to convey a meaning through its exact, explicit image. If American Sign Language were a truly iconic language, it would deal only with direct, specific meaning and eschew implied or associated meaning.

But iconicity is only one way to communicate meaning. Another way is to communicate through metaphor, a figure of speech in which one symbol is expressed as if it were another. Metaphoric communication expresses an idea by replacing its literal representation with words or signs that suggest a likeness or analogy. Metaphoric communication is a way of communicating through resemblance and similarity. It is a method of expressing an idea by comparing it point by point with something else.

It is well known that a sign can convey more than the meaning or concept it explicitly names or describes. ASL's rich metaphoric characteristics can assist the student in both learning and interpreting visual information accurately. Imagine a hand formation consisting of two extended fingers that form the V hand with the palm and the two fingers facing down. In this position, the hand metaphorically resembles a pair of legs. The metaphor of little legs is an effective mnemonic device to remember such associated signs as STAND, MOUNT (horse), LIE-DOWN, and DANCE. Similarly, a bending action to the V hand effectively differentiates such signs as KNEEL and JUMP.

The reason such visual associations are regarded as metaphoric and not iconic is that such analogies require a brief explanation. A V hand held with the palm down for example may not be readily recognizable as two legs. But once the analogy is established, the idea of legs can then serve a useful purpose of association.

A signer can use metaphoric strategies to incorporate the concepts of size and shape into the spatial dimensions of signs. If you analyze all the analogous variations of a sign you will probably identify some fundamental characteristic that agrees with its representative concept, at least partially. A sign such as WINDOW is articulated in its neutral form by first bringing both open hands together (primary atop secondary). The palms are oriented inward while the hands are held at chest level. The hands vertically separate, pause, and then return to the original position. Metaphorically, the sign WINDOW can be considered as a visual representation of a double-hung window. But this same composition might equally conceivably remind someone of a freight elevator, a cutting machine, or a camera shutter. The number of possible interpretations contradicts the definition of an icon since different perceptions may suggest different meanings.

Metaphorically, visual associations can also be represented by movements. Returning to the sign WINDOW, when the hands initially are separate (primary is held above the secondary hand) and the active (primary) hand drops down to meet the stationary (inactive) hand, the movement creates the metaphorical meaning WINDOW // CLOSE. An opposite movement in which the hands begin together, followed by the active hand rising vertically upward a short distance changes the sign's meaning to WINDOW // OPEN.

Metaphoric representation is intertwined throughout ASL vocabulary. A sign's manner of delivery can represent shape and size. The signs TALL GLASS and SMALL GLASS are differentiated by relative vertical movements, and the signs SMALL BOX and LARGE BOX are differentiated by relative degrees of horizontal movement. Similarly, hand shapes can act as metaphors for different forms of visual analogies. The open hand, for example, is associated with such objects as a plate, a bed, or any flat surface. The curved hand, associated with some kind of group, creates the foundation for signs like JOIN or QUIT. Consider, too, the metaphoric association between wiping the forehead and the sign FORGET.

There is a meaningful perceptual association between many ASL signs and their meanings. Visual representation can often connect a sign metaphorically with its fundamental semantic concept. The sign CAR, for instance, is associated to the basic movement and hand position of a steering wheel. The sign UMBRELLA resembles the action of opening an umbrella. Sign parameters can often be regarded as general formations that resemble the associated physical objects that the signs represent. Although a sunset and an arm in a horizontal position have little in common, after a person learns to view the arm as a metaphorical sunset, it is easier to understand a series of time-oriented signs like MORNING, NOON, and NIGHT.

According to Stokoe (1965), ASL signs can be subdivided into six classes based on their representational articulation. The first group comprises "pantonymic" signs, which derive their semantic value by visually reenacting their meanings. Pantonymic signs are generally action verbs such as READ, DRINK, and WATER. Many sport concepts are also expressed as pantonymic signs including SWIM, TENNIS, and FOOTBALL. The second group, the "imitative" signs, reflect an essential feature of their related action or objects. In imitative signs, a part of an object or action serves as a reference for the whole. The grinding action associated with the sign COFFEE exemplifies such a partial representation. Similarly, signs like CAR, DOOR, and TREE use a partial aspect to represent a larger whole concept. A third group, "metonymic" signs, are similar to imitative signs in the sense that both sign groups incorporate a single aspect of a concept to represent the whole. But unlike imitative signs, metonymic signs incorporate a lesser or unessential aspect of the whole concept. The sign HOUSE, which is composed of metaphoric parameters that represent the shape of a roof, exemplifies this group. Other metonymic signs are PIE, FAMILY, and COLLEGE.

In each of the first three sign groups, a characteristic is used to depict a concrete concept. These signs tend to preserve some mimic or metaphoric association with its referent actions and objects.

Stokoe's remaining three classes of signs are oriented to arbitrary expressions. The fourth group consists of "indicative" signs. Indicative signs are not actually formal signs, but instead are a series of predetermined indexing motions used to represent such concepts as self, personal pronouns, and parts of the body. Indicative signs include ME, YOU, HE, WE, and THEY. The fifth group includes all initialized signs. Such signs use the first letter of the English word that best represents its core concept as the initial hand formation of the sign. PEOPLE, GROUP, RESTAURANT, and WATER each use the initial letter of the corresponding English word ("P," "G," "R," "W," respectively) as the initial hand formation. The sixth and last group consists of "name" signs. Name signs are informal, personal signs that are created by a particular individual to represent a specific person or place. The signs PITTSBURGH and NEW YORK are typical name signs. These signs may be derived by any of the above strategies or be created by strictly arbitrary means.

Recent evidence has identified other classes of signs. Such signs as SCISSORS reflect what the concept does. Other signs, such as PHONE, reflect what one does with the referent concept (Hoemann, 1978).

ASL communicates through the visual pathway. To accomplish the goal of visual communication, it uses any strategy that will assist in conveying meaningful communications. Such strategies include iconicity, pantomime, and metaphoric expression. However, ASL signs are inherently constrained both spatially and linguistically. Like a word, a sign can be disassembled into its own definable set of distinguishing components (Klima and Bellugi, 1979).

An Evolution of Movement

The origin of American Sign Language is in part a matter of speculation. It is reasonable, however, to speculate that many signs may have originated from icons. Many newly created signs may have originated in mimesis. Such signs expressed the intended idea so well that the reader without special knowledge or training was able to accurately interpret them. But if all signs were born as icons, generating them must have been quite time consuming. Reproducing an idea like "store," for example, would have entailed an elaborate imitation. As a method of day-to-day communication such iconic signs would have been both time consuming and cumbersome. To convey each referent idea would require a good deal of effort, not to mention the mental effort and fatigue in reading them.

Signers who had to rely on this cumbersome way of gesturing thoughts would undoubtedly have been frustrated by the ineffectiveness and linguistic limitations of the system. Thus, visual communication must have been extremely tedious in its early years.

But as years passed and these visual, iconic patterns were handed down through the generations, individuals discovered different ways to stylize and abbreviate the cumbersome, time-consuming iconic gestures. Prompted by such needs as time-efficient communication and a consistent standard of consistency among signers, the system developed into an efficient language. Many historical changes also came about due to the physical dynamics of the production apparatus, the human body (Battison, 1974).

Signs evolved in a three-phrase process (Mayberry, 1964). In the first phase, signs were generally in a pantomime form. This first phase was motivated by the inherent need of hearing-impaired people to communicate in a channel other than hearing and speech. During the imitative phase, signers developed a primary gestural system that was passed down from one generation of hearing-impaired persons to the next.

Years later, the language evolved into a second phrase, in which imitation gradually transformed into stylized communication. During this stage, signs became more streamlined and less awkward to repeat. Unnecessary components or movement were dropped as the lexical signs begin to be formalized. During this second period of stylized change, certain modifications created new signs while simplifying existing ones. Two, three, and even four separate movement signs were gradually reduced to one or two movements.

As the evolution continued, it reached a final phase in which the language transformed to arbitrary symbols. Inherent pressures and demands to communicate efficiently and succinctly led to a refinement of signs that continues today. This evolution takes its own course of development, as does the evolution of all autonomous languages (Hanson and Bellugi, 1982).

Within the evolution of a sign, it undergoes a form of metamorphosis. Beginning as an elaborate imitation of the visual characteristics of an idea as it is acted out, it streamlines as the physical actions or gestures are repeated over and over again with increasing consistency. This streamlining gives the sign form. As the repeated actions continue, certain unnecessary movements are eventually discarded, and the streamlined action soon becomes recognizable as an abbreviated idiomatic pattern that is associated with a certain semantic understanding. As the process continues, the sign transforms further into a highly efficient, arbitrary set of articulated parameters that always produces the same semantic understanding.

Each change in the articulation of a sign is guided by the principles of perception and production as applied to interpersonal communication. The physical refinement of a sign progressively abbreviates its articulation by eliminating the low perceptual characteristics while retaining the high perceptual elements. Cumbersome movement is replaced with operational precision. The evolution of a sign from pantomime through the various stages of economized movement and standardization of form is usually rather predictable. Information tends to be concentrated in the hands rather than the hands and the body. Information tends to be drawn close to the center of the sign field. Finally, information tends to condense into one hand, but if both hands are involved, the sign tends to be articulated symmetrically.

Since the focal center of signing is the facial region, the area that borders the face represents the peripheral field of signs. To compensate for their lessened focus, peripheral signs tend to use both hands, which adhere to identical patterns. Identical movement parameters make signs easier to produce and easier to read. As signs continue to evolve, those that once occupied the side of the body tend to move toward the center of the sign space.

Though the evolution of signs toward arbitrary symbolism continues, it does not influence all signs equally. To this day, certain signs retain remnants of the essence of their original imitative forms. The shape of a house roof (HOUSE), the action of opening a door (DOOR), the cover of a book (BOOK), or the opening and closing of a window (WINDOW) continue to reflect pantomimes of these objects. Within these remaining visual cues, we can still find iconic traces to the past. There is evidence that the evolution of signs is an on-going process and that signs continue to move actively further away from recognizable iconic depictions, and toward less recognizable but more time-efficient representations.

Training Exercises

A. Are you a visualizer or an auralizer? To find out, take a moment to readjust your posture so that you are quite comfortable. When you close your eyes, imagine as vividly as possible the color and pattern of the interior of your car. Make an internal picture of the seat, the steering wheel and the dash board in your mind's eye to find the answers. Are the doors open? Can you clearly see the windows in your image? Take a few moments to sharpen your mental picture. Go ahead.

Now take a few deep breaths. This time recall the voice of a close friend that you haven't been around for a while. In your mind, listen to his or her pitch, the tonal qualities and tempo of the voice when s/he speaks. Can you recall something specific your friend said and can you hear the words as if your friend were saying them now?

If you found forming the image of your car easier than rehearing a familiar voice, you are likely a visualizer. And if hearing the voice was easier, you are probably an auralizer.

Under the appropriate conditions, even so-called nonimagers can produce visual and auditory images. The capability reflects a practiced effort of reviving sensory experience. The determining factor is not so much whether you can think visually, for there is good evidence that indicates you are capable. Rather, it is a matter of how much attention you pay to such images, and how much effort you expend to practice building visual skills.

B. Nearly all persons can develop their ability to form a visual image. Practice your visual imagery by striving to form a mental picture of the following words. Next, using your visual images, link the pictures together.

   Example: walk, lion, coat, ice cream

Linked together: You might visually imagine someone walking along a sidewalk while enjoying an ice cream cone when suddenly a lion jumps out forcing him to drop his coat.

   1. cup, cola, rope, tulip, pillow
   2. skip, blue, window, crash, sugar
   3. recline, thirst, monkey, sun, green
   4. money, wrench, stroll, pocket, heart
   5. swim, dog, cards, bed, nose
   6. sky, foot, milk, appointment, shower
   7. swallow, skate, neighbor, dessert, desk
   8. office, dress, sausage, jump, newspaper
   9. nap, shoes, steak, store, rose
   10. order, baby, garage, write, train

C. Use a watch with a second hand, and in one minute try to memorize as many words from list 1 that you can. When one minute elapses, turn the list over, wait forty seconds. Now write down as many of the words you can recall. Now repeat the task with each remaining list.

| LIST 1: | unit | attempt | weight | lean | worry | theory | arrive |
| | ask | certain | mention | | element | thing | |

| LIST 2: | sunset | waterfalls | eagle | blue | tire | door |
| | diamond | roses | desk | blush | moon | boulder |

| LIST 3: | strain | need | plan | low | keep | near | code |
| | quality | gradual | sort | particular | matter | |

LIST 4: piano   cry   engine   ring   bark   shout   clang
        horn   tree   crisp   rain   drums

Check your results. If you scored highest on List 2, you have strong visual capabilities. If you scored highest on List 4, you have strong auditory-imagery skills. Sensory-oriented words (Lists 2 and 4) are usually much easier to remember than abstract words (Lists 1 and 3), which rely on a verbal association without a corresponding sensory symbol.

Part 2
Understanding ASL's Linguistic Structure

Years ago, many believed that American Sign Language (ASL) had no homogeneous uniformity and that it was not a well-ordered system. But in recent years evidence has continuously shown that ASL is in fact a highly elaborate and fully expressive language whose structure is determined in part by the articulating dynamics of the body. Research has also shown that ASL's sign patterns are anything but random. ASL's grammatical relations of sign order, together with its grammatically functioning facial and body behavior, operates systematically and uniformly (Liddell, 1978; Supalla and Newport, 1978; Liddell, 1980).

Part 2 investigates ASL syntax: the ways that ASL arranges its signs, the sentence patterns it creates, and the characteristics that differentiate each sentence pattern. Collectively these chapters provide a versatile overview of ASL syntax and describe how a signer intermixes various sentence types during discourse.

It will become apparent that American Sign Language does not adhere as stringently to a linear sequential structure as does English. ASL does have both form and sequential patterning, but its distinctive feature lies in its successful mingling of linear sign order and simultaneous expression through the use of spatial and movement dimensions. To maintain a necessary degree of latitude and flexibility, ASL uses guidelines rather than rigid rules.

Understanding ASL syntax begins with the study of basic sentence patterns and then builds progressively. This book makes every effort to clarify its linguistic composition. It presents the material in ordinary language, avoiding technical jargon wherever possible. To maximize your learning, you should study the chapters in order, since each chapter lays the groundwork for the next. When you complete your study of these chapters, you will have acquired the necessary skills and knowledge to enable you to explore further the many variations, mechanisms, and strategies that collectively make up American Sign Language.

101

6. The Basic Structure

While a single sign in isolation is capable of communicating meaning, its greater contribution occurs when it is part of a sentence that expresses a complete thought. In everyday conversation, true communication of meaningful information occurs within the context of the sentence. Communication depends not just on the selection of signs, but also on how well each sign forms a part of an integrated whole.

The sentence is the basic vehicle of communication. Its components are so interrelated that one element may affect the form or occurrence of another element. "Sentence" can be defined as a relationship among components in which the meanings of individual units interact with one another in such a way as to convey a whole thought. A sentence represents something more than just the sum total of the meanings of its lexical units (words or signs). Sentential meaning is richer than the meanings of each individual component.

A sentence conveys a complete thought, however, only when it is understood by others. And its meaning will be understood only when the signer chooses signs appropriately and puts them into the correct order or visual matrix. The relationship of signs within a sentential framework and the linguistic strategies that these relationships express are referred to as "syntax." The syntax of American Sign Language involves strategies of sign selection, sign formation, and methods of incorporating semantic variations as conveyed in sentential constructions.

Basic Elements

ASL grammatically constrains sign order within a sentence. This constrained framework reduces potential confusion by establishing structural guidelines that define intelligible sentence patterns from meaningless strings of signs. Sign order in ASL is constrained by two major principles: first, by how the signs are arranged within the sentence; and second, by the delivery of that sentence. Sign order provides a means to determine who the subject is and what the action is. It offers a way to know "who" is doing "what" and "to whom."

102

ASL's syntactic structure allows several ways to arrange subjects, verbs, and objects. But according to Fischer (1975), the underlying structure of ASL is based on subject-verb-object (SVO) order. This sequence occurs more frequently in sentences containing a noun-transitive verb-noun sequence (Liddell, 1980). "Transitive verbs" are verbs that require an object to create a complete thought (e.g., "He received the notice.").

Whether SVO order is the basic sign order of ASL or only one of several major patterns is not the issue here. ASL does have a variety of sentence patterns, but the three major parts of speech, the subject, verb, and object, do serve as fundamental elements within the sentence order in ASL, and they will serve as our starting point.

A fundamental linguistic purpose of any sentence is to indicate the relationship between the action (verb) and its referents (person, place, or thing). A basic sentence usually consists of two or three major parts of speech. First, a "subject," which represents the principle focus of attention. While the concept of subject is handled differently in ASL than in English, one similarity is that in both languages the subject provides the sentence's principle focus. The subject is what the sentence is usually about, the dominate idea that is being talked about.

Once the theme or subject is established, related comments follow that describe the action and associated referents. The second major sentence component is the "verb," which makes some statement about the subject matter. The verb describes the action or happening of the sentence. The action can be an abstract (e.g, THINK, FEEL, KNOW) or a concrete action (e.g. WALK, PULL, SWIM). A major difference between ASL and English is that English always requires a subject and a verb to create a well-formed sentence, and ASL does not. Certain well-formed ASL sentences do not require a verb, and other sentence patterns do not require either an overt subject or object.

A third basic part of speech is the "object." A noun concept, the object receives the action of the verb. When a sentence involves a verb that transmits an action, that action is transmitted to the object. It is the object that answers the question "whom or what?" as represented by the sign BILL in a sentence like DAN TELL BILL.

Basic Sentence Patterns

Within the framework of such concepts as statements, questions and commands, there are many ways to construct a basic sentence. The first class of ASL sentence patterns is the declarative sentence. Based on SVO order, the simplest declarative sentence consists of two major grammatical parts, excluding modifiers, markers, etc. While English specifically requires both a subject and a verb to create a grammatical sentence, ASL allows virtually any two signs that represent a subject, verb, object, or complement to form a sentence. The combination of the two signs serves as a sentence in the respect that it conveys a complete thought. An appropriate sign pair together with certain nonmanual signals is sufficient to represent a well-formed sentence in ASL.

Nonmanual behavior refers to the expressive movements of the signer's eyes, face, head, and body (Baker, 1980). These nonmanual aspects shade the meanings of signs depending on context and delivery style. Signing is accompanied by changes in facial expressions, "non-neutral" head positions, and head and body movements, all of which support the grammatical signs in patterned ways (Liddell, 1980).

Diagramming

We can diagram sentence patterns to illustrate the grammatical relations within them. In a sentence that includes a subject and a verb, each major component is located on the base line. The division between these two elements is expressed by double vertical lines that intersect the base line.

Subject ‖ Verb	e.g.	MARY ‖ WRITE
(S) ‖ (V)		(S) ‖ (V)

When the sentence includes all three main components, the verb and its object make up the "comment," which is included on the base line. Double vertical lines divide the main theme of the sentence from its subsequent comment, and an "×" separates the verb from the object within the comment.

	Comment				
Subject ‖	Verb	Object	e.g.	MARY ‖	WRITE × LETTER
(S) ‖	(V)	(O)		(S) ‖	(V) (O)

Pattern 1

The first sentence pattern is a sign pair that consists of a subject and a verb. The distinguishing characteristic of this pattern is the type of noun that serves as the subject and the kind of verb that depicts the action. This subject-verb pattern parallels an equivalent word order in English. An example of this sentence pattern is CAROL TYPE, which can be translated as either "Carol types" or "Carol is typing."

The subject of a Pattern 1 sentence is usually a noun that answers the question of who or what is performing the action or is being referred to by the verb. Generally, Pattern 1 sentences contain an "intransitive" verb, a verb that expresses an action that the subject is performing in and of itself. Such verbs do not need objects.

Pattern 1: subject-verb
ASL: JAY REMEMBER
English: Jay remembers it.

Diagram: <u>JAY</u> ‖ <u>REMEMBER</u>
       (S) ‖   (V)

ASL	*English*
LU ANNE FINISH	Lu Anne finished it.
JOE FORGET	Joe forgets.
MY FATHER SNORE	My father snores.
WINDOW BREAK	The window broke.
FROG JUMP	The frog jumped.

Exercise: Write six Pattern 1 sentences, each with a person as the subject of the communication.

Pattern 2

Pattern 2 is a two-sign pair in which the verb supplies the action and also serves as the main theme of the sentence. This pattern is characterized by a command sentence in which a verb is followed by an object. The subject of such a sentence is understood as "you." The verb involved in Pattern 2 is usually "transitive," a verb that requires an object to complete the sentential meaning. In a Pattern 2 sentence, the action is the principle focus of attention followed by the person, place, or object that is governed by the verb or receives its action. CLOSE WINDOW (meaning "close the window") illustrates Pattern 2. The subject is understood to be whomever is being addressed.

Pattern 2: verb-object
ASL: STOP GAME
English: Stop the game.

Diagram: <u>(YOU - understood)</u> ‖ <u>STOP</u>⤬<u>GAME</u>
           (S)   ‖ (V)   (O)

ASL	*English*
GIVE BUTTER	Pass me the butter.
LEAVE HOUSE	Get out of the house.
LOOK GOOD	It looks good.
FEEL BETTER	It feels better.

Exercise: Write six Pattern 2 sentences, three as requests and three as commands. Write four other Pattern 2 sentences, two with person objects and two with noun objects.

Pattern 3

This pattern represents a three-part relationship and a noun-verb-noun sequence in which a noun concept does something to (or for) someone or something else. In this pattern, the subject and the object are separate lexical signs. The verb is usually transitive, transmitting an action from the subject to the object. JOB PAY RENT (meaning "My job pays the rent.") illustrates this basic pattern.

Pattern 3: subject-verb-object
ASL: KAYE KNOW ANGIE
English: Kaye knows Angie.
Diagram:

COMMENT

KAYE ‖ KNOW ⤬ ANGIE
(S) ‖ (V)   (O)

ASL	*English*
CAR WIN RACE	My car is winning the race.
DOG BITE MAN	The dog bit the man.
FRED REPLACE WINDOW	Fred replaced the window.
TIM GUESS CORRECT NUMBER	Tim guessed the right number.
NURSE HELP PATIENT	The nurse is helping the patient.

Exercise: Write ten Pattern 3 sentences, five with persons as objects and five with non-person objects.

Pattern 4

A final contextual pattern is based on SVO order but is not represented in English. The Pattern 4 sentence is formed as a subject-complement sequence. It is not represented in English because it violates one of the most fundamental criteria associated with English sentences, namely, it has no verb.

The subject complement of a Pattern 4 sentence can be either a descriptive noun (e.g., CAR FLAT *TIRE*) or an adjective (e.g., MORNING *COLD*). The complement tells something about the subject or identifies one of its characteristics. It completes the meaning of the subject. Since a verb in such a pattern does not describe an action, the ASL sentence deletes it, under the principle of economization. Thus, ASL can create a well-formed sentence without a verb, something not possible in English. The initial noun identifies the subject or theme, and the subsequent noun or adjective tells something about it.

In a sentence like BENCH COLD ("The bench is cold"), the subject is followed by a related comment that applies to it. No verb is needed to understand its meaning. The closest equivalent to this pattern in English is a sentence that uses a linking verb, such as "is," "are," "was," etc. Linking verbs are included within English sentences for mechanical purposes, to help the sentence maintain a smooth transition. But linking verbs contribute little semantic content.

Pattern 4 ASL sentences lack such functional verbs. The complement in such sentences assumes the position of an object. If it is a noun, it tells something about the subject or renames it. If it is an adjective, it describes one of the subject's characteristics. Interpretation of Pattern 4 sentences is based both on sign order, and, in part, on the semantics of the individual signs. In other words, the reader sees the sentence, thinks about plausible combinations and then selects one to make an interpretation of the sentence's meaning. For the reader to make sense out of such a Pattern 4 sentence construction, there is usually only one plausible combination.

The purpose of the Pattern 4 sentence is to complete the sense of the subject. Therefore, if a Pattern 4 sentence involves a person, it contains only one person reference, which is then followed by the complement. A Pattern 4 sentence is most commonly used when the person being discussed is not present at the time of the communication. Consider a situation, for instance, where two neighbors are talking and one says to the other, JOE DOCTOR. To make sense of this sentence, only one part can be identified as the subject (the actual person). The other major part must then serve as the complement: "Joe is a doctor." If the sign order were reversed, DOC-TOR JOE, it would be interpreted as either "Dr. Joe," which is not a complete thought, or "The doctor is Joe," which is essentially the same as "Joe is a doctor."

Pattern 4: subject-complement
ASL: SHARON WIN // PERSON MARKER
English: Sharon is the winner.
Diagram: SHARON ‖ WIN // PERSON MARKER
(S)   ‖   (C)

ASL	*English*
CAR FLAT TIRE	The car has a flat tire.
DOUG POLICEMAN	Doug is a policeman.
OFFICE CLOSE	The office is closed.
COFFEE STRONG	The coffee is strong.
NURSE NICE	The nurse is nice.
STORM APPROACH	A storm is approaching.

Exercise: Write eight Pattern 4 sentences, four with persons as subjects and four with non-persons as subjects.

Reversible Sign Order

The SVO sign order is clearly a part of ASL, particularly in sentences with noun–transitive verb–noun sequences. But the SVO order does not dominate ASL as it does English. The SVO order is only one part of ASL's syntactic structure, and is used only when each major grammatical component corresponds to an explicit sign. Constructing actual SVO-ordered sentences in which each major component is overtly expressed by a sign occurs most frequently with nondirection verbs (see chapter 7). But even then, signers tend to use the SVO pattern sparingly, and usually as a means to differentiate the subject and the object in a sentence (Friedman, 1976). SV order and its related modifications (V, V-S, etc.) are used more commonly in ASL discourse than SVO.

According to Fischer (1975), SVO sign order applies in ASL when a sentence contains a reversible subject and object that are represented as full nouns (not substituted with pronouns). One common instance in which a sentence contains full noun phrases occurs when the sentence participants are not present at the time of the communication event. Such references need to be identified. By "reversible, subject and object" Fischer means that even when subject and object are reversed (in their respected positions), each sentence arrangement yields a semantically plausible sentence.

Most reversible sentences are Pattern 3 sentences, containing all three grammatical components. If a sentence contains two persons who are not present during the conversation and who represent the subect and object, these references can be exchanged. In a sentence like RICHARD MARRY ANNETTE (meaning, "Richard is marrying Annette"), Richard is the subject and doer of the action while Annette is the object of the action. If the respective position of the nouns is inverted, the equally acceptable sentence ANNETTE MARRY RICHARD ("Annette is marrying Richard.") results. In this sentence ANNETTE is the subject and RICHARD the object of the action. Thus, RICHARD and ANNETTE are reversible sentence participants. To avoid potential confusion, the location of the subject and the object is predicted by its position in relation to the verb. When two persons occur in a sentence as subject and object, the SVO sign order tells the reader who is doing what to or for whom. Consider a scenario in which one neighbor tells another the latest news:

1st neighbor: ME LEARN NELSON LEAVE WIFE
             (I heard that Mr. Nelson LEFT his wife.)
2nd neighbor: ME LEARN SHE LEAVE HIM
             (But I heard that she left him.)
1st neighbor: ERICK TELL ME
             HE (ERICK) KNOW ALL
             (Erick told me and he knows everything.)

Even a sentence that contains only one person reference can be capable of reversibility. Both Pattern 1 (subject-verb) and Pattern 2 (verb-object) sentences on occasion can be reversible. In a sentence like SAM STUDY ("Sam is studying") for instance, the interpretation is rather straight forward since only one person and one action is involved. But if the elements SAM and STUDY are reversed to yield STUDY SAM ("You are to study, Sam") this, too, is an acceptable sentence of the command type (Pattern 2). Such a sentence, however, usually relies on the context to prevent semantic confusion.

ASL (Pattern)	*English*
LAURA SAY (1)	Laura said so.
SURPRISE BILL (2)	Go surprise Bill.
KEN LOVE SCHOOL (3)	Ken loves his school.
RON TELEPHONE BARB (3)	Ron called Barb.
LAURA RELIEVED (1)	Laura is relieved.

Noun Types

When a noun is used in a sentence to denote a person, place, or thing, the reference is often not physically present and needs to be introduced into the conversation. Under such circumstances, the noun, as subject or object, tends to occur in an SVO sentence pattern.

Three basic types of nouns occur in such sentences: proper nouns, nominal person nouns, and collective nouns. "Proper nouns" are the names of specific persons, places or things such as KAYE, DR. ERICKSON, WILLIAMSBURG, JAY NELSON, NIAGARA FALLS, etc. "Nominal-person nouns" are the general names of particular persons such as, "MY GIRL, YOUR FRIENDS, HIS UNCLE, etc. "Collective nouns" represent the names for entire groups of people or things such as FAMILY, TEAM, BAND, FRATERNITY, etc. A collective noun is a singular name for a whole group of individuals.

Whenever a noun of any of these types is used, the implication is that the reference is a person, place, or thing that is not physically present at the time of the communication. Since the signer must identify the noun, such references are overtly included in the sentence construction.

When a person who is not present is a topic of conversation in ASL, the signer uses the individual's proper name to let the reader know who is being talked about. Since the person must be introduced into the conversation, the person's name becomes the principle focus of the sentence.

The use of proper nouns is common in SVO sentence constructions. Then, too a proper noun might be used in a subject-verb sentence (Pattern 1) when the doer of the action is someone unknown to the reader. Consider a scenario in which a girl asks her brother to recall who went to a recent party she wasn't able to attend. Her brother reflects on it and then states, DAWN ARRIVE ("Dawn came to it."). KAYE ANGIE THERE ("Kaye and Angie were there."). MANY PEOPLE HAVE FUN ("There were many people there having a good time"). Each specific person reference is represented as the subject of the sentence in which it occurs.

When a proper name occurs in a verb-object sentence (Pattern 2), the implication is that the receiver of the action is not present and that his or her identity must be supplied. A scenario that reflects this type of sentence might involve a boss telling a worker what he needs to do: FIRST PHONE MIKE, TELL HIM WASH FLOOR. NEXT WRITE REPORT. SEND JIM HERE. ("First, go call Mike and tell him to wash the floors. Next, go write up that report. By the way, send Jim up here.") The sentence PHONE MIKE uses Mike as the object of the verb.

A third common use of the proper name occurs in subject–transitive verb–object sentences (Pattern 3). One such usage occurs when both the doer and the receiver of the verb's action represent persons not immediately present for the conversation. SVO order is also used when the sentence involves a proper-name doer of the action and an object of the action, regardless of whether the object is a proper name. An illustrative scenario might involve a roommate who returns to her dorm after attending a school dance. As she enters, she tells her roommate: BECKY ARRIVE ALONE ("Becky came alone"); EDDIE PLAY BAND ("Eddie was playing in the band"); TOM DANCE LINDA. LATER HE (TOM) DANCE ME ("Tom danced with Linda. But later on, he danced with me.").

A nominal-person or collective noun is also used to clarify a reference to a person who is not present. A nominal phrase such as MY GIRL represents a specific person. And since the signer needs to identify the person being discussed, the reference is supplied directly. This pattern can be illustrated by a scenario in which two friends talk on campus and one remarks: NEXT WEEK MY GIRL VISIT ME ("My girlfriend is going to visit me next week."). This sentence is in basic SVO order. Similarly, a sentence like MY LITTLE BROTHER READ ("My little brother is reading.") follows the two–grammatical part sentence of Pattern 1 (subject-verb).

When a nominal phrase functions as the object of the action, the sign order signals the function of the nominal in the sentence. In a sentence like JAY HELP MY GRANDMOTHER ("Jay is helping my grandmother"), Pattern 3 (subject-verb-object) is used.

The same order also applies when both the subject and the object are nominal-person phrases, as in MY SISTER KNOW YOUR HUSBAND ("My sister knows your husband."). A nominal-person phrase is treated as an absent person reference and follows the unmarked SVO sign order.

	Subject	*Object*
ASL:	MY BROTHER KNOW KAYE	KAYE KNOW MY BROTHER
English:	My brother knows Kaye.	Kaye knows my brother.

Diagram:

(MY) BROTHER ‖	KNOW ⤬ KAYE		KAYE ‖	KNOW ⤬ (MY) BROTHER
(S) ‖	(V) (O)		(S) ‖	(V) (O)

Similar word orders are used with collective nouns. The use of a collective noun indicates that a group is not present at the time of the communication and needs to be identified for the reader. A collective noun can serve as a subject, an object, or in both capacities of a sentence. Sentences in which it occurs typically follow SVO order. To illustrate this noun type, consider the scenario of two friends from rival schools watching a race. One person remarks MY RELAY TEAM WIN RACE ("My relay team is winning the race."). Such a remark contains the collective noun "team" as the subject of the sentence, and since the subject is overtly supplied, the sentence follows SVO sign order. His or her friend might respond with NO. RACE WIN MY RELAY TEAM ("No, the race is being won by my relay team."). In this case the collective noun serves as the object of the action but SVO sign order is still used. Even when both major components are collective nouns, the SVO sign order is often used: MY TEAM PLAY YOUR TEAM ("My team plays your team.").

	Subject	*Object*
ASL:	BAND WIN CONTEST	DAWN JOIN MY CHURCH
English:	Our band won the contest.	Dawn joined my church.
Diagram:	BAND ‖ WIN CONTEST	DAWN ‖ JOIN (MY) CHURCH
	(S) ‖ (V) (O)	(S) ‖ (V) (O)

Remember that proper nouns and related nouns are used primarily in ASL when the person under discussion is not present during the communication. This criterion also applies to sentences involving more than one person. In a sentence like CHRIS ANN SURPRISE, the use of the two proper names implies that these persons are not present at the time of the conversation. This sentence follows Pattern 1 (subject-verb). The sentence participants are introduced, and a related comment follows: If only one person were absent and the other present for the conversation, the sentence might place the proper name reference in the initial position and use a gesture to designate the second person: CHRIS SHE (gesturing to a second person, Ann) SURPRISE. The proper names can also appear as objects: SURPRISE CHRIS ANN ("Let's surprise Chris and Ann.").

Training Exercises

A. Economize the following English sentences into a succinct form, and then translate them into ASL. Identify each sentence pattern.

   1. A cat is walking on the roof.
   2. Carol met a new friend.
   3. My uncle is a retired lawyer.
   4. Perry likes to jog.
   5. Coke is my favorite drink.
   6. Frank bought a pet snake.
   7. Jack is trying on a pair of new shoes.
   8. Today is a beautiful day.
   9. My cousin is your nephew.
  10. The new coat was free.
  11. That lady is quite famous.
  12. The soup smells awful.
  13. John loves Angie very much.
  14. Sandy opened the letter and read it.
  15. Write it up and send it to me.

B. Identify the basic sentence pattern of each of the following sentences, and then translate them into English.

   1. RAIN STOP NOW
   2. FRED WRITE ME
   3. CAR GAS NONE
   4. MARY CALL YOU
   5. TED MAY PASS TEST
   6. ROGER KNOW BUDDY
   7. GARY MEET YOU?
   8. MR. JONES MAYBE WRITE SCHOOL
   9. TINA FORGET TELL ME
  10. FLIGHT CONTINUE THREE HOURS

C. Diagram the following sentences. Place the modifiers above the main sentence elements they explain. Be sure to distinguish objects from complements.

   1. SMALL SPOT DOG HUNGRY
   2. LANA JIM BUY NEW CAR
   3. TALL GIRL TRUE BEAUTIFUL
   4. GAME WAIT MUCH RAIN
   5. YOUR FATHER MAYBE RICH
   6. BUS ARRIVE AT-LAST

D. The most useful practice is signing sentences in context. In the following scenarios, write out the discourses you feel might occur. If you have a partner, role-play each scenario after you have developed the context.

Scenario 1:

Last night you sneaked out of the house and went out with your friends. This morning you are too tired to go to school. Not realizing your mother knows what you did, you try to convince her that you are too sick to go to school today.

Scenario 2:

You decide to drop a college class and therefore, no longer need the book for the course. You want to return it to the bookstore, but you missed the two-week return deadline period by one day. You plead with the assistant store manager to accept the book back.

Scenario 3:

You are on your way to a piano lesson with an elderly teacher. You performed poorly in your last session, and haven't practiced all week. You try to explain why you are doing poorly without hurting your teacher's feelings.

7. Topicalizing a Sentence

Like English sentences, American Sign Language sentences are based to some degree on a linear sequence of signs. This is reflected by the fact that a signer can produce only one lexical ASL unit at a time. American Sign Language is distinguished from English by its ability to incorporate spatial and temporal aspects into its sentential construction simultaneously. The style of ASL sentences can best be described as "contextual." Compared to English, which is dominated by strict adherence to word order, ASL is a relatively free-style language in which sentence patterns depend on the dynamics of the discourse.

The most common means of expression in ASL is the context sentence. A context sentence is a construction that depends on the sentences around it either for semantic support or for part of its essential semantic elements. The use of context sentences is a principle factor accounting for the relatively infrequent use of SVO sign order in ASL.

American Sign Language is considered a "topic-prone language." When arranging the sign order of a sentence, it adheres to the principle of "strongest emphasized information first." The strategy of placing the heaviest weighted lexical item at the beginning of the sentence is referred to as "topicalizing" the sentence. Topicalizing sentences is far more common in ASL than in English (Baker and Cokely, 1980).

To topicalize a sentence, a signer must first determine the sentence's central idea and then draw attention to it by positioning it in the beginning of the sentence. In a sentence like PARTY, WE GO, the main idea of the thought is "party." The priority position of "party" in this sentence informs the reader what the sentence topic is. The comment, WE GO, then continues. An equivalent English translation might be, "There is a party, let's go to it."

The strategy of topicalizing places the main focus of a thought at the beginning of a sentence, and thus many topicalized sentences do not adhere to a SVO sentence pattern. A common phenomenon in manual conversation, topicalization reflects the influence of the ongoing discourse and specifically, how sentences are influenced by context. Topicalizing invites the signer to construct each sentence according to the contents of the discourse up to that point. The purpose of topicalizing is to supply additional new information first; supportive or complementary information follow.

The strategy of topicalizing is appropriate to ASL because manual conversation is a visual event. Imagine a sentence as a train that carries an idea from one person to another. The main theme serves as the engine of the sentence and the other grammatical components link up as the box cars. The main theme is the foundation for pulling the sentence along. Once the reader recognizes the engine or topic of immediate interest, the rest of the train or comments that follow supply the complementary details. The "headsign" (first sign of the sentence), however, focuses the reader's attention on the main purpose of the sentence.

Consider the role of the subject in a standard SVO sentence. The subject is the foundation of an SVO sentence, functioning to identify who or what the principle object of attention is in the sentence. The subject routinely occupies the initial position of an SVO sentence. But if each semantic unit in a basic sentence were weighed in terms of the relative degree of information it supplies, the subject would not always represent the greatest semantic substance. The same proper name, for example, used repetitiously in several sentences provides at best only secondary information. This is one reason ASL relies so heavily on personal pronouns in discourse. A pronoun eliminates constant repetition of a proper name. But pronoun substitution also implies that the person reference within a sentence is not the main theme of that sentence. While the pronoun often assumes the main focus as the underlying subject ("I am sleeping," "I am worried," "You look good," etc.), it is not always the proper focus of informative attention.

When the most useful information in a sentence is placed in the beginning, that unit is referred to as the topic. A topic is the theme or momentary object of interest of a contextual sentence. "Topic" is defined as the nominal(s) that is established first in a sentence and as such becomes definite (e.g., a proper noun) (Friedman, 1976). A nominal is any lexical unit that takes a noun construction or is placed in a noun position of the sentence. In ASL, any grammatical component can serve as the topic of a contextual sentence.

On one level, a topic and a subject share certain grammatical characteristics; on another, they serve distinctly different functions. A topic, for instance, is not necessarily found in a sentence with SVO order, but a subject may be found in a topicalized sentence. Both topic and subject inform the reader what a sentence is about. But within the framework of ASL, the importance of who is performing the action is only one consideration influencing sentence construction.

American Sign Language is a visual phenomenon. Ideas, thoughts, and emotions are communicated by a combination of physical articulation of the hands and such nonmanual elements as facial expression, head position, and head movement. The reader perceives these manual and nonmanual dimensions collectively, and collectively they define the communication process.

To communicate in a manual-visual language, a minimum of two persons must be physically present within a reasonable proximity of each other, and their view of each other must be unobstructed. Movement serves as the medium to transmit manual information through visual perception. Mandatory person-to-person contact is a distinguishing characteristic of manual language. Verbal language, on the other hand, does not require visual contact as a prerequisite to communication with someone. Communication can also occur by telephone radio, or even through a closed door. TDD (Telecommunication Device for the Deaf), does not constitute an exception because such an instrument though used by hearing-impaired people, is not a manual communication system. It is based on a written word format, usually English, rather than ASL.

An ASL topic is different from a conventional subject because the topic complies with the principle of strongest information first. In a sentence like ME LIKE MUSIC, the subject is ME and it tells who likes music. But in terms of information, the sentence is about music, since that is the new information. The idea of ME LIKE is complementary information. Manual language topicalizes a sentence by weighing each major sentential element according to its informative value within the context of ongoing discourse. The topic informs the reader of the most important idea by placing this idea in the beginning of the sentence. Topics in ASL are less frequently represented by pronouns than in English.

The persons involved in a visual/manual conversation, are undeniably present and accessible. Because of this, all references to a person who is present is regarded as complementary information in ASL. Thus, the topic of an ASL sentence is usually what the doer of the action is doing. Therefore, a pronoun gesture toward someone present seldom acts as the headsign of an ASL sentence. Rather, new information assumes the headsign position. Repeating a reference to someone who is present is not new information, so such references most often appear as a part of the comment section of the sentence. Overt proper names, on the other hand, usually occupy the topic position in a SVO pattern. In other words, only pronoun references usually do not serve as the topics in ASL. In an earlier example, ME LIKE MUSIC, the reference ME represents someone involved in the conversation. In terms of priority, this pronoun reference is regarded as complementary information, and the corresponding topicalized sentence is MUSIC, ME ENJOY.

The topic of a topicalized sentence is represented by such concepts as persons, objects, or places (not immediately present), or actions. In topicalized sentences what takes priority over who. As a result, it is more common to find a verb serving as a topic than a pronoun. In topicalized sentences new information comes first, and is followed by old, established information. Old information is knowledge that the signer assumes to be known already by the reader at the time of the discourse. New information is knowledge that the signer assumes that is being introduced to the reader.

Topicalizing is not common in English. As a result, translation between English and ASL cannot always be based on sentence-to-sentence correspondence. But even in English, certain sentence patterns reflect topicalizing. One example is the sentence that begins with an adverbial phrase. In a sentence such as "Among the people walked a stranger," the subject is "stranger." But in terms of word order, a general scene of many people is first established, followed by the action of the sentence. The subject is supplied last. In this sentence, the phrase "among the people" serves as the topic. Another example of a topicalized sentence in English is a sentence in which a temporal adverb such as "Saturday" leads off a sentence as in "Saturday, I went to a ball game." The day sets the time frame in which the comment that relates to it follows.

One of the more common ways to topicalize a sentence in English is to introduce a sentence by a prepositional phrase, as in "In Cleveland, people love their sports." The topic "Cleveland" acts as the theme, which the subsequent sentence complements. The only difference between ASL and English is that English requires a preposition; ASL does not. But in an English sentence like "The movie, I saw it yesterday," a preposition is not required. Other examples of this form of topicalizing an English sentence include, "In math, you learn to divide and multiply"; "By summer, you need to lose the weight"; "About the party, I can't go"; "For Mary, I will do it," and "About the meeting, where is it being held?"

Another strategy for placing an idea other than the subject in the initial position in English occurs in passive-voice constructions. In a passive-voice sentence the what of the sentence is expressed first, followed by the who. In a sentence such as "The portrait was painted by him," the lead position is occupied by the object: "portrait." Although "him" is the logical subject, it is momentarily thrust into the role of the complement.

American Sign Language differentiates topicalized sentences from SVO sentences by including what is referred to as an intonation break in the topicalized versions (Fischer, 1975). To create an "intonation break" you tilt your head up and back as you raise your eyebrows. You perform this nonmanual signal while you manually execute the sign of the topic, in effect marking it for topicalization. The head tilt implicitly separates the moved constituent (topic) from the rest of the sentence. In written form this is identified by a comma, which indicates, the division between the topic and its comment, as in BILL, ME HELP ("I am helping Bill"). In addition, a topic sign is usually performed with an extra-long duration, which gives an added impression of the break or pause (Liddell, 1980). All topicalized sentences are marked by an intonation break.

ASL Specific Sentence Patterns

Topicalized sentences represent an alternative to SVO sign order. Diagrams can highlight the different grammatical relations in these sentences. In a diagram of a topicalized sentence, the topic is lifted above the base line, and an extended double vertical line connects the topic with the rest of the sentence. The grammatical role of the topic is labeled underneath.

Pattern 5

The most basic topicalized pattern consists of two grammatical items: a noun and an action. Sentences of Pattern 5 mark the action as the topic of the sentence. Marking the action calls attention to it. The comment, which follows, consists of the subject as in a sentence like REMEMBER, ME (meaning "I remember."). In written form, a comma separates the topic from the subsequent comment and is communicated in ASL as an intonation break. If this same sentence were not marked for topicalization, it would convey the idea REMEMBER ME as a command. Similar to Pattern 1, Pattern 5 commonly uses an intransitive verb. An object is not needed to complete the thought. Another example of a Pattern 5 sentence is TYPE, SHE which is translated as either "She types" or "She is typing," depending on the context.

Pattern 5: Topicalized verb, subject
ASL: WORK, SHE
English: She works.
Diagram: $\dfrac{\text{WORK}}{\text{(T-V)}} \parallel \dfrac{\text{SHE}}{\text{(S)}}$

ASL	*English*
SWIM, HE	He swims.
BOWL, ME	I bowl.
WIN, SHE HE	They won.

Exercise: Write three Pattern 5 sentences.

Pattern 6

When a two-part sentence consists of only two main nouns, the complement is topicalized and followed by the subject. This arrangement represents Pattern 6. This construction represents no action and hence, no verb. The topicalized complement renames or identifies one of the subject's characteristics. Its referent noun is then supplied (subject). Pattern 6 is similar to Pattern 4 (subject-complement) except that the complement assumes a position of greater emphasis than the person it applies to.

A complement is topicalized when it presents the reader with new information. The topicalized complement informs the reader of a new characteristic or quality and then tells the reader who it applies to.

A sentence like GRADUATE, ME ("I graduated.") illustrates Pattern 6. No action is involved, simply a condition. Another example is a scenario in which two men are walking down an alley. As they pass a man lying on the ground, they notice he is drinking from a paper bag. The one person remarks to his friend: "SMELL BAD, HE ("He really smells bad."). Or imagine two women standing together at a dance. As one woman notices a good-looking man standing by the punch bowl, she remarks to her friend: LOOK MARTHA. TRUE HANDSOME, HE (meaning "Look over there, Martha. He is really handsome.").

Pattern 6: Topicalized Complement, Subject
ASL: HAPPY WIN PERSON // MARKER, SHE
English: She is a happy winner.
Diagram: $\dfrac{\text{(HAPPY) WIN PERSON MARKER}}{\text{(T-C)}} \parallel \dfrac{\text{SHE}}{\text{(S)}}$

ASL	*English*
DOCTOR, HE SHE	They are doctors.
TRUE WORRY, ME	I am really worried.

NEW HAIRCUT, SHE   She just got a new haircut.
SURPRISE, YOU   You were surprised.

Exercise: Write four Pattern 6 sentences. Keep in mind each would be part of an on-going conversation.

Pattern 7

Pattern 7 includes all three of the main grammatical parts arranged in the sequences: O, SV. This pattern is most often used when both the subject and the object are separate lexical items and the subject is present during the conversation. The object is topicalized as the sentential theme and is separated from the comment by an intonation break. In a sentence like COLLEGE, ME GRADUATE ("I am graduating from college."), COLLEGE sets the scene. The subsequent comment, ME GRADUATE supplies the complementary details. The doer of the action (subject) is repositioned into the intitial position of the comment, but overall is now in the middle of the sentence. Another illustration of the topicalized O, SV pattern is BOOK, SHE WRITE (She is writing a book.) When the object is the topic of attention, the comment serves as a sentence within a sentence and follows the standard subject-verb sequence. Consider the scenario of two students having lunch together. One remarks, YOUR SALAD, YOU FORGET EAT. ME EAT INDEX (SALAD)? (You forgot to eat your salad. Do you mind if I have it?"). The topic is established first, and comments about it follow.

Pattern 7(a): Topicalized Object, Subject-Verb
ASL: UMBRELLA, ME FORGET
English: I forgot my umbrella.
Diagram:

	Comment
UMBRELLA (T-O)	ME ✕ FORGET (S) (V)

ASL	*English*
BOOK, ME READ	I read the book.
CHRIS, ME KISS	I kissed Chris.
CAR, WE CAN REPAIR	We can repair the car.
HOUSE, WE BUY	We bought the house.
TABLE, ME FINISH AGAIN	I refinished the table.
YOUR GRADE, TEACHER CHANGE	Your teacher changed your grade.

Exercise: Write eight Pattern 7(a) sentences, four with the object as a person not present and four as a non-person noun.

A variation of Pattern 7 is represented by a sentence with an indirect object. An "indirect object" indicates to whom or for whom the action received by the direct object is completed. According to Friedman (1975) indirect objects are uncommon in an ASL sentence. Direct or definite object construction dominates the language.

But when an indirect object is included in an ASL sentence, certain changes in the sentence pattern are made to accommodate it. Consistent with Pattern 7, the direct object (the lexical item that receives the action of the verb) is topicalized. The comment now consists of three main elements: subject (the doer of the action), the verb (the action), and the object (the object of the action). With the topic established, the comment acts as a sentence within a sentence, in which the subject, verb, and object are arranged in the basic SVO sign order. In a sentence like, "Ed is giving Tracy a beautiful necklace," the direct object "necklace" along with its modifiers becomes the topic, followed by the SVO-generated comment: BEAUTIFUL NECKLACE, ED GIVE TRACY.

Pattern 7(b): Topicalized Object, Subject-Verb-(Indirect) Object
      ASL: BIRDHOUSE, JAY BUILD CAROL
    English: Jay is building a birdhouse for Carol.
    Diagram: <u>(BIRD) HOUSE</u> ‖ <u>   COMMENT   </u>
             (T-O)

                                ‖ <u>JAY</u> ‖ <u>BUILD</u>✗<u>CAROL</u>
                                ‖ (S) ‖ (V)   (O)

ASL	*English*
MORE MONEY, BOSS GIVE ME	My boss gave me a raise.
LARGE PIZZA, CHILDREN REQUEST FAMILY	The children called for a pizza for the family.
BATH CLOTHES, MOTHER GIVE ME HE	Mother gave us our bathing suits.

Exercise: Write four Pattern 7(b) sentences.

Pattern 8

Another variation of the three-part sentence occurs when the verb assumes the initial position. In such a Pattern 8 sentence the verb and anything that follows to modify or complement it are topicalized, thus forming a topicalized verb phrase. As a result, the comment usually consists of only a subject reference. Pattern 8 can also be described as a postpositioning of the subject while the verb and object remain in their standard sequence. A Pattern 8 sentence in effect moves the subject to the end of the sentence.

In a sentence such as TELL MARTY, YOU ("You tell Marty.") the topicalized order of verb-object, subject (VO, S) places greatest emphasis on the action. Reflecting the flexibility of contextual sentences in American

Sign Language, this pattern generally occurs when two conditions are met: the subject is a person who is present during the conversation, and the action represents new information. In an earlier illustration of Pattern 7 COLLEGE, ME GRADUATE, the emphasis was placed on the idea of graduating from college as opposed to high school, junior high, etc. But in the sentence GRADUATE COLLEGE, ME ("I am graduating from college.") the emphasis shifts from where the person is graduating from, to the idea of a personal accomplishment, "I am really graduating." The different topicalizing patterns create subtle shifts in meaning. If you want to draw attention to the idea that it is "I" who am graduating as opposed to anyone else, you might use a standard SVO sign order as in ME GRADUATE COLLEGE.

Pattern 8: Topicalized verb-object, subject
ASL: CALL YOU, SHE
English: She called you already.
Diagram:

CALL ⟋ YOU	‖	COMMENT
(T-V) ⟍ (T-O)	‖	SHE
	‖	(S)

ASL
LOVE YOU, ME
READ YOU, ME
CHANGE MIND, SHE
GET JOB, YOU
DECIDE FORGIVE HE, SHE

English
I love you.
I am reading to you.
She changed her mind.
You need to get a job.
She decided to forgive him.

Exercise: Write five Pattern 8 sentences.

The Meaning of a Topicalized Sentence

A topicalized sentence can be represented by such sentential patterns as noun, noun verb; noun, noun; and verb noun, noun. To differentiate the subject (who is doing the action) from the object (who is receiving the action) in such patterns, an ASL reader must first determine whether the sentence is topicalized. This is accomplished by determining whether the sentence is marked by an intonation break. If there is no intonation break, then the sentence follows the SVO sign order, as in ED SELL CAR ("Ed is selling his car.").

When the sentence is marked for topicalization, however, the intonation break alerts the reader that a weighted sign order is being used such, as in CAR, WE SELL ("We are selling our car.") The combined effect of sign order and marking for topicalization by an intonation break means that another method must be used to differentiate the object from the subject (Liddell, 1980).

ASL admits a variety of different sentence patterns that include both subject-verb-object orders and topicalized orders. The following sentences illustrate the differences between unmarked (standard order) and marked (topicalized) sentences.

Unmarked (Pattern)	*Marked* (Pattern)	*English*
TOM WAIT (1)	WAIT, ME (5)	Tom waits.
		I am waiting.
JOYCE FRIEND (4)	FRIEND, YOU (6)	Joyce is a friend.
		You are a friend.
ERIN BREAK	WATCH, SHE	Erin broke her watch.
WATCH (3)	BREAK (7)	She broke her watch.
NANCY KISS JIM (3)	KISS HER, HE (8)	Nancy is kissing Jim.
		He is kissing her.

Training Exercises

A. Translate each of the following English sentences into ASL. Determine whether the sentence is topicalized, and identify the appropriate pattern.

1. The work was assigned by me.
2. They have the jobs.
3. The man is standing out on the sidewalk.
4. The song was composed by him.
5. I am looking down at grandmother's quilt.
6. Give the ball to your brother.
7. The teacher assigned several pages of homework.
8. Tony left his toys in the living room.
9. I am trying to start my car.
10. Soon, we could feel the thunder.

B. Rewrite each of the following English sentences in at least two different ways using different ASL strategies.

1. I like my new job.
2. She is very hungry.
3. Martha's new house is beautiful.
4. You know Gina. She is my best friend.
5. Sheila gave us a drink.

C. Identify the pattern in these ASL sentences and then rewrite in equivalent English sentences.

1. HER CHEEK, ME KISS
2. WHOLE TRACK, ME RUN
3. DOCTOR, SHE
4. SMOKE STOP, HER

5. ME LOVE YOUR NEW COAT

6. ALONE, SHE FEEL

7. COME-HERE, HE SHE SHE

8. FRANK KNOW ME

9. SNAKE, THEY BOTHER MY SISTER

10. NURSE SHOOT // ARM ME

D. ASL communicates in context. Create useful dialogues for the following scenarios. Highlight your dialogue with topicalized sentences. Remember to use topicalization to introduce new information.

Scenario 1:

You really want to go out with a certain person, but you are shy and haven't found the nerve to make the first move. As a last resort, you ask your best friend to drop a hint with the guy/gal of your interest. But the object of your affection misunderstands the message and thinks it is your friend who wants to go out. Since your friend is already engaged, he/she makes you straighten the mess out with this important other person.

Scenario 2:

You are eight years old, and you decide you just have to have a dog. After two weeks of putting constant pressure on your parents, you get your wish, a young puppy.

But three weeks later, you discover you are just too busy to care for the puppy as you so solemnly promised. You like the dog, but you just can't keep up with the responsibility. You discuss this matter with your best friend, who agrees to take the puppy. Now convince your parents.

Scenario 3:

While waiting to be interviewed for an important job, you decide to get a drink at the snack shop. While carrying your drink, you walk around the corner right into someone spilling the drink on both of you. Nervous about the interview, you overreact and yell at this other person, blaming him/her for the accident. After a while, you privately regret your outburst, but since the other person was a stranger and you will probably never see him/her again, you forget about it. When it is finally time for your interview, you walk in and discover that the interviewer is the same stranger you bumped into. Handle the situation while trying to salvage your chances for the job.

8. Spatial Indexing

An ASL sign is a multidimensional entity whose parameters are produced not linearly, but simultaneously. Similarly, ASL sentence production does not proceed as a predictable series of successive distinct units arranged in time. American Sign Language makes full use of the dimensions of space to produce linguistically constrained movements that reveal their semantic meanings. The spatial mode represents a major part of the underlying structure of ASL. As applied to the construction of sentence patterns, spatial referencing serves a number of semantic functions, among them the expression of pronouns. In ASL, pronominal references are supplied by a set of arbitrary points within the sign field.

The basic function of a pronoun is to serve as a substitute for a noun. Use of a pronoun eliminates the need to constantly repeat the same noun in discourse. Person pronouns enable someone to refer to another person without constantly repeating his or her name.

Person pronouns are used to distinguish the person speaking ("I" [first person]), a person being addressed ("you" [second person]), or a person or thing being talked about ("he, she, it" [third person]). Since a person pronoun functions in the place of a noun, it can act in a sentences as subject, object, or noun complement. The noun that the pronoun replaces is referred to as its "antecedent."

Pronoun signs are not a separate classification of signs in ASL. Instead, ASL makes pronominal references through a strategy called "indexing" (Friedman, 1975, 1976). In indexing, the index hand representing the neutral or basic hand formation conveys a person reference through its movement and palm orientation within the neutral sign space. When a signer points or indexes toward someone who is physically present, for instance, the gesture constitutes the pronominal reference "you."

ASL expresses all pronominal references (including many locative references) with indexing, especially when the main verb is nondirectional (Friedman, 1976). Indexing allows the signer to refer to any person, object, or location that is real, hypothetical, or contextually established.

In spatial referencing, the communication event is viewed as an imaginary stage empty of props or backdrops. The actor (signer) is a narrator who is communicating to an audience (the reader). An imaginary line joins

125

the signer to the reader, and this "sign line" is an imaginary stage on which spatial references can be created (Klima and Bellugi, 1979). The orientation of the signer's body represents the location of the neutral or communicative space (Friedman, 1975).

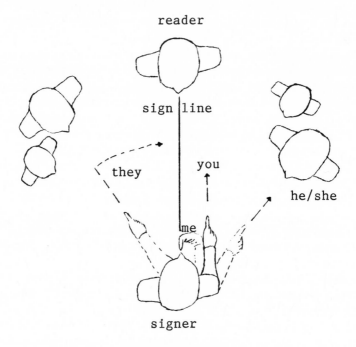

Figure 1. The sign line

American Sign Language uses prearranged locational points on the sign line to mark particular references. A movement in one of four directions from the sign line conveys the basic pronominal references: (1) for a first-person reference, the index hand moves directly inward on the sign line, usually touching the signer; (2) for a second-person reference, the index hand moves directly forward on the sign line toward the reader; (3) for a third-person singular reference, the index hand moves indirectly forward while slanting to either side of the signer (in relation to the sign line); and (4) for a third-person plural reference, the index hand moves forward to one side and then arcs across the sign field, intersecting the imaginary sign line as it passes from one side to the other.

These pronominal references are constant. A direct outward reference for instance, always refers to the second person, YOU. Similarly, indirect indexing toward either side always indicates a third person (HE/SHE/IT).

ASL pronoun referencing does not differentiate the subjective/nominative form of person pronouns ("I," "she," "he," "they") from the objective/accusative pronoun cases ("me," "her," "him," "them"). When someone is translating a sentence between ASL and English and wishes to make such distinctions, he or she must rely on the context to determine the case of the pronoun. In addition, unlike English, which uses three different pronouns ("he," "she," "it") to express the gender of the third-person singular ASL makes no linguistic distinction for gender (male, female, or neuter), economizing the reference into one indexed gesture.

The third-person locational points on the sign line are not used when a person referent can be seen by the sign reader. In such a case, the signer will point directly to that person, and the reader will interpret the motion by visual association. ASL signers always refer to persons (or objects, or locations) physically present by gesturing directly toward them.

When a person referent in a discourse is actually present, the signer will indicate the referent directly. But when a person referent is unknown to the reader, the signer must provide a description or explanation of that person. This condition prompts another dimension of indexing: contextually established pronoun references. To make a contextual reference, the signer introduces the person to be discussed as new information. The signer then gestures with the index hand to an arbitrary point in space. After that, whenever the signer indexes to that arbitrary position, the reader interprets the action to mean the preceding concept. This type of indexing reserves that spatial location for the referent just introduced into the conversation. The reader will now recognize and understand the meaning of this specific spatial location by visual association. Henceforth, when the signer indexes toward that point, the action will be interpreted as a specific pronominal reference. The reader will recall the reference and associate the appropriate person, object, or location represented by that point in space.

The strategy of contextual association is used only for references to persons not immediately present. It is used when a signer raises a point about a person (or topic) not present. Planning to talk further about the subject or person, the signer indexes the name to reserve a point of reference for future association.

A signer can introduce a person reference either subsequent to, after, or before establishing that person's contextual index (Friedman, 1976). When contextual indexing occurs before the reference is introduced, the reader must see the index and remember it later when the specific person reference is established. A reader must internalize the signer's frame of reference into his or her own perspective in order to understand the different positions and related references.

Once a contextual index is established, indexing is performed with essentially the same motion used for an actual reference. During the remainder of the conversation, whenever the signer points to the location now reserved for a contextual referent, the reader will understand the gesture as if the signer were pointing directly toward the referent. It is as if that imaginary referent were physically present, but instead of gesturing toward an actual person, the signer points toward a certain point in space understood to represent that certain person. Contextual indexing establishes a metaphoric understanding of association between the signer and the reader.

To express the indexing strategy in written form, this book will use two classifications. If the index gesture is actual or preestablished, the pronoun references will be designated in capital letters (e.g., HE, YOU, ME). A sentence like "I know," for instance, will be written as KNOW, ME, in which ME indicates an actual indexing reference. But if the pronominal reference is contextually established, a second method will apply. The word INDEX will be written, followed by its antecedent in parentheses. For instance, TED (index to establish location) CALL. INDEX (TED) PLAN LATE translates in English to "Ted called. He will be late."

Indexing can also apply to multiple-person references. As each person's name is introduced, a contextual index is established for that person by gesturing to a different arbitrary point in space. Usually the first reference is placed on the signer's right side, and the second on the signer's left. The reader remembers the reference reserved at each point and interprets the gesture accordingly. To illustrate, imagine two campers waiting for friends to join them. One of the late campers arrives and says, "We have to wait for Tom. He is bringing his friend Barney. You'll like Barney. He is a good camper." In ASL, the first sentence is performed in a basic SVO order, drawing attention to the persons involved: WE MUST WAIT TOM. The next sentence is topicalized since it is providing new information: BRING NEW FRIEND BARNEY (index to establish location), HE. The indexing action immediately follows the target noun. The next sentence illustrates two forms of indexing, first in a contextually established reference (INDEX) and then in an actual reference (YOU). The topicalized sentence stresses the relationship between referents: ENJOY INDEX (BARNEY), YOU. The final sentence can also be topicalized to emphasize the new information: GOOD CAMP PERSON // MARKER, INDEX (BARNEY).

Ambiguity in Sentence Referents

A particular advantage of indexing is its ability to express explicit communications. Indexing is less vulnerable to ambiguity than a pronominal reference in English. When the antecedent of an English pronoun (the referent it represents) is not clear to the listener, the sentence becomes confusing and difficult to understand. Such ambiguity is illustrated by a sentence like "When Kaye told Angie, she was pleased." In this sentence, it is not clear who was pleased: Kaye, Angie, or someone else. The manual equivalent is written in two sentences; KAYE (index to establish location) TELL ANGIE (index establish location). INDEX (ANGIE) PLEASE. As a result of indexing, no ambiguity occurs. The reader understands the message as "When Kaye told Angie, she (Angie) was pleased." Pronominal indexing could have been used to gesture toward the location representing Kaye or to a totally different location indicating a third person. In this case ASL communication is much more explicit than English. Indexing is a substitution for a proper noun, but it also reminds the reader of the specific reference. Indexing eliminates the potential for ambiguity and does so without necessarily changing the sign order.

All languages need to have a way to distinguish sentence subjects from objects. When a sentence construction involves a transitive main verb, as in "Larry likes green apples," both a subject and an object are required to create a well-formed sentence. But when the sentence components can be reversed while retaining a plausible utterance, semantic ambiguity can arise.

The major consideration is whether the sentence arrangement is reversible. Some sentences are referred to as semantically "fixed": there is only one sequence possible that will make a plausible sentential meaning, and no potential interpretative confusion can arise. When a sentence has an intransitive verb, for instance, as in "Bill reads well," there is only one person referent, and limited possibility of alternative interpretation. "Good reads Bill," for example, has no intelligible meaning.

Another combination that is semantically fixed is the verb-object sentence in which the subject "you" is understood. In such a sequence, only one sequential arrangement creates a meaningful message, regardless whether the verb is transitive or intransitive. Such sentences include "Show Bill," "Write me," and "Remind her."

The sequence can be fixed even when the sentence contains both a subject and an object that are overtly supplied, as long as the sentence can express only one reasonable meaning. Generally, sentence patterns are regarded as definite or fixed when only one of the two main nouns can reasonably function as the doer of the action (subject) and maintain a meaningful sentence. Consider a sentence such as GINA READ BOOK ("Gina is reading a book."). This sentence is nonreversible because books, after all, cannot read. If a sentence contains two nouns but only one person the sentence is usually fixed. This is regardless of whether the person is the subject (e.g., MARY RIDE BICYCLE) or the object (e.g., BRIGHT LIGHT SCARED LARRY). A fixed semantic sentence can be arranged either in SVO order or a topicalized pattern without creating interpretative misunderstanding. ME WANT COFFEE or COFFEE, ME WANT are both understood the same way: "I want some coffee."

But when sentences consist of a transitive verb and two person references, which serve as subject and object, the grammatical roles of each reference is not automatically identifiable. Such sentences are said to be "reversible": either person referent could be placed in either grammatical position and the result would be a meaningful sentence. In other words, if the subject and the object were reversed, the result would be a reasonable thought. When a sentence can be reversed, the potential for ambiguity is high. A simple reversible sentence is illustrated in the sentence pair "Otto knows Tina" and "Tina knows Otto." Either sequence conveys a meaningful thought.

ASL indexing reduces the potential for interpretational ambiguity. Indexing always supplies a clear antecedent, for a pronominal reference. This promotes clear, explicit communication. Pronominal indexing involves establishing of a specific location for each referent through indexing. Indexing is arranged according to the context (Friedman, 1976).

To lessen ambiguity in a reversible sentence such as SHE REMEMBER YOU, the signer first supplies the person's actual name (representing the third-person reference) and then indexes it. The signer can now manually express the sentence "She remember you" as SHE (PERSON'S NAME) REMEMBER YOU. Indexing eliminates the need to constantly repeat certain person nouns and also serves to reduce the chance of ambiguity.

Consider a scenario in which two ladies visiting each other one afternoon. As the discussion turns to mutual friends, one lady remarks, "You know Mary, don't you? Carol was surprised that I wrote to her. She never expected it." The lady's remarks are ambiguous. To understand its meaning, the listener must make certain decisions about the probable antecedents of the pronouns. Who did the lady write to? Who never expected it: Mary, Carol, or someone else? The following is the equivalent in ASL:

> MARY (INDEX to establish location), YOU KNOW?
> ME WRITE INDEX (MARY).
> CAROL (INDEX to establish location) SURPRISE.
> INDEX (MARY) EXPECT NEVER.

Within a two-person reference sentence, when the object is topicalized, a nonmanual signal serves to identify the principle actor of the sentence. This nonmanual signal consists of a head nod, which accompanies the second person reference as it is performed. An example of this is a sentence such as SHĒRRY, ME TELL ("I told Sherry"). The marker "hn" (written in lowercase) is placed above the sign it applies to.

Additional Spatial Referents

Another dimension of indexing is its handling of spatial directions. Spatial directions such as up, down, left, and right are conveyed by the index hand gesturing in the actual direction relative to the signer's body position. Indexing gestures to the left and right are directional concepts ("Turn left" as opposed to "I left home").

Lateral indexing has other productive purposes as well. The index gesture RIGHT (relative to the signer), for instance, can convey three different references: (1) if pointing upward, it refers to something up high and to the right (e.g. "up there on the shelf"); (2) if pointing directly sideways, it conveys a direction to the right, or (3) if pointing sideways, it conveys a third person. When an arc motion is superimposed on this gesture, it refers to a locative referent other than "here" (as in "I live *there* in the city.") THERE consists of the index moving to one side in an arcing, up and to the side gesture. THERE refers to an unmarked, unspecified distance from the signer, including the idea of "not here, but somewhere else" (Friedman, 1975).

UP and DOWN locative indexing is also multifaceted. An upward index gesture can mean UP or HIGH. But when the gesture is modified to move in an up, forward, and toward the reader motion, it conveys the idea of "a location far from here." A downward directed gesture conveys either DOWN or HERE, depending on the context. The meaning is determined by the relative angle. When the indexing gesture is formed down and toward the reader, it conveys a locative referent that means a "location close to here, but not precisely here."

Indexing is also used to express relative distance. Distance is conveyed by the relative angle of the index movement in relation to the ground. At the extreme, the index hand gestures straight downward. This reference indicates "right here, at the place we are right now." If the hand arcs forward a bit while it continues to gesture downward, the location is farther away from the signer. Its interpretation is "over there, close to us." As the angle is extended farther forward, but still downward, the angle extends farther forward until it arcs almost to create a near straight forward. Each angular modification means "a little farther away from us." An extended straight forward and then downward gesture means "way over there, quite a distance from us here."

Another meaningful index pattern occurs when the hand rises in a nearly straight up and slightly forward manner in an abbreviated arc (as if pointing above the reader's head). This gesture is interpreted as "far, far away from here." The greater the angle between the rising hand and the ground, the farther the signer from the locative referent (Friedman, 1975). The strategy of locative indexing operates on a continuum of associations.

When a locative referent is known and visually apparent, the index gesture is directed toward the actual location. Real-world referents supersede grammatically established spatial referents. Any person, object, or location in the immediate environment will be indexed directly, not by establishing an arbitrary symbol. Similarly, a person reference takes precedence over a direction reference. In a sentence using both, the directional gesture occurs on the intended side but adjusts itself by moving to a level that is either higher or lower than usual.

Nondirectional Verbs

A particularly important use of indexing occurs with nondirectional verbs. A "nondirectional ASL verb" expresses an action or state of being, and is identified by its fixed parameters. In forming a nondirectional verb's base composition, the signer must rigidly adhere to each physical parameter or the verb's recognizable identity will be destroyed. Any substantial deviation from the core formation distorts the essence of the sign of a nondirectional verb.

Nondirectional ASL verbs include those verbs whose core parameters involve direct contact or defined movement toward the body. Because any apparent alteration would create distortion, the signer must retain all of its fundamental parameters if the verb is to remain linguistically intelligible and meaningful. The verb EAT, for instance, which consists of the modified O hand moving inward until the fingertips touch the mouth, is a nondirectional verb. It has no optional variations.

Regardless of the content within the sentence or the nature of the discourse, a nondirectional verb is always performed in the same way. KNOW, for example, is a nondirectional verb that involves the open hand with the palm inward moving toward the head so that the fingers touch the forehead. Any attempt to alter its articulation base would substantially distort the sign's structure and result in unintelligible, meaningless nonsense.

The chief factor that prevents alteration of a nondirectional verb's parameters is physical contact with the body. The following nondirectional verbs all include body contact (general location of the body contact or proximity is in brackets):

DECIDE (forehead)	KNOW (forehead)	TASTE (mouth)
SURPRISE (near the	FORGET (forehead)	DISAPPEAR (chest)
eyes)	LISTEN (ear)	HOPE (forehead)
BELIEVE (forehead)	SMELL (nose)	GUESS (across face)
THINK (forehead)	SEARCH (face)	REFUSE (over the
REMEMBER	HEAR (ear)	shoulder)
(forehead)	ACCEPT (chest)	TRUST (forehead)

TELEPHONE (side of
face)
EAT (mouth)

WONDER (face)
LOOK-LIKE (face)

HAVE (chest)
VOLUNTEER (chest)

Many nondirectional verbs are used to express either emotion (e.g., SCARED, ANGRY, FEEL, LIKE, LOVE, WORRY, NERVOUS, APPRECIATE, SORRY, ENJOY) or cognitive-oriented concepts (e.g. INTERESTING, STUDY, SURPRISE, WANT, WONDERFUL). Many nondirectional verbs are semantically transitive. Another group of nondirectional verbs feature one person doing something to another person, as in WRITE, REQUEST, and PHONE.

Because the parameters of an ASL nondirectional verb are so rigid, pronominal references in sentences that take them are always supplied with indexing, which supplies actual, hypothetical, and contextual references. In a sentence like "I wonder who you are," the main verb, "wonder," is nondirectional. In this sentence, indexing supplies the pronominal references, which in this case are based on actual location: WONDER WHO YOU.

ASL	*English*
BILL (INDEX) ARRIVE PARTY	Bill made it to the party.
BRING MORE FOOD, INDEX (BILL)	Bill brought us more food.
INDEX (BILL) SURPRISE ME	He surprised me.
TRUE REMEMBER BRING FOOD, INDEX (BILL)	He actually remembered to bring the food.
TELEPHONE INDEX (BILL), ME FORGET	I even forgot to call him.

Training Exercises

A. Translate the following sentences with prearranged pronominal references into English.

1. CAR SIGN (BUMPER), ME NOTICE
2. SILLY, THEY BEHAVE
3. ME MUST WRITE ALL PAPER
4. BASEBALL, SHE PLAY GOOD
5. RACE GOOD, SHE HE
6. E-C-L-I-P-S-E, CAN SEE YOU
7. HE TRY STEAL STORE
8. NEW SUIT, ME GET

B. Translate the following sentences that contain temporarily established references.

1. MR. BROWN (INDEX LOCATION) SICK.
   LIE BED, INDEX (MR. BROWN)

2. YESTERDAY MY FAMILY (INDEX LOCATION) GO-TO BEACH. INDEX (FAMILY) STAY ALL-DAY
3. KAREN (INDEX LOCATION) FORGET BOOK-BOOK LIE ON DESK, INDEX (KAREN) LEFT
4. MY CHURCH (INDEX LOCATION) BUILD NEW SCHOOL ROOM. INDEX (MY CHURCH) BEGIN BUILD SOON
5. ASK TRACY (INDEX LOCATION) SET TABLE DINNER. INDEX (TRACY) TURN
6. LARRY (INDEX LOCATION) MUST HURRY. TRAIN LEAVE. 10 MINUTE. INDEX (LARRY) MAYBE LATE
7. KNOW CHRIS (INDEX LOCATION), YOU? INDEX (CHRIS) YOU SCHEDULE PLAY TENNIS FOR SCHOOL
8. MR. GREEN (INDEX LOCATION) MY UNCLE. INDEX (MR. GREEN) NEW PRINCIPAL YOUR SCHOOL

C. Translate the following English sentences into ASL. Be aware of how you express the pronominal references.

1. Tom, he asked me to go to the pizza parlor.
2. She left her room to go to dinner.
3. Dr. Jones arrived at the football game. He sat on the bench by the sidelines.
4. I saw Fred the other day. He was studying at the library for a long time.
5. When I heard what Karen said to you, I suggested that she see a counselor.
6. Maybe you have a quarter to spare.
7. She can still remember the first television show.
8. The customer smiled at me. I think she likes me.
9. The clerk sold the book. But later, he wished he had the book back.
10. You will always be my best friend.

D. Scenarios provide a good context for developing practice with the various indexing strategies. Use ASL to provide a conclusion for each of the following scenarios.

Scenario 1:

An orderly comes to your hospital bed and tells you he is in a hurry and needs to get you to surgery ASAP. But you are sure your surgery is not until next week. When you try to explain this, he insists on carrying out his task. He's moving for the bed.

Scenario 2:

You go to see a new doctor about a health problem in a very personal part of your anatomy. When the doctor walks in to see you in the examination room, you are shocked to find the doctor is not just the opposite gender but also young and very attractive. To complicate the situation, when you get embarrassed, you usually faint. The doctor instructs you to disrobe and begins to leave the room.

Scenario 3:

It's your parents' thirtieth wedding anniversary, and your whole family has gathered to throw a big surprise party. Although you suspect that your folks may already know about the party, you have been assigned to get them out of the house on the night of the party, and then bring them back without them finding out the reason. It's the night of the party, and it's time for you to make your move.

9. Multidirectional Verbs

One of the most effective characteristics of ASL as a visual-gestural system is its application of the spatial dimension in verb production. Most such activity is in association with multidirectional verbs. The core parameters of an ASL "multidirectional verb" are performed in neutral space without any substantial physical contact with the body or head. Such a verb can move in many different directions without distorting its semantic identity. The flexibility of a multidirectional verb gives the signer several alternative ways to unambiguously convey the subject and the object of a sentence without needing separate lexical signs.

The core parameters of an ASL sign are defined according to the phonological composition of a sign as it appears in neutral isolation—not as it appears in discourse. As part of the core articulation base, verbs can be classified according to their position relative to the body. Verbs are either anchored or free-style. "Anchored" verbs have a position parameter that include actual contact with the body. Examples of anchored verbs are nondirectional verbs, with their fixed position. "Free-style" verbs, on the other hand, are performed completely within the neutral signing space, making no physical contact with the body. Free-style verbs are defined phonologically predominately by two parameters: hand formation and relative body position. The remaining parameters, hand movement and palm direction, are defined only loosely. Free-style verbs are also referred to as "multidirectional" verbs because they can superimpose changes in space and movement on their basic composition.

Most ASL verbs are multidirectional (Friedman, 1975; Fischer and Gough, 1978; Klima and Bellugi, 1979; Padden, 1981). Selected multidirectional verbs include ASK, GIVE, PREACH, LOOK-AT, TELL, BOTHER, SEND ADVISE, COMMAND, MEET, URGE, INFORM, CATCH, DEPEND, CHOOSE, RECEIVE, TEACH, BRING, SEE GO/COME, SHOW, HELP, INTRODUCE, INQUIRY, ENCOURAGE, CONTINUE, STAY, and WAIT.

A major linguistic function of a sentence is to indicate any relationship that may exist between the main verb and its referents (Liddell, 1980). Using its free-style movement capability, a multidirectional verb uses spatial location, real or grammatically established, to unambiguously convey the relationship between the referents of a sentence. It uses linear movement to convey the participants of a sentence, differentiating between the doer of the action and the beneficiary of the verb's action. Superimposing these movements on the verb alters its visual form, and the reader interprets the extra movement as pronominal information (Hanson and Bellugi, 1982). This occurs without substantially altering the identity of the base verb (Padden, 1981).

Regardless of whether a verb is directional, all ASL nominal signs are articulated when the referent is not present. Nominal signs can inform the reader of who is being discussed and/or establish spatial locations for future referencing. Whenever a proper noun is introduced into an ASL discussion, the reference is assigned a space for future use, either by indexing or by an equivalent strategy. In subsequent conversation the reserved spatial point will be used instead of the proper name. When the main verb is multidirectional, the signer will incorporate these indexes into the direction of the verb's movement, moving from the source location (subject) toward the location of the goal (object) to indicate the major sentence participants. Because the direction of the verb's movement can indicate what is happening in the sentence, and to whom, the need for certain signs is eliminated. Instead of supplying a pronominal sign for the subject and/or object reference, the signer will use the direction of linear movement of the verb to indicate the basic sentential relationships. This results in great sentence economy.

The verb's spatial endpoints represent the specific grammatical units of its related nouns. The initial point in space at which the verb begins to be formed is the "source" location. It represents the initiator (or experiencer, doer, agent) of the action. The spatial point where the verb finishes its movements signals the "goal" location. It represents the recipient (or beneficiary, patient) of the action (Friedman, 1975). The point-to-point movement of the verb between these sources indirectly supplies information on who is doing what to or for whom.

Directional verbs can also use prearranged movement to incorporate pronominal referents into the locational endpoints of its movement parameter. A verb moving directly inward, for instance, signals the first-person reference (ME). In contrast, a forward movement along the sign line refers to the second-person reference (YOU). A slanted verb movement along either side of the sign line conveys a third-person reference (HE, SHE, IT).

Multidirectional verbs thus incorporate the indexes for pronominal references directly into their movement parameters. This includes the referencing of persons, objects, or locations. The signer in effect is to gesture toward the sentence's pronominal references. He uses the starting and finishing endpoints of the verb's linear movement. Specifically, the initial location of the hand(s) as it begins to perform the verb signals the initiator/experience reference (the source endpoint). If, for example, the initiator of the action is the signer, as in the basic sentence ME TELL, the multidirectional verb TELL supplies this reference within its movement. In its neutral form, TELL consists of the index hand positioned in front of the chin with the palm inward. Its neutral movement is a small forward-arcing motion. But when TELL incorporates a first-person pronoun, it begins its articulation near the signer's chin and moves forward into neutral space until the arm is near full extension.

The spatial location in which the verb concludes its articulation (if outside of the immediate neutral space) signals the recipient/beneficiary of the verb action (the goal endpoint). In the case of a command such as TELL ME, the first person (ME) is the recipient. The verb TELL incorporates the reference ME into its movement by beginning with the index hand positioned forward and the palm facing upward, and the index hand now rotates inward with the index finger rising to make contact with the chin. Thus, ME TELL and TELL ME differ only in the direction of the verb's movement.

Since the linear movement of a multidirectional verb can supply pronominal references to both subjects and objects, a multidirectional verb can represent a complete sentence in and of itself. A basic three-part sentence, such as YOU TELL ME can be conveyed solely with the verb TELL. This single-sign sentence begins with the index hand of TELL extended directly forward just beyond the neutral space with the palm slanted up and inward (this location represents the second-person pronoun reference YOU). Now the hand begins to perform its sign composition, and as it does so, it moves inward toward the signer's chest (a location representing the first person, I/ME). The result is equivalent to (YOU) TELL (ME). Reversal of the direction of the verb movement changes the participants' roles in relation to the action. To reverse the participants as in (ME) TELL (YOU), the index hand reverses its linear movement and its endpoints. The index hand now moves from the signer's chin (representing the first-person reference) in a direct arc motion just beyond neutral space (representing the second-person references).

Multidirectional verbs can be either single-handed or two-handed. Consider the two-handed verb HELP, which involves a primary S hand (palm oriented toward self) resting on top of the secondary open hand (palm up) at chest level. The basic movement consists of the hands touching or moving up and down slightly. Outside of a momentary contact of both hands, this type of a verb is free-style by definition—neither hand makes actual contact with the body. To convey (YOU) HELP (ME), the hands make initial contact together near the body and then immediately move directly forward a moderate distance. (SHE) HELP (THEM), the hands make initial contact at one side of the sign line and then move across and

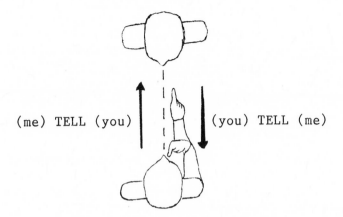

Figure 1. Direction of Movement with the Multidirectional Verb TELL

forward, swinging across the sign line in an arc motion. Other two-handed multidirectional verbs include DEPEND, CONTINUE, BOTHER, and PROTECT.

Multidirectional verbs always unambiguously indicate the initiator (or experience) from the recipient (or beneficiary) within a sentence regardless of whether overt pronominal markers are used (Friedman, 1976). Even sentences that use overt signs to introduce the persons being discussed usually index them for future reference. So long as the verb has multidirectional capability, its linear movement will be used to indicate the initiator from the recipient of the verb's action. In a sentence like MARGARET TEACH FRAN ("Margaret is teaching Fran."), the use of proper names assumes the reader does not know the persons being discussed. The signer thus conveys MARGARET INDEX (to establish location) TEACH (beginning at side of establish location and moving across the sign line to the location planned for second referent) FRAN INDEX (to establish planned location).

In written form, the sentence referents within a multidirectional verb are written in arabic numbers directly below the verb. The order of these numbers or "markers" distinguishes the initiator from the recipient and the numbers themselves signal which pronominal referent is used. When an arabic number comes at the beginning of the verb, as in TEACH, it signifies that the first-person pronoun initiated the action. In this case, the marker supplies the subject yielding "I teach." An arabic number at the end of the verb, as in TEACH, denotes the recipient of the action. In this instance, the marker expresses the object as in "Teach me." Thus, the position of the marker in relation to the verb designates the function of the pronoun in the sentence, and the arabic number supplies the particular personal pronoun.

$$\underset{1 \quad 2}{\text{TEACH}}$$

Sign: Supplies the verb
Number: Supplies the particular personal pronoun
Position of Number: Designates the part of speech. An initial marker denotes the subject and a final marker denotes the object.

The verb's movement can denote three prearranged references to personal pronouns. In written form, an arabic number signifies the location and corresponding pronoun reference.

1 - the location is signer's chest and refers to the first person (I/ME). Example: $\underset{1}{\text{MEET}}$ ("Meet me.").

2 - the location is a moderate distance directly forward and refers to the second person (YOU). Example: $\underset{2}{\text{HELP}}$ ("You help.").

3 - If the location is either side of the sign line, it refers to the third person singular (HE/SHE). Example: $\underset{3}{\text{GO}}$ ("She is going."). If the location is a horizontal arc movement intersecting the sign line, it refers to the third person plural (THEY/THEM). Example MEET: ("meet them").

Now consider the interpretative effect of changing $\underset{1}{\text{BOTHER}}$ to $\underset{2}{\text{BOTHER}}$. Such a reversal changes the meaning from "I bother you" to "You bother me." If a verb has full directional capability, any of the three arabic numbers can be substituted in any combination; $\underset{2}{\text{BOTHER}}$ ("You bother them."), $\underset{1}{\text{BOTHER}}$ ("I bother her."), $\underset{3}{\text{BOTHER}}$ ("He bothers them."), etc. Other verb signs demonstrate a similar linguistic flexibility: $\underset{1}{\text{DEPEND}}$ ("I depend on him."), $\underset{2}{\text{DEPEND}}$ ("You depend on them."), $\underset{3}{\text{DEPEND}}$ ("They depend on me."), $\underset{3}{\text{GIVE}}$ ("She gives you."), $\underset{3}{\text{GIVE}}$ ("They give him."), etc.

The written descriptions of the movement parameters of verbs supply the initial and concluding endpoints to denote pronoun referents. A few descriptions illustrate this movement dimension.

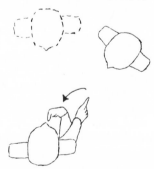

Figure 2: $\underset{3 \quad 1}{\text{ASK}}$ **(HE ASK ME):** **Hand begins at the side of the sign line (point of third-person singular) and moves inward towards the signer (point of first person).**

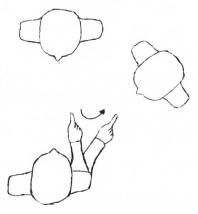

Figure 3. ASK (YOU ASK HER): Hand begins directly and moderately forward
_{2   3}   (point of second person) and moves to the side
                                             of the sign line (point of third-person singular).

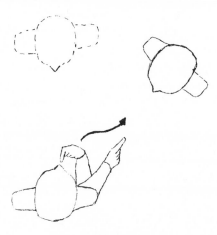

Figure 4. ASK (ME ASK HER): Hand begins near the signer (first person and
_{1   3}   moves indirectly to the side of the sign line
                                            (third-person singular).

Additional ASL-Specific Sentence Patterns

The following patterns are created by the optional movement
capabilities of free-style verbs. Conveying referents spatially through verb
movement is used whenever: (1) the references are established or being
established through indexing; (2) the spatial locations are prearranged according to the understood relation of the sign line and neutral space; and

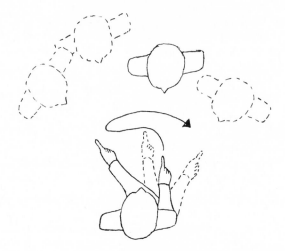

Figure 5. **ASK (YOU ASK THEM):** **Hand begins directly and moderately forward**
    2   3   **(point of second person) and moves slightly**
                                   inward and then to a side of the sign line and
                                   then swings across the sign line point of third-
                                   person plural).

(3) the spatial locations are established as the actual persons (or objects) present during the communication.

To assist your understanding of how verb movement influences the basic sentence framework, this book once again uses diagrams to highlight the general grammatical relations. Verb movement provides an excellent example of how a manual sentence can convey grammatical information not linearly, but simultaneously. To distinguish separate overt lexical items from indirectly conveyed referents, diagrams in this book represent all implied referents in parentheses. A few examples include:

(SUBJECT) ‖ VERB	(YOU) ‖ TELL
(S) ‖ (V)	(S) ‖ (V)

VERB ⤬ (OBJECT)   TELL ⤬ (HER)
(V)   (O)   (V)   (O)

(SUBJECT)‖ VERB ⤬(OBJECT)   (YOU)‖ TELL ⤬(HIM)
(S) ‖ (V)   (O)   (S) ‖ (V) (O)

Pattern 9

Pattern 9 denotes a basic subject-verb sentence in which both main elements are conveyed simultaneously within the verb's parameters. The underlying framework is that of the subject-verb-object sequence.

In Pattern 9 sentences, the subject is indirectly conveyed by the initial location of the verb's movement. This pattern is unmarked in the sentence that is not topicalized. A sentence like "You ask" is written as (YOU) ASK or simply ASK. Since the marker comes at the beginning of the verb, it represents the subject. The number 2 denotes a second-person pronoun.

If the same sentence included a person who needed to be introduced to the reader, as in "Carla asks," the proper noun is performed first, followed by indexing to establish a location. The verb movement then begins from that newly established location. This sentence would be written as CARLA ASK. Another example is TYPE. The position of the arabic marker indicates that the pronoun is the subject and the actual number 3 signifies a third-person reference: (HE/SHE) TYPE, meaning "He or she types."

> Pattern 9: (Subject)-Multidirectional Verb
> ASL: TEACH
> English: He is teaching.
> Diagram: (HE) ‖ TEACH
> (S) ‖ (V)

ASL	*English*
CHOOSE	I am choosing.
TELL	You tell.
STOP	You stop that.

Exercise: Write six Pattern 9 sentences, three with proper nouns and three with pronominal references.

Pattern 10

Pattern 10 represents a reversal in the noun-verb sign order. Pattern 10 signifies an economized version of the basic command sentence. The object is supplied by the movement of the verb and the subject is understood as "you" by the framework and context.

Pattern 10 sentences begin with the verb initially forming within the neutral space. But the movement is toward a predetermined location that visually conveys the recipient of the action (object). This sentence pattern cannot be topicalized, and therefore is never marked by an intonation break. In the case of the simple command "Close the door," manual expression depends on whether the object (door) is actually present or has been established grammatically. If it is actually present within the immediate visual field, then the sentence is written CLOSE, in which the marker indicates that the movement of the verb points toward the actual door as it finishes its movement. If the door has been grammatically established in the sign field, then the verb moves to finish at or near that location. As this example illustrates, referents can be persons, places, or things.

Pattern 10: Multidirectional Verb-(object)
ASL: SHOW
English: Show her.
Diagram: SHOW $\diagdown$ (HER)
(V) $\diagup$ (O)

ASL	English
CATCH	Go catch up with her.
TELL	Tell me.
BELIEVE	Believe me.
GIVE	Give it to me.
INFORM	Let me know, or Keep me informed.

Exercise: Write eight Pattern 10 sentences, four with person referents and four with non-person referents.

Pattern 11

When the movement of the verb incorporates both major grammatical references and their relationships to the verb, the sentence is in Pattern 11. The underlying sign order of a Pattern 11 sentence is (subject)-verb-(object), in which the subject and the object are nonreversible. In written form, the marker that comes at the beginning of the verb always represents the subject (initiator) of the action. The marker that immediately follows the verb always represents the object (recipient) of the action. Thus, the English sentence, "You show me" is written as SHOW in ASL notation.

Pattern 11: (subject)-Multidirectional Verb-(object)
ASL: GIVE
English: I am giving it to you.
Diagram: (I) ‖ GIVE $\diagdown$ (YOU)
(S) ‖ (V) $\diagup$ (O)

ASL	English
GIVE	I am giving it to him.
INFORM	I am letting him know.
HELP	You help me.
CAN HELP	I can help you.

Exercise: Write four Pattern 11 sentences.

Reversed Directional Verbs

Certain multidirectional verbs contain a movement that requires the hand(s) to begin in neutral space and then move inward toward the signer. The sign BORROW has such a composition, and it fundamentally means "I borrow from you." To reverse the sentence referents to yield "You borrow from me" or "I lend you" the movement parameter reverses in direction. The hands now begin near the signer and move forward toward the recipient. Thus in "reversed" directional verbs, the base movement conveys the opposite of the intended associated reference. Other fundamentally reversed verbs include: TAKE, CHOOSE, COPY, INVITE, APPOINT, and AVOID.

Multidirectional movement illustrates how the roots of ASL are in actual discourse rather than in isolated signs or sentences. The economy of ASL syntax is best illustrated by a multidirectional verb such as MEET. To convey the complete idea of "He is meeting her," English uses four words. But through American Sign Language uses economization to express the equivalent thought by a single sign with spatial dimensions: MEET_3. Not only is the ASL sentence more succinct, it is less ambiguous since the spatial indexes inform the reader who, specifically, each referent is.

Changing Palm Direction

In addition to the linear movement of the verb, palm direction can also show the reader who is doing what to whom (Fischer and Gough, 1978). Most multidirectional verbs have free-style palm direction, which can be intentionally changed to "face" the location of a pronominal reference. Like directional movement, palm variations can denote sentence referents.

A sentence like $_2\text{ASK}_1$ (meaning "You ask me.") involves a palm change. In its neutral form, ASK uses a forward palm orientation; but in $_2\text{ASK}_1$, the palm direction or orientation reverses to face inward. The hand then moves inward toward the signer. Another example is $_3\text{ASK}_3$ (meaning "He or she is asking them.") in which the palm direction starts by facing sideways and later swings forward.

Changing palm orientation is especially prevalent in two-handed multidirectional verbs, in which each hand can be used to represent a person referent. The two hands might, for example, face each other to represent two persons looking at each other. Or the palm orientation of only one hand might show a first-person reference, as in WORK_1 ("I am working."). Still another option involves both hands in actual movement, as in WE WORK ("We are working."). And in still another option, one hand remains stationary as if representing someone "waiting" while the other hand

performs the movement to represent another person approaching, as in
HELP WILL ("I will help you."). In this example, since one hand moves
to touch the other stationary hand, the sign movement metaphorically
represents someone moving to help another person. Two-handed verbs that
can be used for this metaphoric representation include CALL, COPY,
WORK, START, BLAME, ARRIVE, and LEAD.

The two-handed verb MEET illustrates the metaphoric representation
created by combining palm orientation with movement. In its core composition, MEET is a two-handed symmetrical verb formed with both index
hands facing (but not touching) each other at chest level. Its basic movement consists of the hands coming together and momentarily touching. It
conveys the basic idea of two people meeting. But since MEET is a
multidirectional verb, various reference options are available.

The first method is to keep one hand stationary while the other hand
moves. While the secondary hand remains in place, the primary hand
moves to meet it, thus metaphorically conveying the idea of one person
meeting another. To express MEET, the stationary index hand is held outward toward the reader, palm facing inward, representing the second-
person pronoun. The active index hand faces the secondary hand (palm forward and hand position close to self) and moves forward to touch the
stationary hand, which means "I meet you." To convey the reversed meaning MEET, the stationary index hand is held close to the signer with the
palm oriented outward. The active index hand begins moderately forward
with the palm facing inward. As the active hand moves inward to touch the
stationary hand it conveys "You meet me."

Whenever a verb is a two-handed symmetrical multidirectional sign
with an active-stationary hand option, the stationary hand always
represents the recipient of the action (object) and the active hand always
represents the initiator of the action (subject). Metaphoric representation
is sufficient to express either the idea of a mutual meeting in which two persons converge or a meeting in which one person moves toward the other.
Palm orientation is used to express pronoun references whenever possible.
If the verb is reversible and the referent marking requires the palm change,
that referent marker must also be reversed. Movement and palm direction
are interrelated in multidirectional-verb signing.

Palm direction conveys pronominal references to the initiator (subject)
and the recipient (object) by its relative location or orientation (Friedman,
1976). Consider a verb like HATE, which involves both 5 hands with the
middle finger touching the thumb. When the hands are held side by side in
neutral space, the hands make a sharp flicking motion with the middle
fingers springing outward. In HATE, as in all verbs of this type, the direction of the palms face the beneficiary of the verb, and the back of the hand
represents the initiator of the verb. If the signer wishes to convey HATE

("I hate you.") the palms face forward and the back of the hands inward. To express HATE₁ ("I hate it."), the palms are directed to one side. To convey HATE₂₁ ("You hate me."), the signer rotates the hand direction so that the palms face the signer and the back of the hands face outward. Multidirectional verbs that rely heavily on palm direction include such signs as HATE, PITY, and TEASE.

Locational Verbs

Some ASL verbs are neither fixed nor multidirectional. Because these verbs have a limited degree of optional movement, they can convey the recipient of the action (object). These verbs, called "locational" verbs, can incorporate a spatial location into their articulation without distorting their semantic identify, but only into their final endpoint. They do this by positioning the hands strategically in the sign space to supply the recipient of a verb's action. Rather than assuming the neutral position, the hand position is arranged according to the recipient pronominal reference's location. The reference may be actual (person physically present), prearranged (in relation to the sign line), or contextual (a point established by indexing to represent a specific person).

An example of a locational verb is MEAN ("intend" or signify"). To convey the recipient reference such as (ME) in YOU MEAN₁, the secondary hand is placed unusually close to the signer's chest. When the verb is performed, the active hand moves to make contact with the stationary hand, which is being held closer than usual to the signer. This placement is a sufficient cue to designate the recipient. Similarly, the sentence ME MEAN₂ ("I mean you.") is conveyed by first performing ME and then deliberately holding the stationary secondary hand moderately forward in the neutral space. As the active hand moves forward to make contact with the secondary hand, the action marks the recipient reference (YOU).

Directional verbs incorporate pronoun references into sign articulation by using the actual linear path that the hands move along. Locational verbs, on the other hand, rely on the positioning of the stationary secondary hand just prior to the sign actually being executed (Fischer and Gough, 1978). This stationary secondary hand is positioned to denote the verb's recipient. Locational verbs do not mark initiators of the action (subject), only the recipients of the action (object). Locational verbs are often two-handed verb signs that are prohibited by their base movement parameters to function multidirectionally. Locational indexing works because with such verbs the secondary hand is positioned prior to sign articulation, and does not affect the actual movement of the sign. In command-type sentences in which the subject "you" is already understood, locational verbs work exactly like multidirectional verbs to mark the recipient of the action.

All locational verbs involve both hands and an asymmetrical articulation. One hand is passive. The other is active and performs the movement of the sign. The verb OWE, for instance, requires the active index hand to tap the palm of the secondary open hand in neutral space. To convey the sentence ME OWE₂ ("I owe you."), the signer first indexes ME. Then the stationary hand is positioned moderately forward with the palm oriented inward to face the signer. The active index hand moves forward and taps the secondary palm to convey the idea: OWE (YOU). To convey the reciprocal sentence, YOU OWE₁ ("You owe me."), the signer first indexes YOU. The stationary open hand is then held unusually close to the signer's chest with the palm facing forward toward the reader. The active index hand moves inward and touches the secondary palm, expressing the present direction of obligation.

In each of these examples, the palm direction of the stationary hand uses location to convey the idea of who owes the obligation. Thus OWE is not really a nondirectional verb, it is a locational verb, which means it can modify its secondary palm direction and use limited spatial location to mark the recipient of the action. Locational verbs include MEAN, OWE, SHOW, LOCK, START PRACTICE, EAGER, EXCUSE, and DEMAND.

The movement parameters of a locational verb may be either horizontal or vertical. Vertical locational verbs locate the stationary hand to mark the recipient reference but maintain a vertical movement. In a vertical locational verb, the active hand moves horizontally (to convey the referent) and then vertically (to complete the verb's articulation). Vertical locational verbs include REMEMBER, BELIEVE, HOPE, PROMISE, LEARN, TRUST, NOTICE, DECIDE, DISAPPEAR, AGREE, and JUDGE.

Body-Oriented Verbs

A variation of the locational verb is the body-anchored verbs that conveys either direct or implied information on one's state of physical health (Fischer and Gough, 1978). These verbs use location to focus the reader's attention on an anatomical site of the body. In other words, while a verb's neutral position parameter may be the general chest area, this position may be relocated without interfering with the essence of the sign's composition.

Consider a sentence like "I hurt." In and of itself, the message is vague and open-ended. The reader does not know what kind of pain or where the pain is located. But a locational verb in this sentence can convey specifically what part of the body hurts. Thus, a locational verb can transform "I hurt" into ME HURT (HEAD), in which the verb HURT is positioned not in the neutral sign space, but instead in front of the head or whatever site is being referred to. Other locations include ME HURT (LEG), ME HURT (STOMACH). In each case, the verb HURT uses relative location of the hands to express the involved area.

A sign like ACHE in its neutral form involves both index hands held in front of the signer with the fingertips facing and palms inward. The fingers move closer together in a twisting or jabbing motion. To convey a general idea of "ache," the twisting motion is performed in neutral space. But when a signer wishes to designate an actual site of the ache, the relative location of the hands performing the twisting motion changes from neutral space to a specific site on the body. Thus location is used to convey such concepts as HEADACHE, BACKACHE, and TOOTHACHE. This form of verb locationality economizes a sentence by supplying additional information within a sign's parameters without using extra signs. Such verbs maintain their hand formation, palm direction, and movement parameters according to the core definition. But they vary the position parameter relative to the signer's body to convey extra information. An injury resulting from a dog bite, for instance, can be expressed by moving the hands to show the location of the mishap. Body-oriented locational verbs include HIT, ACHE, BLEED, HURT, CUT, REMOVE, and WASH.

The basic form of the sign WASH, for example, involves both A hands, palms moving in an alternating manner as if rubbing together. The core position is in neutral space. But when the signer positions the hands on another spatial point of the body, the meaning of the sign will change. If the sign WASH is performed while the hands are touching the signer's chest, for instance it loosely means WASH-MYSELF. But if the same sign is positioned elsewhere, such as near the head (WASH-HAIR) or near the face (WASH-FACE), it conveys other information.

Direct and Indirect Objects

In English, a direct object is a noun that receives the action of the verb, and an indirect object indicates the target of the transaction. The indirect object states to or for whom something is done. "Mary" in "I bought Mary a present" tells for whom the present was bought. "Mary" serves as the indirect object.

American Sign Language uses its spatial dimension to convey this type of relational information. One way it does this is to index multidirectional verbs. Consider how you might express a sentence like, "Tina is giving Erick a haircut" in which "Erick" is the indirect object. One strategy is to topicalize the sentence as: HAIRCUT, TINA GIVE ERICK.

Another strategy is to sign each participant's name while indexing to establish spatial-referent locations. Since two referent nouns are involved, the signer will probably want to assign one referent to either side of the sign space.

reader

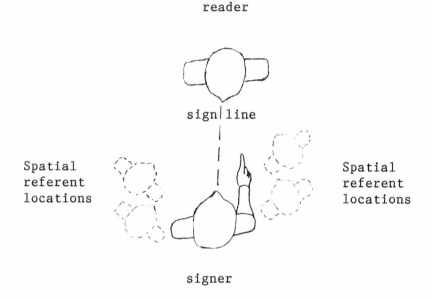

sign line

Spatial   Spatial
referent   referent
locations   locations

signer

Figure 6. Assigning spatial-referent locations

Thus, TINA might be assigned to the signer's right side and ERICK to the left side. Once these spatial-referent locations are established, the sign GIVE (which is multidirectional) is performed beginning on the signer's right side (TINA), and moving across the sign space to finish on the signer's left (ERICK). The verb's movement conveys who is giving something to whom. The signer executes the sign HAIRCUT and the sentence is complete. It can be written TINA (INDEX) ERICK (INDEX) GIVE HAIRCUT. The reverse "Erick is giving Tina a haircut" is accomplished similarly except the movement of the verb is reversed.

When the participants are present during the conversation, as in "He is giving her a haircut," the initial act of establishing referent locations is unnecessary, and the actual location of the persons is used: GIVE HAIR CUT.

In a sentence such as, "I am showing the lady our baby," three different persons are involved. But since the verb SHOW is multidirectional, this sentence presents no real communication problem. First, LADY and BABY are signed and indexed to establish separate spatial locations, typically on the right and left of the signer. Once these locational references are established, the verb SHOW is performed, beginning very near the signer (to denote "I"). The movement then moves out to the right momentarily (LADY) and then finishes at the signer's left (BABY). The directional movements of the verb SHOW indicate who is being shown to whom. The written form of this sentence would be SHOW. Using the direction of verb movement is a common way to convey such participant-participant distinctions in ASL (Bellugi and Fischer, 1972; Hoemann, 1978).

reader

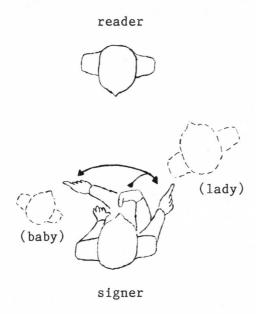

signer

Figure 7. (ME) SHOW (LADY) (BABY)

This same spatial strategy can be used to communicate certain prepositional phrases. A preposition is a connective that shows a relationship between the object of the preposition and another main element in the sentence. In a sentence like, "Paul is meeting Vicky at the movies," the preposition "at" connects "movies" with the sentence, "Paul is meeting Vicky." ASL uses prepositions only infrequently, and usually only when highly informative, but "movies" is informative and must be signed.

To sign "Paul is meeting Vicky at the movies," the signer begins with the fact that MEET is a multidirectional verb. The signer first executes PAUL (index to establish a location) VICKY (index to establish a location). For discussion, Paul is assigned the right side, and VICKY the left side. Now that the referents are in place, this thought can be conveyed any variety of ways. One way is to place the index hands to represent the participants metaphorically. The left index hand is positioned on the left side (VICKY) while the right hand is positioned on the right side (PAUL). Since the idea is that Paul is meeting Vicky, the right hand becomes active and moves across to touch the stationary left hand. The sign MOVIE is then performed: MEET MOVIE.

To reverse the meaning to "Vicky is meeting Paul at the movies," the signer holds the hands first at their respective locations to represent the participants. Now the left hand becomes active, moving to touch the right stationary hand. This reversal is also written: MEET MOVIE. To convey the idea of "Paul and Vicky are meeting at the movies," the hands then move simultaneously and meet in neutral space. The signer then performs the sign MOVIE. Since this is also a visual distinction and not a grammatical one, its written form is also MEET MOVIE.

But suppose the scenario expands to "When Paul met Vicky at the movies, he kissed her." To express this in ASL, the sentence is divided into two underlying sentences, PAUL MEET VICKY AT MOVIE, HE KISS HER. The signer first establishes the referent locations as discussed above. The right index hand (PAUL) is the active hand, and it moves to touch the stationary left index hand and then performs the sign MOVIE. The first sentence is written MEET MOVIE. But the strategy changes for the subsequent sentence HE KISS SHE, which contains the nondirectional verb KISS. Since a nondirectional verb cannot supply pronominal referents through verb movement indexing is used to yield INDEX (PAUL) KISS INDEX (VICKY). If the signer wishes to emphasize the act of kissing as new or surprising information, then the sentence is topicalized as KISS SHE, HE and is performed as KISS INDEX (VICKY), INDEX (PAUL).

Training Exercises

A. Economize the following sentences into information-only sentences. Be sure each sign you choose to represent the words conveys the most exact meaning of what you intend to communicate. Reject any sign that does not enhance semantic specification.

1. You seem to be a very kind person.
2. There really appears to be a mistake here.
3. I have not done anything wrong.
4. There is nothing to be done now.
5. You have too much on your mind.
6. I just put a pizza in the oven.
7. You may be in college forever.
8. The prize is worth all of the effort.
9. He put his theory into practice.
10. She jumped off the diving board into the water.

B. Locate the main verb and translate these sentences using multidirectional verbs.

    1. I stopped over at Tina's house.
    2. You start with these papers.
    3. The children depend on their uncle.
    4. When Sherry received the notice, she cried for joy.
    5. Alice urged her family to come.
    6. Dinah teaches deaf children.
    7. I hate washing my dog.
    8. Grace is asking her to phone.
    9. I depend on good friends.
    10. I really like you.

C. Diagram the following sentences. Simply place any modifier above the main sentence element it refers to. Be aware of all eleven ASL syntactic patterns.

    1. HELEN SELL RED CAR
    2. TEACHER WAIT THREE HOUR
    3. YOU MUST BELIEVE HER
    4. I TEACH SEVEN GRADE CHILDREN
    5. SHE BUMP HER HEAD
    6. JUNE HELP BILL FIX DINNER
    7. NEW SONG, SHE WRITE
    8. RETURN OLD BOOK SHE

D. Write out the likely outcomes of the following scenarios. Be sure to experiment with the various strategies available to you. If possible, act out the written dialogues with a partner.

Scenario 1:
    The paper boy knocks on the door. He asks for the money that is owed for the last four weeks. You are sure that you paid him already, and he is equally sure you have not. Work it out.

Scenario 2:
    A single parent is called out of town on unexpected business and needs to hire a babysitter quickly. At the last minute one is reached. But when she arrives, she explains that something has come up and that she can babysit for only one hour. What does the parent do?

Scenario 3:
    You are a doctor and have just delivered a baby. But you discover that the baby for some unknown reason will never grow hair. You have to explain to the young parents about this unforeseen problem.

10. Asking a Question

There are three fundamental ways to ask a question in American Sign Language. The format of an inquiry is dictated to the sort of information the signer seeks. The most basic question pattern calls for a simple "yes" or "no" response. This pattern includes all questions that can generally be answered with a one-sign response. "Are you going to the dance?", "Do you remember Mork and Mindy?" and "Did you talk with him about your grade?" all illustrate this first type of pattern.

The second type of question is the interrogative question. An "interrogative question" is distinguishable from a yes/no question by two criteria: (1) the inquiry requires a more detailed response than "yes" or "no"; and (2) the inquiry contains an interrogative sign (e.g., WHAT, WHO, HOW, WHEN, WHERE, WHY). Examples of the interrogative question include "Why are you going home now?" "Who are you going to the dance with?" and "How did you manage to win all that money?"

A third sentence pattern of inquiry used in ASL is the rhetorical question. The "rhetorical question" is a question that is both asked and answered by the signer. The reader is not really expected to respond to a rhetorical question. An example of such a question is "Why do I keep going out with Gary?"

The Basic Yes/No Question

The basic yes/no question is any question that prompts a "yes" or "no" response or reaction. The basic yes/no question format is distinguished from a declarative sentence by neither sign order or sign positioning. If both patterns were written side by side, there would be no distinctive feature to separate the two. The declarative sentence GO YOU ("You are going.") and the basic inquiry GO YOU ("Are you going?") are expressed with identical signs and sign order.

In English, declarative and question sentences are generally distinguished by word order. The hallmark of the English question is inverted word order. In an English question, the main verb or one of its auxiliary verbs is intentionally placed before the subject to mark the question, as in "Was Virginia here last night?" or "Should we ask him?" The position of the function word acts as a marker to signal the spoken question.

Since American Sign Language uses no strictly functional elements, inverting sign order is not a plausible way to mark a sentence. As a result, many ASL statements and questions appear on the surface level to be the same entity. An English question like "Is Earl here?" is arranged in ASL as EARL HERE? This ASL question has the same sign order as the corresponding statement of fact: "Earl is here." Since the surface level characteristics of yes/no questions are identical to their corresponding declarative sentences, ASL sentences are marked as questions by other means, usually by the delivery and the use of specific nonmanual signals.

A yes/no ASL question is distinguishable by two elements of delivery: (1) nonmanual facial and body signals; and (2) an inquiry marker. Of these two strategies, the most prevalent is the use of nonmanual signals.

We begin our study of ASL question by studying the delivery of an ASL declarative sentence. An ASL statement is performed with a relatively neutral facial expression. Eyebrows remain relaxed and unremarkable. The speed of delivery is moderate, consistent with the signer's average signing speed. The overall body stance is relaxed and straightforward. Eye contact is not defined, but casual. Unlike other sentence patterns, the declarative sentence is distinguished by no specific grammatical signal. In fact, it is the absence of any special grammatical signals that marks an ASL sentence as a declarative statement. The declarative sentence is signified by an utter lack of any characteristic facial and body signals.

The yes/no question, on the other hand, is characterized by distinctive delivery signals, the most fundamental of which are the use of facial features at the end of the question. Eye contact is usually sustained throughout the performance of the sentence. And the signer completes the question by raising the eyebrows, which in turn widens the eyes, and by tilting the head slightly forward or to one side. This is similar to raising the pitch of one's voice at the end of a spoken question. Facial signals are critical markers for ASL questions.

Since diagrams of ASL sentences do not reflect such facial features as raised eyebrows, widened eyes or head tilt, the graphic depiction of an ASL yes/no question is identical to the corresponding declarative sentence.

ASL: GOOD TIME, YOU ENJOY?
English: Did you have a good time?
Diagram: GOOD

ASL	*English*
TENNIS, GOOD EXERCISE?	Is tennis a good exercise?
TELL SIT? ₃ ₃	Did he tell her to sit down?
CHAIR BREAK?	Did the chair break?
HEALTH, SHE IMPROVE?	Is she feeling any better?
TIME, YOU AWARE?	Are you aware of the time?
SHE PLAN ARRIVE?	Does she plan to come?
TEAM, THEY TRY JOIN?	Will they try to out for the team?

Exercise: Write six ASL sentences that can be delivered as either a question or as a statement of fact.

A second strategy for marking a yes/no question in ASL is the YOU-QUESTION MARKER. A supportive device for the nonmanual signals, the YOU-QUESTION MARKER is a separate sign consisting of the index hand pointing to the person who is being asked a question. The hand points a bit longer than usual and then rises up and back to finish in the X hand position with the palm facing forward. In the YOU-QUESTION MARKER, the hand metaphorically forms a question marker, which is added at the end of the question. When this question marker is used simultaneously with the nonmanual signals at the conclusion of the question, the reader knows clearly that the sentence is an inquiry. The signer awaits a response or reaction.

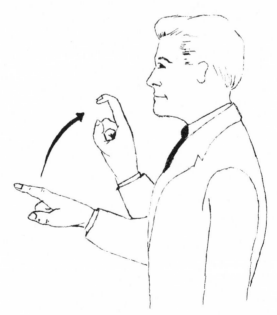

Figure 1. YOU-QUESTION MARKER

The YOU-QUESTION MARKER can also mark a single sign or sign phrase as a question. Examples of single-sign questions include UNDER-STAND? (Do you understand?"), EASY? ("Is it easy?"), EXPENSIVE? ("Is it expensive"), TIME ("What time is it?"), FEEL // YOU? ("How do you feel?"), NOW? ("Do it now?"). Brief sign-phrase questions include FLY HERE SMOOTH? ("Was the flight here smooth?") WANT YOU? ("Do you want it?"), TRUE BAD? ("Is it anything serious?").

An alternative to using the question marker is to hold the last sign of the question longer than usual. Instead of relaxing the hands as is done after a declarative sentence, the signer maintains the position of the last sign to signal the reader that a request for a response is being made. The prolonging of the sign accompanied by facial indicators implicitly signal a question.

When prolonging a sign to signal an inquiry, the signer often repeats the movement of the last sign. This strategy effectively conveys a "waiting" posture, letting the reader know what is expected. A slight forward lean of the body gives a question extra emphasis.

To ask a question that is formed by a single sign or brief sign phrase, the signer can either use the YOU-QUESTION MARKER or prolong the last sign. Consider a question like HE PHONE? ("Did he call?"). Since the YOU-QUESTION MARKER is an independent marker, it can be added to a question even when the question does not end with the sign YOU: HE PHONE YOU-QUESTION MARKER? Prolonging the last sign will also work: HE PHONE-PHONE? You might want to incorporate both methods into your communication. The specific type of yes/no question will determine the appropriate strategy. If a question concludes with the sign YOU as in NEW MOVIE SEE YOU? ("Have you seen the new movie?"), the additional YOU-QUESTION MARKER could be incorporated as a smooth extension of the YOU sign. If the question finishes with another sign as in HE LEAVE? ("Has he left?"), prolonging the final sign's movement might be the more effective choice. Regardless of the method used, the question must always be delivered with an appropriate nonmanual signal.

Another contextual strategy available to distinguish the question is use of the auxiliary verb CAN. Positioning the verb CAN in front of the main verb forms a verb phrase that implies a declarative sentence: SHOE STORE, WE CAN GO ("We can go to the shoe store."). But positioning the auxiliary CAN after the verb denotes a question: SHOE STORE, WE GO CAN? ("Can we go to the shoe store?").

The Interrogative Question

Many questions in American Sign Language ask the reader for a more substantial response than simply "yes" or a "no." The interrogative question asks the reader for substantive information. The interrogative sentence is highlighted by the presence of an interrogative sign such as WHO, WHAT, WHY, WHERE, WHEN, WHICH, HOW, etc.

On the surface level, the interrogative question assumes a basic sign order identical to that of a declarative sentence. It is distinguished from a declarative sentence, however, because it concludes with an interrogative sign and is accompanied by specific nonmanual behavior. Adding an interrogative sign to a declarative sentence like HAPPEN HERE ("It happened here."), for instance, changes the sentence into the inquiry HAPPEN HERE WHAT? ("What is going on here?").

A signer also accompanies an interrogative question with certain nonmanual facial signals. As the signer asks the question, the eyebrows are squinted downward with the eyes drawn in to convey an interested, inquisitive expression. The eyes being drawn in along with the eyebrows being drawn together conveys the message, "Well, what can you tell me about this matter?"

Unlike ASL, the English interrogative question places the interrogative word in front of the sentence. In addition, all English interrogative signs are based on the SVO word order, while ASL often topicalizes even interrogative questions. But interrogative questions in both languages can be distinguished from yes/no questions based on manner of delivery. English interrogative questions do not raise the voice pitch on the last word as is done in a yes/no question, but they do mildly stress the last word. ASL interrogative questions are distinguished from yes/no questions by facial expression. In the yes/no question, the eyebrows raise, opening the eyes wider. But in the interrogative question, the eyebrows squint downward drawing the eyes inward.

To translate an English interrogative question into its equivalent ASL form, consider first whether the question is asked with emphasized interest. For instance, in a sentence like "When are you playing ball?" the sentence can be topicalized as BALL, YOU PLAY. The interrogative unit is then repositioned from the front to the back to complete the translation: BALL, YOU PLAY WHEN? But if the signer is more concerned about the actions of a particular person, the SVO order is used. To translate the question "Why are you late?" the sentence is first economized to YOU LATE, and the interrogative is then repositioned: YOU LATE WHY? In both cases, nonmanual signals complete the congruent delivery of the interrogative question.

In a diagram, the interrogative sign is an independent component that is presented on a "T" line placed at the end of the base line.

ASL: WASH DISH WHO?
English: Who is going to wash the dishes?

Diagram:

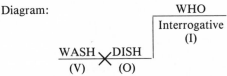

ASL	*English*
TIME WHAT?	What time is it?
DOOR, HERE WHO?	Who is at the door?
YOUR APPOINTMENT WHEN?	When is your appointment?
LEARN, YOU HOW?	How did you find out?
GO CAN WE WHERE?	Where can we go?
MEET, KNOW-YOU WHEN?	Do you know when the meeting is?
PARTY TIME, DECIDE FINISH YOU WHEN?	Have you decided on a date for the party?
BORN, YOU WHEN?	When were you born?

Exercise: Write six interrogative questions, three formed in the SVO order and three with topicalized order.

Specific Interrogative Signs

WHICH

The sign WHICH conveys the idea of choice and is loosely equivalent to the English conjunctions "either/or." WHICH asks the question "what one(s)." This sign conveys the idea of making a choice through the use of spatial relations.

WHICH can be used to bracket choices. Although the ordinary position of WHICH is at the end of the sentence, under certain circumstances, WHICH is positioned both at the beginning and at the end of a sentence. Use of WHICH depends on the type of choice. Bracketing a sentence with WHICH (at both ends of the question) is most often used to ask a question that involves either a comparison of some type or a closed set of choices. When WHICH brackets a sentence such as WHICH PREFER SUMMER WINTER WHICH? ("Which season do you like more, summer or winter?"), the choice is a closed set. In this case, the phrase "closed set" refers to the idea that the only choices involved in the present inquiry are included within the sentence. The use of bracketed WHICH implicitly conveys that since the choices have been directly presented, the reader is to choose from them. The signer has limited the possible choices and closed them to other alternatives. In the question WHICH YOU WANT SANDWICH HAMBURGER WHICH ("What do you want to eat, a sandwich or a hamburger?"), the question supplies the selection and asks the reader to make a selection.

Bracketed WHICH also eliminates the need for a conjunction like "either/or." The initial WHICH alerts the reader to anticipate a choice coming, and the second WHICH signals the choice has been presented. A sentence like WHICH CLASS SPANISH MATH, YOU PLAN ATTEND WHICH? ("Which course are you going to take, Spanish or math?") illustrates how the double WHICH effectively replaces the need for the conjunction "or."

Bracketed WHICH implicitly signals that the boxed choices are the only available options. To diagram the bracketed WHICH, each sign is treated as an independent component and is represented on a "T" line at both ends of the question.

ASL: WHICH LIKE COKE PEPSI NONE WHICH
English: Which do you like: Coke, Pepsi, or neither?
Diagram:

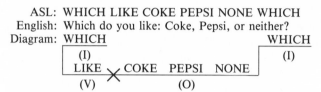

ASL	English
WHICH MORE EXPENSIVE, CAR HOUSE WHICH	What costs more, the car or the house?
WHICH BOOK GONE WITH WIND MOBY DICK READ YOU WHICH?	Which book did you read, *Gone with the Wind* or *Moby Dick*?

Exercise: Write two interrogative questions involving the bracketed WHICH pattern.

WHICH is used without bracketing when the sentence presents an open choice. Such a sentence does not supply a list of preference or choice within its surface structure. In a question like REPORT, YOU NEED WHICH? ("Which report do you need?"), the question does not explicitly supply a list of reports in its content. Instead, it assumes the reader knows which choices are being referred to. It therefore represents an open set. Open-ended questions usually require only one WHICH, and this WHICH is positioned at the end of the question. As a general guideline, when a question supplies the elements of choice, bracket it with WHICH. When the question raises an open-ended choice, use a single WHICH placed at the end of the question.

In sentences in which English would use the conjunction "or" to signal a choice in a yes/no question, ASL will simply rely on the context. In such questions, the yes/no question signaled by the appropriate nonmanual behavior is sufficient to imply the choice. An example is the question: HUNGRY THIRSTY, YOU?

ASL: TEAM, YOU WANT WIN WHICH?
English: Which team do you want to win?

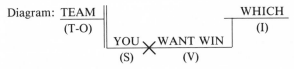

Diagram:

```
TEAM ‖                          WHICH
(T-O)  |                         (I)
       | YOU ⟍ ⟋WANT WIN |
       |     ⟋ ⟍          |
        (S)  ✕    (V)
```

ASL	*English*
CAR, YOU BUY WHICH?	Which car did you buy?
PARTY DRESS, YOU WEAR WHICH?	Which dress did you wear to the party?
PANCAKES EGGS, WANT?	Do you want some pancakes and eggs?
BOOK (INDEX TWO), YOU WANT USE?	Do you need to use either of these books?
TV PROGRAM, YOU ENJOY MOST WHICH?	Which TV programs do you like the most?

Exercise: Write four sentences, two with open-ended choices questions and two that contain more than one choice.

When a signer introduces new information to the reader, he or she might elect to index a spatial location for it for future reference. Combining an interrogative question with indexing is an effective strategy for raising certain questions and then discussing them during the discourse. This strategy can be expressed in a question like "Do you like to bowl or swim better?" To express this thought in ASL with spatial referents, the signer expresses WHICH BOWL (index to establish location) SWIM (index to establish location), ENJOY MORE WHICH? To signal the question even further, the signer now places one of each of the hands near the location assigned for each choice when performing the final WHICH sign. When the hands alternatively move up and down at the position of each reference, the movement emphasizes the choices. When the actual topics are physically present as in the question "Are you going to buy this tie or that one?" indexing the actual objects is the preferred strategy: INDEX (first tie) INDEX (second tie), YOU WANT BUY WHICH?

When the choice involves more than two items, signing depends on whether the subject matter is real or hypothetical. When the items are real and present within the visual area, the signer indexes toward each item. This strategy is illustrated in a scenario where two people are dining out together. As they look over their menu, one signs WHICH INDEX (steak) INDEX (chicken) INDEX (seafood) WANT EAT WHICH? ("What do you want to eat, steak, chicken, or seafood?").

In a case where the topics are hypothetical, each item needs to be grammatically supplied. The signer first introduces each item STEAK, CHICKEN, SEAFOOD and immediately indexes each item. The signer is now ready to ask the question: WHICH INDEX (steak) INDEX (chicken) INDEX (seafood), YOU ENJOY EAT WHICH ("What kind of food do you like steak, chicken, or seafood?").

WHAT'S // UP

Considered a compound interrogative, WHAT'S // UP consists of an abbreviation of the sign WHAT followed by a shrug of the shoulders and relaxed open hands, palms up. When expressed in isolation, WHAT'S // UP asks the question "What is happening?" or "What is going on?" When used in a sentence, WHAT'S // UP functions as an ordinary interrogative sign. It is positioned at the end of the sentence and works with the simultaneous nonmanual signals to create an interrogative question. WHAT'S // UP asks "What or why is this happening?" In a communicative sequence like, "You're late. Any special reason why?" for instance, the question follows a statement of fact. It asks for information that pertains to it: LATE, YOU. WHAT'S // UP?

Figure 2. The interrogative sign WHAT'S // UP

ASL: MUCH NOISE WHAT'S // UP
English: Why are you making so much noise?
Diagram: MUCH
     (M)   WHAT'S // UP
     NOISE   (I)
     (S)

ASL   *English*
PEOPLE LAUGH WHAT'S UP?   Why are all these people laughing?
                                 What's going on?
WHAT'S // UP?   How about it?

Exercise: Write two interrogative questions that include the interrogative WHAT'S // UP.

HOW

The interrogative HOW is used chiefly when the signer wishes to know information that relates to manner, method, or condition. In a question like "How did you find it?" the request for information specifically asks "What steps did you take that led you to discover this?" It therefore asks a question of manner: DISCOVER, YOU HOW? In contrast, when a speaker verbalizes a question like "How do you like the pie?" the speaker is not using "how" as defined in ASL. This English question could be paraphrased to yield "Do you like the pie?" In this case, ASL used a yes/no question: PIE, YOU ENJOY?

HOW as an interrogative sign in ASL is used only to inquire about the manner, method, or condition of something or someone. A sentence like TELL SHE, ME HOW? ("How am I going to tell her?") clearly seeks conditional information. In effect, the question asks, "What manner or method could I use to tell her this without having her become upset?"

ASL: FEEL, YOU HOW
English: How do you feel?
Diagram:

FEEL		HOW
(T-V)	YOU	(I)
	(S)	

ASL   *English*
KNOW, HOW?   How do you know him?
  3
TELL, ME HOW?   How am I going to tell her?
  3

Exercise: Write two questions using the interrogative HOW.

HOW // MANY and HOW MUCH

The compound HOW // MANY is formed from the source signs HOW and MANY and is expressed as an interrogative. The compound interrogative HOW // MANY prompts a comment on degree, number, or price. The sentence PEOPLE COME-HERE HOW // MANY? ("How many people are coming?") illustrates its use and its position at the end of the question.

HOW is also used in the phrase HOW MUCH, which prompts a response concerning extent. But the phrase HOW MUCH usually is economized by dropping the sign HOW as in LEAVE WILL, YOU MUCH?

("How much will you leave?"). Although the phrase is economized, the sign MUCH retains the interrogative meaning and is placed in the final position of the sentence.

ASL: MALE FRIEND, YOU KNOW HOW // MANY?
English: How many boyfriends do you have?
Diagram:

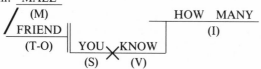

ASL: YOUR HOUSE WORTH MUCH?
English: How much does your house cost?
Diagram:

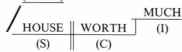

ASL	English
VACATION DAY, YOU HAVE HOW // MANY?	How many days of vacation do you have?
MONEY, EARN YOU MUCH?	How much money did you make?
GUESS OLD ME HOW // MANY?	Guess how old I am?
NOW // DAY BECOME WARM MUCH?	How warm will it get today?

Exercise: Write six questions, three using HOW // MANY and three using MUCH.

Since HOW asks for information on manner, method, or condition, there are many instances where English does not use the equivalent lexical unit as ASL. When translating between American Sign Language and English, you must often use dissimilar semantic units (words and signs) to express a given meaning. In English for instance, the word "how" is often used in a functional capacity to mark a question. In an English sentence like "How cold is it?" the speaker is not asking in what manner is it cold. Rather, the speaker is either asking if it is really cold (TRUE COLD?) or to what degree it is cold (TEMPERATURE WHAT?). The sign choice depends on the explicit meaning being expressed. The intent is to convey the most precise thought possible. Other everyday examples include: "How old?" (OLD HOW // MANY?), "How come?" (WHY?), "How about it?" (OK?), etc. ASL sentences always strive to use the signs that will convey the most precise meaning possible.

ASL	English
ARRIVE HOME, TIME GUESS YOU?	How long will it be before we get home?
TIME FIX GUESS YOU?	How long will it take to fix it?

TIME AWAY HOME GUESS YOU?   How long do you think that
                                 you will be away?

WHAT

The interrogative WHAT prompts an answer concerning the condition, process, status, or role of someone or something. In English, the word "what" is often used for "who" as in "What do you think I am, a genius?" or "why" as in "What did you do that for?" or "where" as in "What is your address?" ASL, however, restricts the use of WHAT to those instances when its precise meaning is applicable: YOUR ADDRESS WHERE? BEHAVE YOU WHY?

ASL: NEXT ROOM, ME CLEAN WHAT?
English: What room should I clean next?
Diagram: NEXT

$$\diagup \begin{array}{c} \text{ROOM} \\ \text{(T-O)} \end{array} \Big\| \underset{\text{(S)}}{\text{ME}} \times \underset{\text{(V)}}{\text{CLEAN}} \underset{\text{(I)}}{\overset{\text{WHAT}}{}}$$

ASL	*English*
WANT ME DO WHAT?	What do you want to do?
YOU WANT FIRST DO WHAT?	What do you want me to do first?
PAINT NEXT, WANT YOU WHAT?	What do you want to paint next?
NOW // MORNING HE DO WHAT?	What will he do this morning?

Exercise: Write three questions containing the interrogative WHAT. Next write three English questions that use "what" inappropriately and then translate each one into ASL.

WHY // NOT

A compound formed with the interrogative WHY, WHY // NOT is performed by signing WHY and then swinging the open hand forward and down. The movement parameter is similar to DON'T // LIKE or DON'T // KNOW. The compound WHY // NOT is the negated counterpart to WHY as in a sentence like PRESIDENT, WONDER APPLY YOU WHY // NOT? ("Why don't you consider running for president"). WHY // NOT is often expressed in English as "why don't," and is placed at the end of a question: WORRY, YOU WHY // NOT? ("Why are you worried?").

ASL	*English*
GO, YOU WHY // NOT?	Why are you going?
YOU DRIVE WHY // NOT?	Why are you doing the driving?
INDEX (object), HE GIVE ME WHY // NOT?	He gave it to me, so what's the matter?

The Rhetorical Question

A question that is raised not for a response but merely for effect is a "rhetorical question." Although no response is expected, the rhetorical question does have a purpose. The rhetorical question gives the signer (or speaker) a chance to raise an issue. Since the receiver does not respond, the communicator then has the opportunity to speak further on the issue. Thus, a rhetorical question introduces a topic, and gives the communicator a chance to supply a comment, statement of fact, or an opinion. The rhetorical question "What would your father say if he were here right now?" allows the speaker to raise the question, pause, and then use the opportunity to respond.

Some rhetorical questions pose questions that only the speaker can answer. An example of this type of rhetorical question is, "Am I going to pay this tax? You bet I am." Still others need no answer as in "Do you believe what you just saw?" or "Are you kidding?"

Rhetorical questions in ASL are accompanied by the nonmanual markers of raised eyebrows and tilting of the head. Such nonmanual markers signal the reader to reflect a moment as the signer continues. The composition of the rhetorical question usually includes an interrogative sign. The sign REASON often serves as an interrogative in this type of question, expressing a semantic concept similar to WHY.

Figure 3. The interrogative sign REASON

In terms of sign order and sentence pattern, the rhetorical question follows a base pattern similar to the interrogative question but builds upon a three-part sentence. Rhetorical questions can also be differentiated from interrogative questions by context and nonmanual markers. Consider a scenario where a class of students are dining out and a student comments on how expensive the restaurant is. The teacher responds: EAT FINISH YOU-ALL. PAY DEBT GUESS WHO? YOU-ALL. ("When you finish eating, guess who gets to pay for this? You all do.").

Signing a rhetorical question is a three-stage process. First, a general statement is expressed, such as TRUE HAPPY, SHE ("She is really happy."). This statement is followed by a rhetorical question such as REASON? ("Why is she happy?"). After a pause, the signer supplies the response to the raised question, TOMORROW MARRY ("She is going to be married tomorrow."). The three stages of the rhetorical question are accompanied by the nonmanual signal of raising the eyebrows to mark the question. An example of this is a scenario in which two men are sitting on a park bench. A woman approaches, and as she sits down, one of the two men remarks to the other: TRUE HAPPY SHE. REASON? TOMORROW HER MARRY DAY. ("She is really happy. Why? Because she is getting married tomorrow.")

In terms of diagramming, each part of the three-part construction is treated as a separate sentence.

ASL: TRUE HAPPY, SHE
English: She is really happy.
Diagram: TRUE

(M)

HAPPY ‖

(T-C) ‖ SHE

(S)

ASL: REASON
English: Why?
Diagram: WHY

(I)

ASL: CONTEST, WIN
English: BECAUSE SHE WON THE CONTEST.
Diagram: CONTEST ‖

(T-O) ‖ WIN

(V)

ASL	*English*
TRUE TIRE, ME. REASON? NIGHT WORK LONG	I am really tired. Why? I worked nearly all night long.

MY STOMACH HURT. REA-SON? PAST // NIGHT EAT MUCH	My stomach hurts. Why? Last night, I ate too much.
FINISH PAY EAT. WHO? YOU-ALL	When you are finished eating, who is going to pay for this? You all are.

Another way to pose a rhetorical question in ASL is to assert a declarative statement and immediately follow it with a one-sign question. With the sentence SHOP-SHOP, YOU PREFER, the signer makes the statement "You prefer to go shopping." But immediately afterward, the signer adds RIGHT? along with the nonmanual features that signal a question: SHOP-SHOP, YOU PREFER. RIGHT? The resulting inquiry can be translated as "You prefer to go shopping, am I right?" or "You prefer to go shopping, don't you?" The composition of this sequence is a form of a rhetorical question. In this form, the signer raises a statement that is presumably a statement of fact and then follows up with a request for confirmation. The follow-up question requests for a response. As an example, the signer notices a fellow worker looking his best. Curious why, the signer raises the point FEEL GOOD, YOU. REASON RIGHT? ("You are obviously feeling good. There is a particular reason, isn't there?")

The following dialogue includes all three of the basic types of questions. First posed is a yes-no question. An answer follows. Next posed is a rhetorical question, and after that an interrogative question. A comment completes the dialogue. In the scenario, two friends (Ann and Sue) are talking about a recent event during which one of their friends had a fight with her date.

Ann: TRUE BECOME ANGRY, SHE? (Did she really get upset?)
Sue: YES. SHE THROW DRINK HIS FACE. (Yes. She even threw a drink in his face.)
Ann: KNOW HIM, ME.$\overset{hn}{}$ ANGRY, SHE. REASON? HE BEHAVE TRUE BAD. (Well, I know him. Do you want to know why she got mad? Because of the way he behaves — he deserved it.)
Sue: HE DO WHAT? (What did he do to her?)
Ann: TROUBLE, HE (He is nothing but trouble.)

Training Exercises

A. Translate the following English questions into ASL and then identify the type of question each represents.

1. Will you stop teasing the cat?
2. Why is your little sister crying?
3. Can you stop talking just for a minute?
4. Are you going skiing next week?

5. Do you need me to drive?
6. Whose gloves are those?
7. Why are some teachers so boring?
8. What is your brother going to say about this?
9. Who bought Pat's car?
10. Do you know him?
11. Who was that masked man?
12. Which of these programs do you prefer?
13. What can I do for you?
14. How many players made the team?
15. Am I to believe you said that?

B. Diagram the following questions. Place any modifiers above the main sentence element they refer to.

1. LATE, YOU. REASON? YOU FORGET TIME.

2. FINISH, YOU SOON?

3. TIME, YOU HERE WHEN?

4. YESTERDAY, YOU ENJOY SWIM?

5. FAVORITE ACT // PERSON WHICH?

6. NICE RING, GIVE YOU WHO?

7. RECENT MOVIE, YOUR FAVORITE WHICH?

8. YOUR CAR STOP. GAS NONE?

C. Translate the following sentences and questions into an ASL sentence pattern that can be delivered either as a statement of fact or as a question.

1. Will the meeting adjourn before noon?
2. Will you join me after the show?
3. Did Jim buy the store?
4. Did the nurse bring him the paper?
5. She is my favorite sister.
6. Everyone in town calls her Aunt Sally.
7. Did he hurt himself?
8. It was misty down by the river.
9. This car is my pride and joy.
10. Am I late for dinner?

D. Work as many questions as possible into the dialogues you create for the following scenarios. Afterward, identify each type of question used.

Scenario 1:
As you are getting your hair styled for an upcoming business meeting, your beautician sneezes and accidentally cuts a large notch into the side of your hair. Your beautician is in tears and very upset. Respond.

Scenario 2:
You are a steward(ess) on a small commuter plane. The pilot and copilot become terribly sick and unable to fly the plane. You must go into the passenger cabin and find out if there is a passenger on board who can fly a plane.

Scenario 3:

You agree to watch your neighbor's much-loved little puppy for the weekend. But while they're gone, the puppy gets lost. You spend all weekend looking, but you now have to explain what happened to your neighbor. Three weeks later, one of your friends finds the missing puppy. Now you return the puppy to the rightful owner. (Two scenarios here.)

11. Modifying a Sentence

American Sign Language makes use of space, movement, and separate lexical signs as morphological mechanisms for modifying other signs, thoughts, and ideas within sentences. The purpose of an ASL modifier is to specify, limit, or describe the semantic meaning of another sentence element. Modifiers provide a phrase or sentence with more specific detail and precision. Although ASL modifiers are similar in function to English adjectives, adverbs, etc., there are distinctive strategies for producing ASL modifiers. Since ASL is based on visual perception, an ASL modifier is often characterized by vigorous and animated movement, which compels attention and interest. ASL modifiers help to build sentences that are strong in imagery and vivid in content.

The underlying principle of modifying is to restrict the meaning of the referent concept. For example, BOOK is a general inclusive sign that can mean any book — big, small, thick, or thin. But when a modifier such as COLOR is added, the combined phrase, *COLOR* BOOK, limits the possible meaning. An ASL modifier always gives information that creates a more vivid, sharp communication. Thus, in ASL, concrete modifiers are usually preferred over abstract concepts. Concrete signs describe an object in sensory terms. In other words, a concrete sign invites the reader to understand the concept using the human senses (see, hear, touch, taste, or smell). An example of a concrete sign is HOT in the phrase HOT BREAD. Since it is clear how a concrete sign modifies a concept, the reader can easily translate the phrase into meaningful terms. Abstract modifiers, on the other hand, tend to be more awkward and harder to understand (e.g., "a bashful wine"). The more abstract the term, the fainter the visual image. The more concrete and specific the term, the sharper and brighter the visual image.

Since the function of ASL is clear, specific communication, an ASL signer must be on guard against superfluous modifications. English speakers often make extravagant use of qualifying words that add relatively little to the meaning of a sentence. For example, the English sentence "It is really rather nice" contains several qualifying words that contribute little information. Because of the principle of economization, ASL deletes lexical items that do not add meaning to a sentence. Thus, the sentence, "I

171

am very terribly sleepy-eyed" is expressed manually as simply TIRED, ME or *TRUE* TIRED, ME, depending on the intensity of the fatigue. ASL uses modifiers only when they are informative and specific. Concrete modifiers are much more common than abstract modifiers.

This chapter identifies three classes of ASL modifiers and gives guidelines for arranging them in ASL sentences. The modifiers to be discussed are adjective modifiers, auxiliary verbs, and possessive modifiers.

Adjective Modifiers

The adjective modifier is an ASL sign that qualifies, describes, or limits a noun. It answers such questions as "Which?" "What kind?" or "How many?" about the sign it modifies. Such signs as CLOUD, GOOD, FINE, NEW are typical examples of adjective modifiers, as in *CLOUD* SKY, *GOOD* FOOD, *FINE* HOME, and *NEW* HAT. Such modifiers build strong, vivid images and make it easier for the reader to understand the sentence. The usual adjective modifier is an independent component that precedes its target noun.

One type of adjective modifier is the "comparative modifier." Comparative modifiers include such signs as MORE, MORE-THAN, LESS, and LESS-THAN. A sign like MOST is a "superlative" modifier. A comparative or superlative modifier usually precedes its target noun. A sentence such as *MORE* MONEY, ME WANT ("I want some more money.") illustrates this placement. But in some contexts, the modifier follows its target. In the sentence MY MONEY *LESS-THAN*, ME HOPE ("I have less money than I hoped."), the modifier follows its target noun.

When a signer does not wish to specify clear limits, she might choose to use an "indefinite adjective modifier." Indefinite modifiers include such signs as FEW, SEVERAL, and ENOUGH, as in *FEW* PLAY-PERSON ("few players"), *SEVERAL* BOOKS ("several books") and *ENOUGH* PAPER ("enough paper"). An indefinite adjective modifier usually precedes its target noun.

An adjective modifier is diagrammed on a slanted line positioned above and before the target noun it modifies:

ASL: OLD CHURCH RECEIVE MANY IMPORTANT IMPROVEMENT.
English: The old church has undergone many important changes.

ASL	*English*
WIND CITY	the windy city
ANGRY FACE	angry expression
BRAVE SENTENCE	a bold statement
MORE HELP	more helpful
MISTAKE LESS // THAN	fewer errors
ENOUGH TIME	enough time

Exercise: Write six ASL sentences, two with adjective modifiers, two containing indefinite modifiers and two containing comparison modifiers.

The adjective modifier plays an important role in the basic ASL sentence pattern. In a subject-complement sentence pattern, the adjective serves as an adjective complement and is a main sentence element. In such sentences as BROWN *TALL* ("Mr. Brown is tall.") and MY GRAND-MOTHER YOUR *NEIGHBOR* ("My grandmother is your neighbor."), TALL and NEIGHBOR act as adjective complements that serve to modify the subject noun.

In a subject-complement (S-C) pattern ASL sentence in which the complement is an adjective modifier, the adjective complement serves to complete the sense of its target sign. In a sentence like VACATION // PERSON MARKER *HOME-SICK*. ("The tourist is homesick."), the adjective complement HOME-SICK tells something about its target, VACATION // PERSON MARKER, to complete the whole thought. In another example, DENTIST *DEPEND* ("The dentist is dependable."), the modifier qualifies the attributes of its target noun. In cases when the main verb is a "sense" verb such as FEEL, LOOK, SMELL, SOUND, or TASTE, the adjective complement serves as part of the main complement to complete the meaning associated with the subject it modifies. An example is the modifier BAD as in WET CLOTHES FEEL *BAD*.

When an adjective modifier serves as part of the basic sentence pattern as the complement, it is diagrammed on the base sentence line.

ASL: ME PROUD
English: I am proud of myself.
Diagram: ME ‖ PROUD
(S) ‖ (Complement)

ASL	*English*
FOOD TASTE GOOD	The food tastes good.
NURSE NICE	The nurse is nice.
SHE TRUE WORRY	She is really worried.

Exercise: Write six sentences in which the complement is an adjective. Include an example of each sentence pattern that includes a complement.

The typical function of a noun in an ASL sentence is as a main grammatical part of speech such as subject, topic, object, or noun complement. But in a sentence like MY PARENT BUY *ALASKA* HUSKY DOG ("My parents are buying an Alaskan husky."), the noun ALASKA is more like an adjective than a noun. Nouns sometimes modify other nouns. In such phrases as *DRESS* DESIGN // PERSON MARKER, *PEANUT* FARM // PERSON MARKER, *BASEBALL HAT*, the modifiers DRESS, PEANUT, and BASEBALL are all nouns acting as modifiers.

Like the adjective modifier, the noun modifier qualifies or specifies a noun. Also like most adjective modifiers, the noun modifier immediately precedes its target sign. Examples of noun modifiers include *SHOE* SALE, *APPLE* PIE, *STORM* WINDOW, *TAXI* DRIVE // PERSON MARKER and *TELEPHONE* NUMBER. ASL treats a noun that supplies useful information to a basic sentence like an adjective modifier. In terms of diagramming, such a noun is written on a slanted line above and before the sign it modifies (A).

Another feature that the noun modifier shares with the adjective modifier is its ability to serve as a complement. In the sentence MY BROTHER *FIRE // PERSON MARKER*, ("My brother is a fireman."), the noun complement FIRE // PERSON MARKER modifies the subject. When a noun modifier acts as a complement, it is positioned on the base line of a diagram (B).

(A) ASL: MY HOME OLD POLICE HOUSE
English: My home is an old police station.
Diagram:

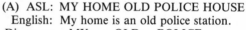

```
       MY        OLD       POLICE
       (M)       (M)        (M)
      /HOME ||  /     /    /HOUSE
       (S)    ||             (C)
```

(B) ASL: MY UNCLE NEW DENTIST
English: My uncle is the new dentist.
Diagram:

```
       MY          NEW
       (M)         (M)
      /UNCLE ||  /DENTIST
       (S)    ||    (C)
```

ASL	English
PAINT FISH BOAT	Paint my fish boat.
TABLE TENNIS CONTEST, SHE	She won the table tennis contest.
ME LOSE BOOK MARK	I lost my book marker.
TENNIS SHOE, ME BUY	I am buying some tennis shoes.
CAR KEY WHERE?	Where are my car keys?

Exercise: Write six ASL sentences, three containing at least one noun modifier and three containing a noun modifier as a complement.

Still another possibility is that a verb will be used to qualify a noun.

When an English verb is used in English as an adjective to modify a noun, it is called a "participle" and requires a suffix, as in "I bought a *swimming* pool," "This is my *swimming* time," or "I learned a new *swimming* technique." But in ASL, which does not use suffixes to change the form of lexical items, there is an opportunity for semantic confusion. When an ASL verb is used as an adjective in front of a target noun, it creates an ambiguous phrase that could be interpreted in different ways. The phrase DANCE GIRLS, for example, might be: (1) a command: "Start dancing, girls!" (2) a topicalized sentence, DANCE, GIRLS: "There are girls here who are dancing," or (3) a noun phrase: "the dancing girls are . . .".

When an ASL verb is used as an adjective, positioning is of paramount importance. When the verb modifier appears to have only a single, reasonable interpretation, as in *RUN* SHOE ("jogging shoes"), the modifier usually precedes its target noun. But if the verb modifier might be interpreted as a verb and not as a modifier, the signer is likely to place the modifier after the target sign. In conjunction with this positioning, the neutral pronoun reference (ITS) is usually added between the target and the modifier to help signal that the verb is a modifier. For example, a confusing command-type phrase would be created if a signer placed WRITE in front of a target noun as in *WRITE* EXAM. Instead, the signer places the modifying verb after the target and precedes it by the neutral pronoun: EXAM *ITS WRITE* ("written exam").

This post–target sign arrangement also occurs with certain event modifiers, such as CHRISTMAS. To avoid confusing phrases like *CHRISTMAS* DAY ("Christmas is the day that. . ."), CHRISTMAS can be repositioned to yield DAY *ITS CHRISTMAS*.

When a verb acts as an ordinary adjective modifier, it is diagrammed accordingly (A). But to differentiate the specially treated verb/event modifier graphically, a line extends below the base line (B).

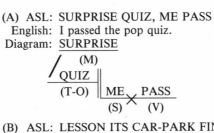

(A) ASL: SURPRISE QUIZ, ME PASS
English: I passed the pop quiz.
Diagram: SURPRISE

(B) ASL: LESSON ITS CAR-PARK FINISH
English: The parking lesson is finished.
Diagram:

ASL	*English*
GIFT ITS CHRISTMAS	Christmas presents
SCHOOL ITS DRIVE	driving school
RUN SHORT-PANTS	jogging shorts
PARTY ITS NEW // YEAR	New Years Party
SWIM CLOTHES	bathing suit

Exercise: Write four sentences containing verb modifiers.

Auxiliary Verbs

Auxiliary verbs, or helping verbs, represent another class of modifiers. Auxiliary verbs act as modifiers by combining with main verbs to create specially understood meanings. They semantically shade another verb's meaning with such ideas as obligation, willingness, or capability. The sentence ME STUDY ("I am studying.") means something very different from a sentence containing an auxiliary verb as in ME *MUST* STUDY ("I need to study."). HELP ("I am helping you.") is changed substantially when an auxiliary verb is added to yield *CAN* HELP ("I can help you"). Auxiliary verbs supply semantic detail as to how the main action should be interpreted. The semantic change created by an auxiliary can be quite noticeable or very subtle, as in the conversion of ME STUDY ALL-NIGHT ("I am studying all night.") to ME *CAN* STUDY ALL-NIGHT ("I can study all night"). Auxiliary verbs include such verbs as MUCH (conveying strong necessity), CAN (conveying ability), MAYBE (conveying uncertainty), ALLOW (conveying permission), TRY (conveying effort), NEVER (conveying not under any condition). An auxiliary verb precedes its target, the main verb. ASL allows the use of auxiliaries because they make a major semantic contribution, affecting the meaning of the main verb.

Because of economization, ASL often translates English nominal infinitives into ASL main verbs. English infinitives are formed by placing the word "to" in front of a verb so that it can serve as a noun. When the sentence is reduced to its essential parts, the infinitive becomes a major part of the verb phrase. The result in ASL is a phrase that includes an auxiliary and a main verb. To translate a sentence like "I don't want *to challenge* him" into ASL, the signer economizes the infinitive "to challenge" into the verb phrase: ME $\overline{\text{WANT } CHALLENGE}$ HE. The infinitive is now represented as the main verb. Another sentence, "I wanted *to win*" becomes WANT *WIN*, ME and "He hopes *to live* there" becomes HE HOPE *LIVE* THERE.

Within a diagram, the auxiliary verb is represented as part of the verb phrase (A). Since auxiliary verbs are treated as part of the main verb phrase, their use is not affected by the directionality of the other verb. Regardless of whether the main verb is directional or locational, the auxiliary modifier precedes the main verb (B).

(A) ASL: BILL MAYBE HIRE CINDY
English: Bill may hire Cindy.
Diagram: <u>BILL ‖ MAYBE HIRE ⤬ CINDY</u>
       (S) ‖   (V)   (O)

(B) ASL: CAN ASK
           1 3
English: I can ask her.
Diagram: <u>(ME) ‖ CAN ASK ⤬ (HER)</u>
       (S) ‖   (V)   (O)

ASL	*English*
NEVER FORGET	I will never forget.
KEY MUST FIND	I must find the key.
CAN TELL, WE	We can tell him.
TRY HELP	Try to help.
ME WANT SPEAK	I want to speak to her.
ME WANT PLAY	I want to play.
SHE ENJOY LISTEN ME	She likes to listen to me.

Exercise: Write six sentences with auxiliary modifiers, three with nondirectional main verbs and three with multidirectional verbs.

Possessive Modifier

Signs such as MY, YOUR, HIS/HER, ITS, and THEIR, which are used to convey ownership, are called "possessive modifiers." Possessive modifiers are generally used only when the context is insufficient to supply the necessary reference. Even when a sentence involves several different participants, indexing and multidirectionality in ASL assure clear identification of each reference, so ambiguity is usually avoided. In a sentence like CAR KEY, UNCLE (index actual person) GIVE ME ("My uncle gave me the car keys."), no possessive modifier is needed because the context together with indexing is sufficient to indicate the possessive.

Another reason that possessive modifiers are seldom used in ASL is natural conversational congruity, which allows heightened understanding. An example of a congruent sentence is "You should watch your weight." Although this sentence has two pronouns (the nominative "you" and the possessive "your"), in conversation it is easy to see that they both refer to the same person. Because the agreement of the two pronouns is clearly understood in conversation, ASL omits one of the two: *YOUR* WEIGHT, CAREFUL.

Whenever pronouns or person references within a particular sentence agree in their respected pairs, ASL will economize them (e.g. ME and MY; YOU and YOUR; HE and HIS). In each case, ASL omits one of the pronoun references, usually the possessive modifier: BOOK, ME BUY ("I bought my book"). A reflection of the commonness of this economizing strategy is that no sign exists in ASL for the word "our."

When only a single person reference occupies a sentence, there is little chance for ambiguity, so a possessive modifier is unnecessary. An example of a sentence with a single-person subject is "The teacher changed her mind." Since the context involves only one person, no possessive modifier is required: TEACHER CHANGE THINK.

ASL	English
REMEMBER BRING TICKET, YOU-ALL	*All of you* remember to bring *your* tickets.
YOU MUST TURN OFF LIGHT	*You* need to turn *your* lights off.
UMBRELLA, ME FORGET	*I* forgot *my* umbrella.
BOOK-BOOK, ME BRING	*I* am bringing *my* books with *me*.
COAT, HE REMEMBER	*He* remembered *his* coat.

But possessive modifiers are occasionally used in ASL sentences. When an ASL sentence involves several participants and pronoun references, a possessive modifier may be included to identify the accurate ownership associations and eliminate ambiguity. A possessive modifier precedes its target sign and is diagrammed like an adjective modifier.

ASL: YOUR UMBRELLA, ME FORGET
English: I forgot your umbrella.
Diagram:

ASL	English
MY BOOK, GIVE LEE	She gave my book to Lee.
YOUR COAT, ASK BRING	He asked me to bring your coat.

Exercise: Write four sentences, two omitting the possessive modifier and two retaining the possessive modifier.

The Plural

Another expression of modification is distinguishing a plural form from a singular form. In English, distinction between singular words like "lady, boy, truck" and plural words like "ladies, boys, trucks" is usually made by the addition of a suffix. In some cases, regarded as irregular in English, the plural is marked by a change in the internal sound of a vowel, as in "woman-women," "tooth-teeth," "goose-geese," "child-children." Some English nouns do not change their articulatory form at all to mark a plural (e.g., "sheep," "fish," "deer"). In such cases, the auditor must rely on context and the use of articles ("a," "the," "an") for clarification.

Instead of using suffixes to distinguish the plural from the singular form, ASL incorporates morphological alteration into the spatial dimension. Among the mechanisms that can be used to pluralize an ASL noun, the signer may use a plural modifier, indexing, and reduplication.

Pluralizing strategies in ASL are confined to nouns. English, on the other hand, adds suffixes to some verbs to mark number. For example, third-person singular verbs add an "s" in English. But ASL does not mark verbs. Furthermore, ASL marks only nouns that represent a concrete object or person, while English pluralizes abstract concepts such as situations, feelings, or experiences.

Plural Modifier

Consider a sentence like "the lawyers gathered for a meeting." Since the noun "lawyers" is a concrete noun, it works well to demonstrate some of the methods available to manually express pluralization.

One way to pluralize a noun is to use a sign whose meaning relates the idea of two or more units. One such sign, GROUP, serves well as a plural modifier. When placed next to a noun, it defines the target concept as more than one. When a plural modifier is used to pluralize a noun, it generally follows its target noun: LAWYER *GROUP* CONVENE MEET.

To shade the semantics of a target noun, a signer has several articulation options available. A signer can convey the relative size of the target noun by the detailed execution of its modifier. To convey "a small group," for instance, the signer restricts the relative movement of the sign's parameter. The compact size tells the reader that only a few lawyers gathered. On the other hand, to convey "a very large group," the signer exaggerates the relative movement of the sign. Thus, as a plural modifier, GROUP serves two purposes simultaneously: it pluralizes its target noun and it incorporates information about its relative number. The plural marker GROUP is limited to person nouns. It cannot be used, for example, to pluralize BOOK as in DROP BOOK GROUP, ME. In such a context the plural marker MANY would be used: DROP MANY BOOK, ME ("I dropped a lot of books.").

As Hoemann points out (1978), another sign that frequently functions as a plural modifier is the verb HOARD. Its neutral composition involves holding both open C hands side by side at chest level with the palms down. The hands simultaneously move forward a short distance, while the eyes squint (as if it were difficult to see through the many items). HOARD implies a very large number of items. It is used only to convey a large amount or degree; FOOD *HOARD* MINE ("All of this food is mine."). HOARD follows its target noun.

Signs such as MANY, FEW, SEVERAL, SOME, and ALL represent indefinite plural modifiers. Unlike a plural modifier that is also a base noun (e.g., GROUP) or a verb (e.g., HOARD), an indefinite plural modifier typically precedes its target noun as in *MANY* drink ("drinks"), *MANY* STREET ("streets"), *FEW* TEST ("tests"), *ALL* FRIEND ("friends"), *SEVERAL* PLAY ("plays"), etc.

Another variation of the separate plural modifier is the use of a number. A specific number that precedes a target noun conveys a specific plural. *TWO* ROOM, WE PAINT FINISH ("We have finished painting two rooms already."), When a signer wishes to emphasize that a commodity is singular, they can add numeral ONE preceding the target noun.

In a diagram, the plural modifier is represented in parentheses. This shows that the information it provides is secondary.

ASL: MANY BOOK, ME RETURN
English: I returned the books.
Diagram: (MANY) BOOK ‖
              (T-O)   ‖ ME ╳ RETURN
                                    (S)   (V)

ASL	English
TEACHER GROUP SICK	The teachers are sick.
GIVE ME YOUR TWO TICKET	Give me your tickets.
ONE GOOD REASON, ME WANT	I need just one good reason.
WASH ALL CAR	Wash all of the cars here.
YOUR NEW SHOE, I ENJOY	I like your new shoes.

Exercise: Write eight sentences that include examples of each of the various plural strategies discussed to date.

Indexed Plurals

A second way to pluralize a noun in ASL is based on the principles of spatial indexing. This strategy uses relative space and location collectively to indicate a plural concept. Spatial indexing immediately follows the execution of the noun. Once the target noun is established, the signer indexes it not once but repeatedly. The repeated indexing is a metaphoric means of informing the reader that more than one of the noun units is present. To pluralize "lawyer" in the sentence "The lawyers gathered for a meeting" by using spatial indexing, the signer performs *LAWYER* and immediately afterward indexes to several different spatial locations. The ASL sentence is then completed with the remaining signs, CONVENE MEET. To express "The birds flew south for the winter," an ASL signer would express WINTER APPROACH, *BIRD* (index several points) FLY SOUTH.

The act of indexing is only one dimension of this pluralizing mechanism. The specific indexing pattern can simultaneously supply additional contextual information. In the above example, plural indexing of LAWYER might create a spatial pattern that visually resembles an imaginary circle, which conveys the idea of a meeting taking place around a table. Similarly, an indexing pattern that resembles rows might suggest a speaker-audience meeting. This latter sentence could be written LAWYER THERE THERE THERE (in a row) CONVENE MEET. The ASL sentence conveys information both by the indexing motion and also the visual pattern formed by the gesturing action. In a similar manner, signing BIRDS might include indexing that points to random points above the head to suggest the idea of flying or to patterned points to express the idea of flying in formation.

To sign the sentence "Your clothes are in your room," the signer might use a random gesturing in space. This random gesturing simultaneously conveys plural as well as locational information: CLOTH INDEX (several downward points) ROOM. The reader understands not just that there are clothes in a room, but also that the clothes are scattered all over the room in a disarray.

As a general rule of thumb, plural indexing tends to follow the target noun. An ASL signer does not index plurality with one hand while performing the sign with the other (Hoemann, 1978).

Reduplication

A third means of pluralization is sign reduplication. Using this strategy, the signer reduplicates the verb to convey the idea of pluralization (Hoemann, 1978). Although this method is similar to indexing in its relative use of spatial dimensions, it is applied not to nouns, but to main verbs.

Reduplication is used only when the verb is multidirectional. Just as multidirectional verbs can supply participant referents, they can also pluralize nouns. Pluralization occurs not along the dimension of linear verb movement, but rather by intentionally repeating the main verb and moving the hands to a slightly different spatial location each time it is repeated.

To apply the reduplication technique to the earlier example "The lawyers gathered for a meeting," the signer would repeat the verb CONVENE several times. Each time it is repeated, the signer moves the hands to a slightly different spatial location. The sentence would be articulated LAWYER CONVENE (move hands) CONVENE (move hands again) CONVENE MEET. Each relocation or spatial change during the verb's repetition implies that another person gathered for the meeting. In other words, each relocation of the hands represents another target noun (e.g., lawyer here, lawyer there, lawyer there, etc.). Three repetitions can mean either "three" or "many."

Reduplicating a sign while changing to different spatial locations can also apply to certain nouns. Although there is not yet a complete list of nouns known to be pluralized by reduplication, such signs as COFFEE, SHOE, BOOK, LESSON, CHAIR, WINDOW, TEA, DOOR, PAPER, and TABLE are often pluralized with this method.

But nouns that involve some type of direct contact with the body (i.e., anchored nouns) are usually too awkward to be pluralized through reduplication. HOSPITAL, PEPSI, APPLE, and ORANGE, for example, cannot be pluralized by reduplication. Compound nouns such as NEAR // PERSON MARKER ("neighbor") are also difficult to pluralize through reduplication.

The repeated-and-shift technique involved in reduplication offers a means of supplying additional spatial information related to the context. By forming a specific pattern while moving the hands during duplications, CHAIRS, for example, can be metaphorically lined up in rows, pairs, or small clusters, or even random arrangements. The sign DRESS can be reduplicated to indicate such ideas as "hung up, all in a row" or "stacked in a pile." TICKET might be duplicated twice to represent a pair.

Reduplication can also be used to convey the idea of duration. If the signer duplicates the same verb but does not change its relative position within the sign space, it conveys the idea of continuance in time. This is a "durative" reduplication, conveying the idea of the time that someone or something exists or continues (Fischer, 1973). The sentence TEST SOON, BILL STUDY-STUDY-STUDY means "Bill studied for a long time for the upcoming test."

As a morphological mechanism for pluralization reduplication has deep roots in ASL, as reflected by the evolution of certain signs. The sign CHILDREN, for instance, was originally derived from a reduplication of CHILD. As the sign gained more and more usage, the reduplicated movement gradually became restricted both in location and direction of movement. Today, the signs CHILD and CHILDREN are listed as two separate lexical items. It seems likely that the sign CITY evolved from the reduplication of HOUSE and the sign FOREST from TREE in a similar shortening of the defined movement parameter.

Dual Expression

A natural extension of reduplication is ASL's method of conveying the idea of duality. Unavailable in English, "dual expression" is a method of associating a dual number simultaneously with the performance of certain signs. Most commonly achieved with one-handed signs, a normally one-handed sign is intentionally performed with both hands in succession. In its base form, for example, the sign THANK consists of a single open hand that moves forward from the chin. But when this sign is performed with both hands, each performing the sign in succession, the revised expression means "Thanks to you both" or "Thanks to all of you." Similarly the single-handed sign AIRPLANE is performed with both hands, one after the other, the newly created expression depicts either an airport, or if the hands follow the same pattern, airplanes flying in formation. Successive production can modify the sign IDEA to mean "all of your ideas," or the sign STAY to mean "All of you can stay." When a one-handed verb such as TELL incorporates the dual use of hands, TELL becomes ANNOUNCE or "Tell everyone."

Certain two-handed signs can also show duality. This occurs when the signer uses each hand to perform the movement of the active hand and does so in succession. The dual expression of the sign SIT consists of executing the primary active hand immediately followed by the secondary hand duplicating the same composition. At the end of the articulation, both hooked H hands rest on imaginary secondary H hands. The result is a metaphoric expression of two people sitting side by side. Two-handed signs expressing duality are generally restricted to those signs that involve a primary active hand and a secondary stationary hand. Another example is the dual expression of NIGHT, which means "Night after night." Such signs as AVOID, FOLLOW, TRIP, ACCOMPANY, and CHASE are other examples of signs that can convey the duality. The fact that the motion is successive rather than simultaneous separates a dual expression from a stressed, emphatic expression.

Training Exercises

A. Pay particular attention to the use of modifiers as you economize the following sentences into clear, briefly stated sentences. Retain all informative modifiers, but discard superfluous ones.

1. I really do plan to slowly start to create a new weed-free garden next spring.
2. Marsha just loves her large, brand-new house with the latest new ideas in modern convenience.
3. It truly makes me happy just to see the small children having so much fun playing together.
4. I first learned how to drive on an old, rusty, blue-and-gray pickup truck.
5. Everyone now has to take a long, written test that is boring and hard to finish.
6. Window shopping can be such fun when you just want to see all of the latest in fashion.
7. The park was dark and gloomy, with large, spooky trees in a darkening sky.
8. Erin really enjoys going to crowded discotheques because they are such a delight for her whenever she can go.

9. I always try to be courteous and polite due to the fact that it just seems to be part of my nature.
10. In my opinion, I think that you need some hot black coffee to help you wake up.

B. Eliminating excessive wordiness is one of the main objectives in learning to use ASL modifiers. Always be economical and direct in your sign choice. Rewrite the following sentences to eliminate any poor choices of words or phrases. Then translate the revised sentences into ASL.

1. As soon as he sat down in the bus, he was sleeping.
2. None of them thought that I would ever really succeed.
3. It takes time to understand how to drive.
4. I enjoy being a student of the language of signs.
5. Helen has a lot of fascinating hobbies such as scuba diving.
6. She would have told him about it a long time ago.
7. It took quite a bit of time to learn how to ask.
8. Mary was startled by the big, brown bear.
9. Randy was thought to have been passed over for promotion.
10. Mike was greatly disappointed at having been left out.

C. Translate the following sentences into ASL and then practice using different strategies to pluralize only the appropriate items.

1. Your friends can come with us.
2. She wears different dresses all weekend.
3. I will remember all of the words.
4. Several of my neighbors told me.
5. It will take years to become an expert.
6. My friend's brother had to work late.
7. You seem to need some dry clothes.
8. My aunt is bringing my cousins with her.
9. Bring your notes, books, and past exams with you.
10. A lot of kissing spreads colds.
11. Our neighbors sold their cars and both trucks.
12. Flowers seem to draw bees and flies.
13. The birds landed on the apple and peach trees.
14. She baked three good pies, but no apple pie.
15. The ice cream melted all over my papers.

D. Incorporate the various modification strategies into improvised dialogues for the following scenarios.

Scenario 1:
You want to go on a trip this weekend with your best friend. Meanwhile, your mother just got a call from your teacher informing her that you are doing poorly in school. As you approach your mom for her permission, you are not aware that your teacher called.

Scenario 2:
You are in the library working late, and you accidentally get locked in a storage room overnight. You hear a noise and discover that a former girl

(boy) friend who you really detest is locked in with you. How will you work together to get out? Or will you?

Scenario 3:

You are at a fancy restaurant with a blind date who has turned out to be a pleasant surprise. You want to make a good first impression, but when your food comes to the table, you find a large bug in it. The waiter is an uppity stuffed shirt. What do you do?

12. Expressing Time

All languages need to have some method to communicate the concept of time. The notion of time is organized into three main divisions: past, present, and future. These three temporal divisions are linguistically represented on the surface level of a language, regardless if it is oral or manual.

English expresses time through a complex inflectional system that uses the tense of a verb to indicate when an action takes place. "Verb tense" is the form of a verb that specifies the time of an action. Sometimes English tense can be expressed with a single-word verb, as in the simple present (e.g., "give," "gives") and the simple past (e.g., "gave"). Sometimes English tense requires a verb phrase as in simple future (e.g., "will give"). An English speaker can also use a verb phrase to express a temporal reference other than the time of the speech act, as in the present perfect tense, for instance, which refers to a past action that is now complete (e.g. "She *has learned* how to sign."). The future perfect tense refers to an action that will occur at some definite point in the future but is not directly associated to the immediate moment (e.g., "She *will have learned* how to sign by next summer."). The progressive verb is still another variation of temporalizing strategies in English. A progressive verb phrase denotes an action that is in progress as in "been giving" (present progressive), "was giving" (past progressive), and "will be giving" (future progressive). Within English's elaborate verb tense system, references to time can be anchored to a period of time other than the time of the speech act.

English equips the speaker with an array of markers and inflections allowing the speaker to refer to several points of relative time. But inherent to any communication event is that it takes place in time; the moment it occurs is the present moment. Although a speaker may not always be actively aware of it, the speaker constantly maintains an association to actual time. Even when conversing in the perfect tense, a speaker must maintain this connection to the present time.

Because ASL is a visual phenomenon that must occur at a moment in time, the temporal strategies used in ASL to express various time references are all anchored to the present communication event. Because a signer must be physically present to communicate, the ability to focus attention on a time reference other than the present moment is severely restricted (Friedman, 1975). American Sign Language does not use verb tense or verb inflections. Rather, it uses its spatial dimension to create its own grammatical mechanisms to express time frame, along with a lexical vocabulary that can express certain time concepts. The spatial aspect is clearly evident in the ASL treatment of temporal references.

Conversational Time Reference

Since two persons must be physically present to communicate in ASL, a time base or "gauge" is inherent in the communication event. Unlike a written letter that can be written one day but not complete the communication chain until hours, days, months, or even years later, manual communication is virtually instantaneous. In ASL, the time base for a temporal reference is the moment of exchange. This time base, which reflects the moment of the linguistic exchange, is referred to as the "conversational time reference." All time divisions in ASL evolve from the actual time of the present communicating act.

As it applies to the actual moment in which the act of communication occurs, time can be classified into three relative divisions: (1) the time of the ongoing communication event itself (the present time frame); (2) time prior to when communication event has occurred (the past time frame); and (3) time beyond the present communication event (the future time frame).

The conversational time reference is illustrated by a scenario in which a young man returns home from a blind date. When he returns, his best friend is waiting to hear the entire story in detail. As the two converse, the subject matter alone is sufficient to supply temporal information. The blind date that has just occurred represents the past. The ongoing discussion between the friends and the young man's actions in relating the events about the experience represent the present. Action the young man is contemplating with this blind date again represents the future. Thus, this example illustrates how context and real time together can represent all of the main divisions of time. The time of the conversation establishes a point of reference so that any activity that has already occurred is in the past; any ongoing activity is the present; and any action yet to be experienced is in the future. As a result, all contextual implications are directly associated to the conversation.

The conversational event is the common denominator between the signer and reader. Both understand that events will be expressed in direct reference to that conversational moment. If the event has already happened, the present moment of conversation logically places that event in the past. If the event is ongoing, it places it in the present, and if it is upcoming, it places it in the future. The use of the conversational time reference is

illustrated by the sentence CLASS FINISH, TIM MEET. The topic of this
sentence is CLASS. The actual time that a signer expresses this sentence to
another person is the conversational time reference. Four possibilities exist
related to that moment of conversation: (1) if the sentence is expressed after
the class in question has already taken place, the conversation implicitly
places the topic in the past; (2) if the sentence is expressed while currently
in class, the conversation implicitly places the event in the present; (3) if the
sentence is performed prior to class, the topic is a future event; and (4) if
the reader does not know when the class meets, the time frame of the
sentence is unknown. More details are needed such as CLASS WHEN? The
combined information generated from context alone can often be sufficient
to supply temporal references in a discourse.

An English sentence consists of a linear series of independent semantic
words arranged to convey a complete thought. In this conceptual framework, temporal information can be supplied in a number of ways, as long
as it follows a standard grammatical structure. A story can be told in any
chronological order, for instance, regardless of when each event actually
occurred in a sequence of events. A sequential sentence such as "I will clean
the garage as soon as I have eaten and finished reading my book" is considered a well-formed sentence in English. As long as the correct functional
elements accurately link English clauses together, they can be strung
together in any order. Thus, the above sentence could also be stated as "I
will finish reading my book and as soon as I have eaten, then I will clean
the garage." Regardless of its chronological order, this is still a well-formed
English sentence. Scrambling of chronological order in English is made
possible by such function words as "before," "after," "during," "then," and
"when," which serve as relative time conjunctions (e.g., "I fell asleep *before*
the movie was over.").

But the temporal structure of ASL is based on real time. A series of
events must be related according to its actual chronological order of occurrence. Each event is arranged in real chronological time relative to the other
events that have occurred or will occur. In addition, each event is anchored
to the immediate conversational event as the point of reference. To
translate the multievent sentence into ASL, the signer must arrange the sequence into its actual chronological order: "I will finish eating and reading
my book, then I will clean the garage." The sequence is then treated as three
separate sentences: FINISH EAT, ME. READ BOOK. CLEAN
GARAGE. Similarly, to translate an English sentence like "I fell asleep
before the movie was over," the signer must first rearrange it according to
the actual chronological occurrence of events: "I fell asleep, the movie concluded," and then translate it to: SUDDEN, SLEEP ME. MOVIE FINISH
SEE NONE. Thus, ASL relies on the conversational time reference and actual chronological sequencing to manage a multievent sentence.

The time base of an ASL sentence changes constantly according to the time the conversation takes place. When the topic of conversation and the conversation itself occur at the same time, ASL uses the present time frame. Otherwise, the event is placed in the past or future depending on its relation to the current moment of the conversation. The concept of a conversational time reference is not grammatical. Rather, it is an understanding shared and utilized by both signer and reader.

Implied Time

Certain ASL verbs are directly influenced by the conversational time reference. Semantic concepts such as FORGET, TIRED, LOSE, and AR-RIVE have an inherent association to the conversational time reference. Such concepts imply a logical association to the past. In English, for instance, when a speaker says "I forget your name," the implication is that the speaker once knew the name but that he or she presently forgets it. But even though the action of forgetting is currently going on, English grammar considers the sentence "I *am forgetting* your milk" is incorrect. Although the action of "forgetting" in this sentence is occurring in the present tense, the sentence fails to account for the ties to the past. Instead, this thought requires the past tense of the verb "forget" to yield "I *forgot* your milk." Similarly, consider a woman arriving for an important engagement. As the woman walks through the door she remarks: "I am glad that I arrived on time." The time frame in this sentence is logically inaccurate. It would be logically correct if it were expressed "I am glad that I am arriving on time," to reflect the present action. But instead, it is expressed in the past tense. In each example, the action is ongoing occurrence but is stated as if it has already occurred. The complication is that these ongoing actions incorporate an implied reference to the past within their sentential construction.

When an ASL verb's action is anchored to the present conversational moment, there is a similar blending of time references. Although the action is currently being completed, its context is understood by the reader to be in the past. In a sentence like ME LOSE INDEX (a specific person reference) PHONE NUMBER ("I lost his phone number."), for instance, while the act of losing something is ongoing, the action itself occurred in the past. In such a case, the ongoing conversation as a temporal baseline reference is sufficient to signal the past time frame. Thus the ASL sentence will be economized by deleting the use of an extra sign to mark the past tense.

In a sentence like BREAD, ME FORGET BUY ("I forgot to buy some bread."), the reader understands that a reference to the past has been conveyed. Since the concept of past time has been conveyed there is no need for a time marker. A time marker is included only when the action has yet to be completed: BUY BREAD, ME FORGET FUTURE (meaning "I will forget to buy some bread."). Other examples of implied time include:

ASL	*English*
MONEY, SHE LOSE	She lost her money.
KEY, ME FIND	I found my keys.
WORK TIRE ME	I am tired from all of the work.
NEW FRIEND, MEET	I met a new friend.
1 3	
MOVIE, SHE ARRIVE LATE	She was late for the movie.

Exercise: Write six sentences that contain a verb that implies the past tense.

The Time Line

The surface manifestation of time in American Sign Language is structured on an imaginary time reference that is established alongside the signer's body. The ASL "time line" is an imaginary vertical line drawn down the body so that it intersects with the ear. This vertical line is the articulatory center of the time spectrum; it serves to represent the present. Another imaginary line horizontally intersects the time line to represent relative time. These two imaginary lines divide the sign space into the three major time divisions.

Figure 1. The time line

The space coincident with and immediately in front of the signer's body is regarded as the "neutral" space and is reserved for the present time, in accordance with the conversational time reference. Ordinary discourse is performed within this neutral space. Space behind the signer's body is reserved for past time, time that transpired before the ongoing conversational time period. Space extends in front of the neutral space is reserved for future time, time that will occur after the present conversation. A physical movement of one or both hands outside of the neutral space signifies a time frame other than the present: a forward movement indicates the future; a backward movement indicates the past. The spatial boundaries of the time field consists of a near extension of the arms in front of the body (future) and approximately one foot behind the back (past).

The ASL signs PAST, NOW, and FUTURE provide strategy of expressing time through a basic overview of this spatial dimension. The sign PAST involves the hand moving backward over the shoulder with the palm oriented backward. The sign NOW (also identified as PRESENT) involves the hands dropping straight downward immediately a short distance in front of the signer while remaining within the neutral space. The sign FUTURE is performed by moving the hand forward, ahead of the body, extending beyond the neutral space. The spatial region occupied by each sign's movement parameter is located in the temporal domain for that time concept: PAST (backward over the shoulder), NOW (on the time line within the neutral space), and FUTURE (forward and ahead of the neutral space).

When no overt sign or marker is used in a sentence to mark time, the reader relies on the implications of the conversational time reference to understand the time frame. Consider a sentence like EXAM, ME PASS. Since no time sign is used, the actual moment that the conversation takes place determines whether it means "I passed," "I am passing," or "I will pass the exam." But when a time marking sign is used, it supersedes any implication of the conversational time reference. Incorporating a time marking sign such as NEXT // WEEK into the sentence NEXT // WEEK EXAM, ME PASS, intentionally places the idea into the future time frame: "I will pass the exam next week."

There are a variety of linguistic and grammatical strategies to express time either within an ASL sentence or in relationship to other sentences. This chapter discussed several such morphological mechanisms, including use of a specific time marker, indexing, a general time marker, a completion marker, and a time modifier.

Specific Time Marker

A sign that conveys a precise, restricted time frame and simultaneously defines the time period of the action is referred to as a "specific time marker."

Specific time markers include a select group of base signs, but are more commonly represented by compound signs.

A temporal compound in ASL is formed when a time sign is enjoined with a modifier so that the two together can define the time element. The compound NEXT // WEEK, for example, is a specific time marker. It serves to establish the time of the sentence. The time reference provided by a specific time marker can range from a single sentence to the time frame of an entire discourse. A specific time marker must meet two criteria: (1) it must define the time span involved; and (2) it must place the context into an explicit time division (past, present, or future). A specific time marker can also be used with verbs that imply time (e.g., LOSE).

To determine if a sign such as NIGHT, WEEK, or YEAR functions as a specific time marker, you must decide whether the sign under consideration meets both of the above criteria. Each of these signs, for instance, meet the first criteria: they define the time span (e.g., seven hours, seven days, twelve months). But do any of these signs supply an actual time division? The sign NIGHT for example, as seen in a sentence like NIGHT FEEL BAD, ME fails to specify whether the reference is "last night, tonight, tomorrow night, three nights ago, etc." Even in the context of the conversational time reference, the concept of NIGHT is too often vague and ambiguous to establish the time division adequately. The same is true for the signs WEEK and YEAR. Neither is capable of establishing the particular time division without further information.

But the single signs TOMORROW, YESTERDAY, and EVERYDAY satisfy both criteria. TOMORROW, for example, defines the time span (twenty-four hours) and the time division (future). EVERYDAY also meets the requirements of the time span (twenty-four hours) and time division (ongoing day-to-day occurrence) as does YESTERDAY (twenty-four hours and past). These signs are specific time markers.

Most specific time markers are the result of compounding two concepts so that the collective sign meets both time requirements. The single sign DURING, for example, ordinarily conveys the concept of "while at the time of," and is not regarded as a specific time marker. But when DURING is joined with a contextual sign such as TEST, the newly formed compound DURING // TEST meets the criteria as a specific time marker. The compound DURING // TEST defines the time span (an hour or so that it takes to complete a test). The context of the sentence or the entire discourse itself serves to imply which test, according to the conversational time reference. Thus, the context supplies the time division (past, present, future).

Consider the scenario of two students discussing a recent incident at school when someone was rushed to the hospital. One of the students remarks: DURING // TEST SEE AMBULANCE LIGHT ("I saw the ambulance lights when I was taking my test."). DURING // TEST established both the time span ("while taking a test") and the time division (a past event).

When DURING is joined to a context sign such as WINTER, the newly formed compound DURING // WINTER meets the requirements as an ongoing event that occurs within a specified number of months. The conversational time reference in the discourse supplies the time division, as in DURING // WINTER PLAN SKI ("I plan to ski every winter.").

Most specific time markers are created by fusing a base time sign with either a particular context sign or a modifier sign. The two together define the time element. Base time signs include the seasons, days of the week, months, and even holidays. When these are fused with modifiers like NOW, NEXT, and PAST, the result is time compounds. Since the newly formed compounds define both the time span and division, they constitute specific time markers: NOW // DAY ("today"), NOW // NIGHT ("tonight"), NOW // MORNING ("this morning"), NOW // WEDNESDAY ("this Wednesday"), NEXT // FRIDAY ("next Friday"), PAST // SATURDAY ("last Saturday"), PAST // MOVIE ("last movie"), etc.

An independent component within ASL sentence construction, the specific time marker is usually placed at the beginning of the sentence to establish the precise time of the discourse. When a specific time marker is used, it supersedes any other time reference. No additional time marker is required until the signer wishes to change the time reference in the discourse. In a diagram, the specific time marker (STM) is positioned on its own line immediately preceding the headsign (topic or subject) of an ASL sentence.

ASL: NEXT // WEEK SCHOOL, ME DRIVE YOU
English: I will take you to school next week.
Diagram:

NEXT // WEEK
specific time marker (STM)

SCHOOL		ME	DRIVE	YOU
(T)		(S)	(V)	(O)

ASL	*English*
NOW // AFTERNOON RAIN MAYBE	It may rain this afternoon.
TOMORROW NIGHT, MY REPORT DUE	My report is due tomorrow night.
NEXT // TUESDAY CLASS NONE	There will be no class next Tuesday.
PAST // NIGHT LIGHT LOSE WE	Our lights went out last night.
TOMORROW BIRTHDAY	Tomorrow is my birthday.
NOW // SATURDAY, CUT GRASS, PAINT HOUSE, ME PLAN	This Saturday, I plan to cut the grass and then paint the house.

Exercise: Write five sentences, two with single-sign specific time markers and three with compound specific time markers.

Indexing Time

Indexing a time sign is similar to indexing a pronominal reference or a plural. Indexing time involves attaching an index movement to the conclusion of a basic time sign (e.g., WEEK, YEAR). Specifically, the indexing construction could be written as "base time sign and appropriate index hand movement." The particular direction the index hand points depends on whether the intent is to convey the past or future. Since both the time division and the time span are supplied, an indexed time sign represents a specific time marker.

present   future

Figure 2. Indexing the sign NEXT // WEEK

To index the sign WEEK, for instance, the base sign is performed as the active hand slides along the secondary open hand. Then as the sign nears completion, the active hand continues moving forward while changing to an index hand. If the intended concept is LAST // WEEK, the hand then turns and points backward over the shoulder. If the intended concept is NEXT // WEEK, the hand points and moves forward. Similarly, when the S hand of YEAR performs its defined movement parameter and then changes to the index hand as it points backward, it creates the specific time reference LAST // YEAR. When this index gesture points and moves forward, it collectively forms NEXT // YEAR. In either case, past or future, the sign plus indexing blends into a continuous motion in which indexing supplies the time division of the base time sign.

Indexing time applies only to the time signs WEEK, YEAR, and sometimes MONTH. The physical composition of MONTH prohibits certain alterations, however, particularly when the primary hand attempts to move forward along the time line. As a result, MONTH can be indexed to the past (e.g. LAST // MONTH) but not the future. To express "next month," an additional sign modifier, NEXT, is used to create the compound time sign NEXT // MONTH.

A special application of indexing is sometimes used to shade the time element. Under ordinary circumstances, a signer immediately follows the time sign by indexing in a particular temporal direction, but when a signer substitutes a single-digit-number hand shape for the index hand shape the time reference is refined. For example, if a signer follows WEEK with an indexing motion but uses the 2 hand shape, the specific time reference conveyed is TWO // WEEKS // AGO or IN // TWO // WEEKS depending on whether the direction of the hand movement is backward or forward. Any hand shape that represents a number from two through nine can be substituted into the index hand to express a more specific time reference. Thus, numbered indexing is used to express such time concepts as FIVE // WEEKS // AGO, FOUR // YEARS // FROM // NOW, SIX // MONTHS // AGO, etc. In a similar variation of indexing, the G hand can substitute for the index hand to create such signs as ONCE // A // YEAR and ONCE // A // WEEK, coupled with the appropriate directional movement.

Although the time line expresses ongoing action, this action can be extended by repeating a neutral time sign in a to-and-from motion. Reduplicating a sign such as YESTERDAY in a to-and-from movement near the side of the cheek conveys the idea of DAILY or EVERYDAY. This understanding is conveyed by the continuous back-and-forth movement of the A hand intersecting the imaginary, vertical time line. Since the movement is repeated without a pause, it means something repeated in time. Repeating WEEK in this manner, for example, alters the meaning to

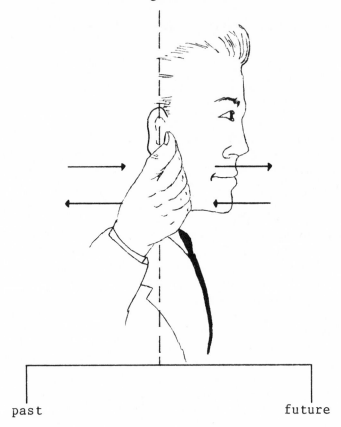

Figure 3: The time sign EVERYDAY

WEEKLY. Similarly YEAR changes to YEARLY, and MONTH changes to MONTHLY.

When the back-and-forth movement is performed in a noticeably slow manner, it expresses the idea of a continuance in time. A slow back-and-forth movement of WEEK for instance, indicates the idea of "for weeks and weeks." Similarly, a slow repetition of MONTH conveys "for months and months," YEAR changes to "for years and years." When the sign ONCE is repeated at normal speed, it conveys the concept SOMETIMES. But when the repetition is slow and circular, the concept is ONCE // IN A // WHILE. Similarly, repeating AGAIN at ordinary speed means OFTEN, but when AGAIN is performed in a slowly and deliberately it changes to OVER // AND // OVER // AGAIN.

Certain multidirectional verbs (Chapter 5) can also derive added meaning from the time line. The directional verb LOOK for instance, basically involves a relatively short forward movement. But when this forward movement is extended in an upward, arcing motion that extends beyond the neutral space, it conveys the sign PROPHECY (a LOOK FUTURE movement). Similarly, when the action of LOOK follows an arc motion that turns backward and moves past the shoulder, it creates the sign REMINISCING (LOOK // PAST).

General Time Marker

When a sentence or conversation pertains to an abstract or vague topic of discussion and does not contain a specific time marker, the time element cannot be understood by the conversational time reference. In the statement MONEY, BORROW ("I borrow some money."), the reader cannot be sure of the time frame. It is unclear whether the signer has borrowed, is borrowing, or will borrow some money. Unless the signer is displaying some evidence (e.g. actual money or a bank application) at the time of the statement, the reader cannot establish the time element by the conversational time reference. Under these circumstances, ASL uses the morphological device of a general time marker, either PAST or FUTURE. These signs incorporate the directionality of the time line to create a shift in temporal understanding and, thereby, establish a change in time. General time markers are distinguished from specific time markers because the former (e.g., PAST) supplies only the time division, while the later (e.g., NEXT // WEEK) supplies both the time division (future) and the time span (seven days).

Present

The present time frame is directly associated with the time of the communication act. Present time is unmarked. Any sentence that lacks time reference, implied or overtly stated, refers to the present tense. Although some present-tense sentences do include a time sign or marker, like NOW // DAY ("today"), this marker functions only to support or emphasize the present time frame. The sentence MONEY BORROW, is a well-formed ASL sentence to convey "I am borrowing some money."

The conversational time reference is a sufficient strategy to express the present tense. READ, ME ("I am reading."), STUDY, WE-TWO ("We are studying."), and YOU CAN QUIT ("You can quit.") all illustrate this unmarked reference. The unmarked present time frame in ASL contrasts to English, which uses various auxiliaries and present tense inflections (e.g., "I *am* eat*ing*," "you *are* eat*ing*," "she *is* eat*ing*," "we *are* eat*ing*," "they *have been* eat*ing*," etc.) to express this time frame.

When conversing in the present time frame, several time signs, such as MONTH, DAY, NIGHT, WEEK, etc., function as single signs. In such a context, such signs become neutral time concepts. In a sentence like WEEK WORK WHEN? ("What week are you working?") WEEK is not a specific time marker. DAY, for instance, expressed as a single sign, means "The day in which the conversation is occurring." or simply "A day."

ASL	*English*
YOUR FRIEND, ME	I am your friend.
HE WORK ME BOSS	He is working for me.
ASK MUCH QUESTION	She asks a lot of questions.
NOW // DAY SWIM, ME HOPE GO-TO	I hope to go swimming today.

Exercise: Write four ASL sentences, two using a neutral time sign and two that are simply unmarked.

Past

An ASL signer performs the general time marker PAST by moving the open hand (or the index hand) with palm oriented backward over and past the signer's shoulder along the horizontal time line. PAST is a general time marker that places a sentence or discourse into the past time division. An independent grammatical element, it typically follows the target verb, as in the sentence CAR, ME LEARN DRIVE PAST ("I have learned how to drive a car."). If the signer who borrowed the money in the earlier example was talking about a past action, the ASL sentence would be: MONEY, BORROW PAST ("I borrowed some money."). In a diagram, the general time marker (GTM) is placed above and after its target verb.

ASL: BREAD MILK, BUY PAST
English: I bought bread and milk.
Diagram:

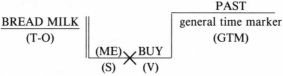

ASL	*English*
BRING PAST WINE	She brought the wine.
TELL PAST STAY	She wore her coat all day.
ADDRESS, ME REMEMBER PAST	I remembered the address.

Exercise: Write six sentences in the past, three with a specific time marker and three with a general time marker.

The sign PAST can also shade or refine the time dimension according to its degree of relative movement. Relative amount of time is indicated by the distance the hand moves along the time line. The base movement associated with PAST is a backward motion in which the hand passes beyond the ear while the fingers extend over the signer's shoulder slightly. When hand movement is restricted in this backward spatial motion, the idea conveyed is recent past. A restricted manual movement just barely past the ear conveys NEAR-PAST. The sentence MONEY BORROW NEAR-PAST means "I just borrowed some money."

But a deliberate and extended backward movement over the shoulder converts PAST into DISTANT-PAST. Another way to indicate the distant past or to emphasize a time long ago is to repeat the movement, yielding PAST-PAST. Either strategy yields MONEY BORROW DISTANT-PAST ("I borrowed some money a long time ago.").

When PAST is bonded to another time sign such as HOUR, NIGHT, or SUMMER, it becomes a part of a compound sign: PAST // HOUR ("last hour"), PAST // NIGHT ("last night"), PAST // SUMMER ("last summer"). In a compound, PAST is a source sign that serves as part of a specific time marker. But as a single sign, PAST is a general time marker. It is also possible to incorporate relative motion into its performance characteristics to provide further temporal shading.

ASL: CAR, SHE LOCK NEAR-PAST
English: She just locked herself out of her car.
Diagram:

CAR (T)			NEAR-PAST (GTM)
	SHE (S)	LOCK (V)	OUT (O)

ASL	*English*
LAMP, ME BREAK NEAR-PAST	I just broke the lamp.
LAMP, ME BREAK DISTANT-PAST	I broke the lamp a long time ago.
TEACH-PERSON CHANGE DISTANT-PAST MIND	The teacher changed her mind quite a while ago.
GREAT IDEA, SHE CREATE PAST	She thought up a great idea.
MANY SALE TICKET, ME USE NEAR-PAST ALL	I used all of the coupons.

Exercise: Write six ASL sentences, three using NEAR-PAST and three using DIS-TANT-PAST.

Future

The sign space immediately and directly in front of the signer is reserved for the neutral or present time frame. The future time frame extends just beyond the neutral sign space. Since such a spatial division is a subjective estimate, these definitions of space serve as arbitrary guidelines.

An ASL signer performs FUTURE by holding an open hand with the palm facing sideways and the fingers facing upward near the side of the temple (or face) and moving it forward in a moderate arcing motion along the horizontal time line. A general time marker, FUTURE is an independent grammatical element that usually follows its target verb, as in CAR, ME LEARN DRIVE FUTURE ("I will learn how to drive a car."). In the sentence about borrowing money, the signer would express the future tense as: MONEY, BORROW FUTURE ("I will borrow some money.").

The sign FUTURE can be refined by the distance the hand travels forward along the time line. The base movement for FUTURE is an arcing forward motion in which the hand travels along the time line a moderate distance. To indicate the near or immediate future, the hand is held near the head, and as it arcs forward, it stops abruptly (distinctive from the typical flowing motion). NEAR-FUTURE is distinguished by a short, restricted arcing motion. The sentence MONEY BORROW NEAR-FUTURE means "I was just about to borrow some money."

To convey DISTANT-FUTURE, the signer makes a deliberately exaggerated movement in which the hand is extended forward to nearly the arm's full length. Another way to indicate the idea of FAR-INTO-FUTURE is to repeat the sign (FUTURE-FUTURE). Thus, MONEY BORROW DISTANT-FUTURE communications the idea, "I will borrow some money, someday."

ASL: PARTY, ME PLAN FUTURE
English: I will plan the party.
Diagram:

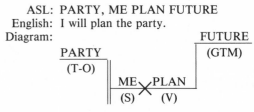

ASL	English
ME WORK LATE FUTURE	I will be working late.
WALLET, HE GIVE FUTURE ME	He will give me the wallet.
GOOD SONG, ME TEACH FUTURE THEY	I will teach them a good song.
CAMP, HE BUILD FUTURE FIRE	He will build a fire in the camp.
PLAY FUTURE GAME WHO?	Who will play in the game?

Exercise: Write six sentences, three using FUTURE in statements and three using FUTURE in questions.

Establishing an ASL Time Frame

Unlike in English, in which each verb in a sentence must be marked for tense, when a particular time frame is established by an ASL signer (e.g., LAST // NIGHT), the reader understands that all subsequent discourse will refer to that time period. Once a time frame is set, it remains in effect until the discourse has concluded or the time frame is intentionally changed. A single time marker is sufficient to serve as the only time expression for an entire communication event. It is the reader's responsibility to remember the time frame and apply it to subsequent sentences.

When a signer establishes a particular time frame (past or future) it supersedes the present-moment reference. Once the new time frame is set, the imaginary time line no longer represents the present. As long as the newly established time frame is in effect, the discourse is understood in that other time frame. The reason for this is that at any given moment the time line can serve as only one time frame. The neutral sign space is reserved for whatever time frame that is momentarily established.

Consider a scenario in which two boys are talking about a recent camping trip. One boy reflects: LAST // WEEK ME GO-TO CAMP. WE STAY AWAKE LATE NIGHT. PLAY MANY GAME. ME LEARN MUCH. ("Last week, I went camping. We even stayed up until late. We played a lot of games. Boy, I sure learned a lot at camp."). The single time marker LAST // WEEK is sufficient to establish the time frame in the past. Once the time frame is established, it is not necessary to repeat it. While it remains in effect, all subsequent discourse is linked to it. Although such sentences as PLAY MANY GAME and ME LEARN MUCH are performed in neutral space, this space momentarily denotes the past tense, the reader understands such associated sentences in the past-tense time frame.

When a signer wishes to return the conversation to the present time, she can introduce an explicitly present time marker such as NOW // DAY ("today") or use a time modifier (e.g., NOW). Once the present is reestablished, it remains in effect until the time frame is changed once again. In every case, all subsequent communications are associated to the particular time frame established by the last time reference. To understand the effect of a time marker on discourse versus isolated sentences, read each of the following examples and notice the difference in the time markers.

Example 1: Connected discourse
PAST // NIGHT PARTY, ME ATTEND. MEET SPECIAL PERSON. DANCE TALK. WONDERFUL TIME, WE ENJOY TOGETHER. NEW FRIEND, MAYBE SEE FUTURE AGAIN SOON.

Example 2: Isolated sentences
    a. PAST // NIGHT PARTY, ME ATTEND.
    b. SPECIAL PERSON, MEET PAST.
    c. DANCE PAST, WE-TWO.
    d. TALK PAST, WE-TWO.
    e. WONDERFUL TIME, WE-TWO ENJOY PAST.
    f. NEW FRIEND, MAYBE SEE FUTURE AGAIN SOON.

The English equivalent of either of these is: "I went to a party last night. I met a special person there. We danced. We talked. We had a great time. Maybe I will see my new friend again some time soon." The first example illustrates how connected discourse relies on a single time marker (PAST // NIGHT) to mark the subsequent sentences by implication, retaining the association to the established time frame. It is not until the signer wishes to comment in a different time frame that any subsequent explicit time marker is necessary. But since no association among the sentences or their context exists in the second example, a time marker is required for each sentence. (The contributive impact of the conversational time reference is intentionally overlooked.)

The Completion Marker

A variation of the general time marker is a sign like FINISH and NOT // YET, which can be used to indicate completed action. Representing two "perfect tense" markers in ASL, these markers enable the signer to establish a secondary reference (past, future) and refer to that time while simultaneously maintaining the present conversational time reference (Friedman, 1975).

Finish

FINISH is a base verb that conveys the meaning "something done, over with." As a verb, FINISH can accept an adverbial modifier as in the sentence ME FINISH SOON ("I will be finished soon.").

FINISH also signals positive completion (Madsen, 1972). In this context, FINISH means something that at the time of the communication act is being completed or will be completed. When FINISH functions as a completion marker (as opposed to functioning as a verb), it is an independent grammatical element that precedes the target verb. FINISH READ ("When he finished reading.") exemplifies the use of FINISH as a completion marker. In an English sentence like "When he had eaten, he left," or "After he ate, he left," the equivalent ASL sentence requires the completion marker to precede the verb FINISH EAT, HE LEAVE. In terms of placement and grammatical function, the completion marker FINISH acts as an auxiliary verb that modifies the main verb. In a diagram, when FINISH is a verb, it is placed on the base line (A). When it is used as a completion marker, it becomes part of the verb phrase, like any auxiliary verb (B).

(A) ASL: CLASS ALMOST FINISH
English: The class is almost done.
Diagram:

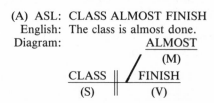

(B) ASL: STORY, ME FINISH WRITE
English: I wrote the story.
Diagram: STORY ‖
(T-O) ‖ ME FINISH WRITE
(S)   (V)

ASL
FINISH EAT, YOU?
WORK, ME FINISH WILL
SCHOOL FINISH, MEET
MOVIE FINISH, WE-TWO EAT
FINISH READ BOOK, PHONE ME

English
Have you eaten?
I will finish the work.
Meet me after school.
When the movie is over, we will eat.
When you are done reading the book, call me.

Exercise: Write eight sentences, four with FINISH as a verb and four with FINISH as a completion marker.

Not // Yet

The other completion marker, NOT // YET, refers to action that has not yet occurred. NOT // YET is a negative completion marker. It involves the nonmanual signal of shaking the head side to side while performing the sign. In the sentence MY LESSON FINISH NOT // YET ("My lesson is not over yet.") the letters "neg" refer to the negative shaking of the head. Another example is the sentence SNOW STOP NOT // YET ("The snow still hasn't stopped.").

As a completion marker, NOT // YET functions to express an action that began or was to begin but up to this moment has still not been completed. NOT // YET follows the target verb and is accompanied by the side-to-side head shake (neg). Since NOT // YET serves grammatically to modify the main verb, it has certain characteristics that are similar to an auxiliary verb. In a diagram, it is placed after the main verb as part of the verb phrase.

ASL: DAY ONE SCHOOL BEGIN NOT // YET
English: The first day of school hasn't begun yet.
Diagram: DAY ONE
(M)
SCHOOL ‖ BEGIN   NOT // YET
(S) ‖ (V)

ASL
MOM BAKE NOT // YET BREAD
CAR NOT // YET OLD
MAN DRY NOT // YET CAR
GRADUATE NOT // YET , ME

English
Mom hasn't baked the bread yet.
The car isn't old.
The man hasn't dried the car yet.
I still haven't graduated.

Exercise: Write four sentences using NOT // YET as a negative completion marker.

Time Modifier

Another morphological mechanism available to modify or refine a temporal concept is a sign that acts as "time modifiers." A time modifier redefines the time element more precisely than the conversational time reference, the time marker (specific or general), or the completion marker. In a simple statement such as STUDY, WE-TWO ("We studied."), the conversational time reference is insufficient for crisp understanding. A general time marker might be added to yield STUDY PAST, WE-TWO ("We *studied*"), or a specific time marker to yield YESTERDAY STUDY, WE-TWO ("We studied yesterday."). After a time element has been marked, a time modifier can be added, as in YESTERDAY STUDY, WE-TWO ALL-NIGHT ("Yesterday, we studied all night long."), to provide additional useful information.

Regardless of the strategy used to established the time frame, the time modifier functions to qualify it. The time modifier can refine virtually any existing time span, but it never replaces or acts as a substitute for another time-marking mechanism. Rather, it refines or emphasizes the established time marked. The time modifier is usually positioned at the end of the sentence.

The conversational time reference applies to a statement such as BEGIN PARTY ("Let's start the party."). But when a time modifier (e.g., LATER) is added, the sentence changes to BEGIN PARTY LATER ("Let's wait a while before starting the party."). Similarly, the sentence YOUR TURN ("It is your turn.") can be changed to YOUR TURN NOW ("It is your turn now.") to intensify the time element.

Common time modifiers include signs such as LATE, LATER, ALWAYS, SOON, STILL, NOW, and EARLY. Each sign serves to qualify time in a slightly different way. And since a time modifier is not a time marker, the established time frame is maintained (by use of indexing, specific time markers, etc). Like any adjective modifier, these time modifiers are used only when the signer wishes to redefine the time involved or to draw attention to it.

The sign NOW serves as a time modifier only when used as a singular sign, as in ME MUST LEAVE NOW ("I must leave now."). When it is part of a compound (e.g., NOW // DAY), NOW functions not as a modifier, but as a specific time marker. The opposite applies to the signs ALL or MOST. As single signs, these give no time reference. But as part of a compound, as in ALL // NIGHT, ALL // DAY, ALL // MORNING, ALL // WEEK, ALL // TIME, MOST // MORNING, MOST // DAY, etc., they function as time modifiers. Depending on position and context the sign LATE can serve either as a modifier or as a main sentence element. In sentences like ME ARRIVE LATE ("I arrived late."), and ME CAN LEAVE LATE ("I can leave late."), LATE functions as the object of the sentence. But in a sentence like MEET, ME ARRIVE LATE ("I arrived at the meeting late."), it functions as a modifier.

The time line also influences the expression of time modifiers. When the secondary open hand is held with the palm sideways and fingers upward, it serves as a metaphoric "hand clock." When the active index hand (palm forward) is placed alongside it and pivots in an abbreviated forward, clockwise direction, it creates such modifying signs as LATER, MINUTE, and AFTER // AWHILE. To convey a past-tense modifier such as AWHILE // AGO or PREVIOUS, the active hand is repositioned with the palm inward. The abbreviated movement then moves in a backward, counter-clockwise direction as the index hand moves toward the signer's body. A full, clockwise, circle motion expresses an HOUR, while a full counter-clockwise motion (palm inward) expresses an HOUR // AGO.

The time modifier is an independent grammatical component that is usually placed at the end of the sentence. But when the time modifier is used in an interrogative question, it is usually positioned just before the interrogative sign. In a diagram, it is placed above and behind the main sentence.

> ASL: ME SLEEP ALL // DAY
> English: I slept all day long.
> Diagram:

$$\frac{\text{ALL // DAY}}{\underset{\text{(S)}}{\text{ME}} \parallel \underset{\text{(V)}}{\text{SLEEP}}} \bigg/ \text{Time modifier (TM)}$$

ASL	*English*
BEGIN NOW	Start now.
JOEY OLD-TWO NOW	Joey is now two years old.
MUST LEAVE SOON	You need to be going pretty soon.
NOW // NIGHT WEATHER CHANGE LATER	The weather will be changing later tonight.
ME WORK WRITE BOOK MOST // MORNING	I worked on writing the book for most of the morning.

Numerical Time Modifiers

A strategy to broaden the application of the time modifier is to incorporate it with numerical hand shapes. Consider a sentence like WAIT, WE THREE-HOUR ("We waited three hours."). The conversational time reference implies a past time period (even if the conversation is occurring while the person was waiting, the time reference is still in the past tense since three hours have elapsed). The use of a numeral hand shape superimposed on HOUR enhances the information conveyed by the modifier by defining the duration of the event (waiting). In a sentence like BUS ARRIVE FUTURE TEN MINUTE ("The bus will arrive in 10 minutes."), both a general time marker (FUTURE) and a numerical time modifier (10 MINUTE) are used to form a temporal sign phrase.

Unlike specific time markers, numerical time modifiers do not supply the time frame and its related division. When a numeral is incorporated into a base sign such as WEEK to form THREE-WEEK, TIME-SEVEN, FOUR-DAY, etc., it intentionally lacks any directional movement along the time line. Because it supplies a time frame without supplying the time division, it remains a neutral reference, a time modifier. Time modifiers that involve a numeral hand shape are generally regarded as neutral sign phrases. In contrast, compounds such as THREE // WEEK // FUTURE ("three weeks from now") or TWO // MONTH // PAST ("two months ago") reflects the added component of temporal indexing. While TWO-YEAR ("two years") is a time modifier, TWO // YEAR // PAST ("two years ago") or TWO // YEAR // FUTURE ("two years from now") are specific time markers. This is because they supply both the time frame and time division.

In an ordinary discourse, it is common to find both time markers and time modifiers, since each sign supplies a different type of semantic information. Consider a scenario in which two young adults are sitting around talking about current events, and one remarks: PAST // WEEK MY PARENT VISIT. STAY THREE-WEEK. TRUE ENJOY, ME. In this discourse, the specific time marker (PAST // WEEK) establishes the time frame (WEEK) and the time division (PAST). The modifier (THREE-WEEK) redefines the time by supplying additional information: "My parents were visiting last week. They stayed for three weeks. I really enjoyed it." Numerical time modifiers are a variation of time modifiers and are positioned accordingly, at the end of a sentence.

ASL: PAPER, GIVE TWO-WEEK LATE
English: You turned your paper in two weeks late.
Diagram: PAPER

PAPER ‖			TWO-WEEK LATE
(T-O) ‖ (YOU)	GIVE (ME)	(TM)
‖ (S)	(V) (O)	

ASL	English
HELEN REMAIN BED FOUR-DAY	Helen has been bedridden for four days.
HOUSE THERE, SHE LIVE FIVE-YEAR	She has lived in that house for five years.
TOMORROW APPOINT, YOU DENTIST TIME-FOUR	You have an appointment with the dentist at four o'clock tomorrow.
NOW // NIGHT COME-HERE ABOUT-TIME-SEVEN	Come on over tonight around seven o'clock.
PARTY CONTINUE BETWEEN SEVEN-NINE	The party will last from seven till nine.

Training Exercises

A. Using various ASL temporal strategies, redefine the time dimensions in the following sentences. First translate each sentence into ASL. Next, rewrite the English either by adding a more defined time element or by changing it to a different time frame.

1. I got these shells at the beach.
2. Where is the Golden Gate Bridge located?
3. The next-door neighbor is playing music very loudly.
4. Several friends will be coming for dinner.
5. What do you pay in interest?
6. The weatherman is predicting a severe storm for later.
7. Your income tax will be due very soon.
8. Your new piece of furniture will be delivered next Wednesday.
9. Karen needs to send out the party invitations.
10. They sent you the wrong books.
11. Our waiter forgot to bring us some water.

B. Using only the conversational time reference, indexing, and specific time markers, translate these sentences into ASL.

1. What is our largest state?
2. Mark will call the florist.
3. Let's make plans to meet for lunch in two weeks.
4. What makes it so easy for me to be late to this class?
5. Fifteen minutes later, everyone got into the car.
6. He copied down a number and then called.
7. Two weeks later my package finally arrived.
8. The baseball game was rescheduled for three weeks.
9. Ben woke up at 7 A.M. and took a shower.
10. You found a dollar lying in the grass.

C. Translate the following discourse into ASL as it would occur in an ongoing conversation.

Discourse 1:
"I told my boss to wait. I would make the dinner reservation for him. Yes, I would call the florist. By closing last night, I had typed twelve letters and filed four reports. I went down to the corner for a newspaper. I even made my boss coffee. But did he ever thank me? Well, if you consider a $100 bonus thanks, you bet he thanked me! I am really lucky."

Discourse 2:
"Baseball is a game. It was invented in the 1800s in New England. People say Abner Doubleday invented the game. It is played by two teams. Each team has nine players. Each player uses a bat, glove, and a ball. The team who scores more runs is the winner. There are nine innings in a game."

D. Diagram the following sentences. Be sure to label all modifiers.

1. SHE REMOVE WILL SOON
   <small>3</small>
2. WRITE REPAIR-PERSON MONEY-CHECK NOW

3. SEE AMBULANCE LIGHT STOP CAR
   ₁
4. FOOD FREEZE-COMPARTMENT SPOIL FUTURE
5. EAT RESTAURANT, YOU HOW-OFTEN?
6. WE DECIDE ORDER DESSERT
7. DOZEN YELLOW ROSE, SHE RECEIVE FUTURE
8. YOU ENJOY MAYBE LIVE WHERE?

E. In context, choice of temporal strategy depends on the established framework and the various shifts in topic. As you create dialogues for the following scenarios, incorporate all of the major strategies as often as possible.

Scenario 1:

Your roommate is very attached to her fish Goldy, which has been a favorite pet for the past three years. Every time your roommate cleans Goldy's tank, she has the bad habit of putting Goldy in the toilet.

One day while your roommate is cleaning the fish tank, you accidentally flush Goldy. You must tell your roommate about Goldy's demise.

Scenario 2:

You are a salesperson in the clothing department of a large department store. A customer who is trying on a top that is obviously three sizes too small is having difficulty getting the top buttoned. The top starts to rip. You want to keep up the good name of the store, but you don't want to be blamed for the damaged top (which would be deducted from your paycheck). You approach the customer.

Scenario 3:

Your car gets stuck in a snow drift out in the country. The only person around is a young child walking by. Since there are no homes in sight, you approach the child for directions to a phone so that you can call for assistance. But when you try to talk with the child, he refuses to talk to you. He has been taught very well not to speak to strangers. You must convince this strong-minded child to make an exception.

13. Negating a Sentence

Negation in ASL is usually conveyed not through explicit signs, but through facial and body signals. Surface-level negation through explicit signs is but a secondary strategy. The usual signal for negation in ASL is a side-to-side shaking of the head. Regarded as an automatic response, the negative head shake is a widely understood signal of disagreement. In a sentence like WOMAN BUY DOG ("The woman is buying a dog."), the action is taking place. But when the side-to-side head shake is added to this sentence, $\overline{\text{WOMAN}}^{neg}$ BUY DOG, the statement is negated, and means "The woman is not buying a dog."

The side-to-side head shake is the most fundamental means of negating a sentence in American Sign Language. Used in all negative sentences, statements, and questions, it is accompanied by a nonneutral facial expression such as a frown or an expression of disapproval. A still stronger negative signal is squinting the brow. This consists of the eyebrows being drawn together and then lowered. A negative facial expression combines with the head shake to form the fundamental ASL negating signal (Liddell, 1980). The ASL negation signal is designated in written form as "neg" (Baker and Battison, 1980). The "neg" is placed over the sign(s) that is accompanied by the head movement. The line above the sentence signifies which portion of the sentence is accompanied by the negating signal.

The nonmanual negating signal is a grammatical component that can negate a sentence without the need for additional signs. When the sentence REMEMBER JOE, ME ("I remember Joe.") is conveyed with a neutral delivery, it conveys the sentential meaning of its signs. But when the same sentence is performed with the negating signal $\overline{\text{REMEMBER}}^{neg}$ JOE, ME, the sentence conveys "I don't remember Joe." Similarly, JERRY THINK SAME KAREN ("Jerry agrees with Karen.") accompanied by the negating signal, JERRY $\overline{\text{THINK SAME KAREN}}^{neg}$, becomes "Jerry doesn't agree with Karen."

The negating signal affects only the signs it accompanies, and the signer uses the strategy according to the intended message. In many instances, this marking is applied to an entire phrase or sentence, and not just to a part of it (Baker, 1980; Liddell, 1980). Whenever a sentence, statement, or question is arranged in SVO sign order, the entire sentence may be

209

accompanied by the negating signal. Thus, the sentence "Jimmie doesn't feel good," would be manually expressed, JIMMIE FEEL GOOD.

The negation signal is applied more strategically to topicalized sentences. When a sentence is topicalized, the topic is set apart by word order and by an intonation break. An ASL signer will use this separation to apply the negation signal strategically. When the topic is not accompanied by the negating head shake, it sets a neutral scene. In such cases, the comment is negated as in MOVIE, ME GO WITH YOU. The sentence can be translated into English as "About the movie—I'm not going with you." On the other hand the topic may be negated, and the comment neutral. In the sentence GO-TO CAN'T, JOYCE ME, the English translation is "We can't go, Joyce and me." In this case, the topic expresses the negative concept, and the comment is expressed in a neutral manner. These different placements of the negation signal among SVO and different types of topicalized patterns illustrate that the negation signal marks the boundaries of the negating force (Liddell, 1980).

When an object or a verb-object clause is topicalized, it becomes the focus of a sentence, setting the scene of the sentence. The topic will be followed by the comment, which supplies the details or footage to the scene. Thus, placement of the negation signal depends on whether it is the topic or subsequent comment that logically receives the negation. In the sentence BUY CAT, SHE, the negation informs the reader what the person did not do: "*She* did not buy the cat." In a diagram, the negating signal is represented by a line over the targeted signs with the notation "neg."

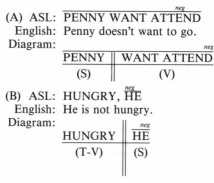

(A) ASL: PENNY WANT ATTEND
   English: Penny doesn't want to go.
   Diagram:

PENNY	WANT ATTEND
(S)	(V)

(B) ASL: HUNGRY, HE
   English: He is not hungry.
   Diagram:

HUNGRY	HE
(T-V)	(S)

ASL	English
WANT ATTEND, ME	I don't want to go.
DOG CAN TALK	Dogs cannot talk.
SNOW ALL SAME	Snowflakes are not all alike.
DOCTOR, YOU MUST GO	You don't have to go to the doctor.
JOHN BILL GO-TO BAND PRACTICE	John and Bill did not go to band practice.

FIREPLACE, $\overline{\text{WE START FIRE}}^{neg}$ We didn't start a fire in the fireplace.

Exercise: Write six negated sentences, three in SVO sign order and three topicalized. Practice delivering each sentence manually.

The Negation Sign

The negating signal is not the only strategy in American Sign Language to negate a message. Another method involves the use of certain ASL signs that express negative semantic concepts. While each of these signs convey its own individual meaning, it also supports the negating signal by expressing negative or negated action. Such signs include NOT ("negation"), CAN'T ("inability"), REFUSE ("won't accept or comply"), and NEVER ("not ever, under no condition"). The negation sign functions as an independent grammatical element, which typically follows the target it negates, usually the verb.

Even in sentences that use a negation sign, the ASL signer always includes a simultaneous negative head shake. In ASL, two negatives do not create a positive, as in English. Rather, two negatives support and intensify each other.

When NOT is used in a sentence, it helps to negate the sentence or serves to emphasize the negation. The fundamental way to negate a neutral sentence like ME LEAVE NOW ("I am leaving now"), is to add the negating head shake, $\overline{\text{ME LEAVE NOW}}^{neg}$ ("I am not leaving now."). But an alternative is to add the sign NOT along with the negating signal: $\overline{\text{ME LEAVE}}$ $\overline{\text{NOT NOW}}^{neg}$ ("I am not leaving now."). NOT does not replace the negating signal; it complements and intensifies it. To further stress the negation, these same strategies are performed with deliberate emphasis in delivery style: $\overline{\text{ME LEAVE NOT NOW}}^{neg}$ ("I am not leaving now!")

Although ASL allows negation signals and negation signs to be used in the same sentence, it does not permit two explicit negation signs to be used in the same sentence. Since NOT and another negation sign such as CAN'T or WON'T cannot be used together, these signs are grammatically interchangeable. An ASL signer will choose which negation sign to use depending on the meaning of the sentence. Thus, the signer can choose a negation sign to express different shadings of semantic negation as in $\overline{\text{HE KNOW NOT}}^{neg}$ ("He doesn't know."), $\overline{\text{HE KNOW CAN'T}}^{neg}$ ("He can't possibly know."), $\overline{\text{HE KNOW NEVER}}^{neg}$ ("He never knows."), etc.

The negation sign (NS) is diagrammed on a line above and following its target sign.

ASL: MONA, $\overline{\text{YOU WAIT CAN'T}}^{neg}$
English: You can't wait any longer for Mona.

Diagram:

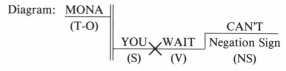

ASL	English
COOK CAN'T, SHE _(neg)_	She can't cook well.
LEARN NEVER LATE _(neg)_	It is never too late to learn.
YOUR NAME HERE NOT _(neg)_	Your name is not here.
ME WORRY NOT _(neg)_	I am not worried.
BELIEVE CAN'T, ME _(neg)_	I can't believe it.
TELEPHONE, SHE ANSWER REFUSE _(neg)_	She refused to answer the phone.

Exercise: Write six sentences that contain a negation sign, three in the SVO sign order and three topicalized.

Negation signs are distinguishable from other ASL signs that represent negative meaning concepts such as ANGRY, AVOID, WORRY, HATE, etc., because negation signs modify the state of action verbs, by negating the verb's action. In contrast, negative-meaning signs like ANGRY and SCARED represent a main sentential element. These two classes of signs serve completely different grammatical roles. In a sentence like ME ANGER AT YOU ("I am angry with you."), the subject ME is expressing the action of the verb ANGER. The verb could have been a "positive-meaning" verb (HAPPY) or a "neutral-meaning" verb (ASSIGN). But in this case, the verb ANGER was used to express a semantic meaning that happens to be negative. Although the meaning attached to these verbs is negative, they remain ordinary verbs grammatically.

Since these two classes of negative-oriented signs function independently of each other, both types can be represented in the same sentence: ME ANGRY CAN'T AT YOU _(neg)_ ("I can't be mad at you."). In this example, the negation marker CAN'T reverses the polarity of the verb ANGRY ("not angry").

Negation markers are also distinguishable from another class of negative-oriented signs: negative modifiers. A "negative modifier" is a sign such as AWKWARD, AWFUL, or SICK that is used to qualify a noun or as a subject complement, and has a negative connotation. The sign BAD, for example, serves as a negative modifier in the sentence BAD FOOD ("This is bad food.") and as a subject complement as in FOOD BAD ("The food is bad."). In either form, the negative modifier functions quite differently from the negation sign. In essence, the negation sign negates a verb, and a negative modifier qualifies a noun. Since these two types of signs function in grammatically independent roles within a sentence, both types can be represented in the same sentence: FOOD TASTE CAN'T BAD _(neg)_ ("The food can't taste that bad."). In this example, the negation sign CAN'T reverses the meaning of FOOD TASTE BAD into "The food tastes pretty good."

Because both general time markers and negation signs usually follow the verb, there is a potential for semantic confusion when they are used in the same sentence. Although context will mitigate this potential ambiguity, when both elements are used in the same sentence, the signer should follow the sequential order: verb —→ general time marker—→ negation sign. To negate "I know," for instance, the nonmanual negating signal is usually sufficient: $\overline{\text{ME KNOW}}^{neg}$. If the negating signal is nonmanual, a different time frame presents no problem: $\overline{\text{ME KNOW PAST}}^{neg}$ ("I didn't know."). But if a signer wishes to use a negation sign along with the general time marker, the sequence V-GTM-NM should be followed: $\overline{\text{ME KNOW PAST NOT}}^{neg}$ ("I didn't know.").

The Negative Compound

In a process Woodward (1974) calls "negative incorporation," an ASL signer can use a limited number of ASL signs to create a negated compound. In general, ASL compounding is achieved by a change in the palm direction and movement parameters of certain verbs and adjectives. To create a negated compound sign, and the palm is turned as the hand moves the movement parameter of the root sign is extended forward. This outward twisting movement of the hand(s) follows immediately after the execution of the root sign.

Figure 1. The negative compound DON'T // KNOW

The sign KNOW, for instance, consists of an open hand (palm inward) moving upward until the fingers touch the signer's forehead. To create the negative compound DON'T // KNOW, the signer performs KNOW, but finishes by moving the hand outward in a twisting motion from the forehead. The reversed palm direction and outward movement comes immediately after the hand touches the forehead. In all negative compounds, the hand or hands complete the base sign and then move away to articulate the succeeding negation without a pause. The following are examples of the negative compound.

DON'T // CARE   HF: primary Modified O hand
                 PD: inward
                 HP: at the forehead
                 HM: fingers touch forehead and rotate around
                       while moving forward/downward and chang-
                       ing into a relaxed 5 hand, palm down
                 (Comment: similar to a tossing or flinging motion)

DON'T // KNOW   HF: primary open hand
                 PD: inward
                 HP: at the forehead
                 HM: fingers touch primary side of forehead and
                       then swing forward/downward, palm down
                 (Comment: similar to discarding KNOW)

DON'T // LIKE   HF: primary touch hand
                 PD: inward
                 HP: chest level; thumb and index finger touching
                       the chest
                 HM: hand moves forward while thumb and index
                       touch together; hand swings downward while
                       relaxing to a 5 hand, palm down
                 (Comment: similar to discarding LIKE)

DON'T // WANT   HF: both bent hands
                 PD: both upward
                 HP: close to chest
                 HM: hands move forward while wrists swing down
                       and out, relaxing to 5 hands, palms down
                 (Comment: similar to discarding a reverse WANT)

All negative compounds involve a verb as a base sign. The negative compound can occupy the same position as a verb $\overline{\text{TOM DON'T // WANT}}^{neg}$ $\overline{\text{DRINK}}$ ("Tom doesn't want the drink."), or it can act as a negation sign and follow another verb; $\overline{\text{TOM DECIDE DON'T // WANT DRINK}}^{neg}$ ("Tom decided he doesn't want the drink."). As a verb, the negative compound can be followed by a general time marker as in $\overline{\text{DRINK, ME DON'T WANT PAST}}^{neg}$ ("I didn't want a drink."). But as a negation sign, it remains as part of the verb phrase, which the general time marker follows, as in $\overline{\text{LEAVE}}$ $\overline{\text{DON'T}}_{\,heg}$ // $\overline{\text{WANT PAST}}$, ME ("I didn't want to leave."). When the negative compound acts as verb, it is placed on the baseline.

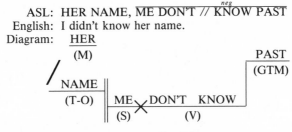

ASL: HER NAME, $\overline{\text{ME DON'T}}$ // $\overline{\text{KNOW PAST}}^{\,neg}$
English: I didn't know her name.
Diagram:

ASL	*English*
$\overline{\text{BUY FORGET}}$ // $\overline{\text{NOT BREAD}}^{\,neg}$	Don't forget to buy some bread.
$\overline{\text{CUT-FINGER}}$, $\overline{\text{YOU DON'T WANT}}^{\,neg}$	You don't want to cut your finger.
$\overline{\text{TRUE DON'T KNOW}}^{\,neg}$, ME	I really don't know.
$\overline{\text{WONDER}}$, $\overline{\text{YOU WHY}}$ // $\overline{\text{NOT}}^{\,neg}$	Why don't you consider it?
$\overline{\text{WE LOOK DON'T}}$ // $\overline{\text{LIKE PAST}}^{\,neg}$	We didn't like to look.

Exercise: Write four sentences involving negative compounds.

Unfinished Action

There are two different kinds of incomplete actions. The first is when something remains incomplete as a steady state. An example is "John did not finish his homework," in which John has failed to complete a particular action, and there is no indication that he ever will complete it. The second is when an action is ongoing or will be completed in the immediate future. An example is "John is still not finished with his homework." The implication of this sentence is that John is continuing to work on his homework.

In American Sign Language, the expression of these two forms of completion are conveyed in distinctly different ways. To convey the concept of unfinished or incomplete, the negation sign NOT follows the positive completion marker FINISH. Thus, "John did not finish his homework" is expressed manually as $\overline{\text{JOHN FINISH NOT HOMEWORK}}^{\,neg}$. To convey an "ongoing" or "to be completed" state, the negative completion marker NOT // YET is used. Thus, "John is still not done with his homework" is manually expressed $\overline{\text{JOHN FINISH NOT}}$ // $\overline{\text{YET HOMEWORK}}^{\,neg}$.

ASL	*English*
$\overline{\text{TALK NOT}}$ // $\overline{\text{YET SHE}}^{\,neg}$, ME	I have not talk to her yet.
$\overline{\text{TOM SEE NOT MOVIE}}^{\,neg}$	Tom has not seen the movie.

$\overline{\text{TOM SEE NOT}} \mathbin{//} \overset{neg}{\text{YET}} \text{MOVIE}$ Tom has not yet seen the movie.

$\overline{\text{TOM SEE FINISH NEVER MOVIE}}^{\,neg}$ Tom never finished seeing the end of the movie.

No/None

The sign NO is often used in American Sign Language as a peripheral expression. This peripheral expression is illustrated by the sentence NO. YOUR MOTHER, $\overline{\text{ME TELL NOT}}^{\,neg}$ (No, I will not tell your mother."). In such a case, NO conveys a denial, rejection, or refusal.

In English, "no" can be used as part of a word phrase, as in "no good, no fun," etc. American Sign Language, does not use NO as frequently or in as many different contexts as English. Rather, it employs specific signs that express the appropriate semantic meaning. To express "no good," ASL uses the sign BAD. To express "You are no different," the ASL sentence is SAME YOU. And "It is no fun" is signed as BORING.

While English frequently uses "no" to express the absence of something, ASL replaces "no" with NONE and positions the sign following its target, as in "There is no class" (CLASS NONE), "There is no more food" (MORE FOOD NONE), "You have no money" (MONEY NONE, YOU HAVE).

NONE denotes the absence or total lack of something or somebody. English frequently expresses this concept by joining the prefix "non" directly to an English word, as in "nonperson" (a person who is regarded as not existing), "nonword" (a word void of meaning), "nonreader" (lacking reading skill), "nonverbal" (lacking verbal skills), "nonsupport" (absence of support).

All ideas that explicitly or implicitly express the absence or lack of something or somebody are manually expressed with the sign NONE. NONE can be classed as a negation sign. As an independent grammatical element, NONE follows its target sign. And as a negation sign, it is always accompanied by the nonmanual negating signal. In a diagram, NONE is positioned as a negation sign.

ASL: CHANGE NONE, ME HAVE
English: I have no change.
Diagram:

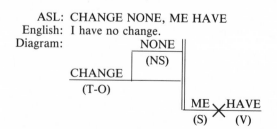

ASL	*English*
TRAFFIC NONE (neg)	There is no traffic.
CHAIR COMFORTABLE NONE (neg)	This chair is not comfortable.
CAREFUL NONE, YOU (neg)	You are being careless.
TRUE PROBLEM HERE NONE (neg)	So there is really no problem here.
ELECTRIC NONE, WE HAVE (neg)	We have no electricity.
TIME NONE, ME HAVE (neg)	I have no time.

Training Exercises

A. Translate each of the following into ASL sentences and then negate each sentence using only the negating signal.

1. You will be awarded a prize.
2. Mr. Benson forgot his wife's birthday.
3. The baby fussed and cried.
4. Jack tried on a new pair of shoes.
5. I like my steak cooked medium.
6. School was cancelled.
7. Mrs. Jones was able to get to work.
8. The child vomited in the wastebasket.
9. Try to start the car.
10. Is anybody here yet?

B. Negate the following sentences by incorporating various ASL negating mechanisms.

1. NOW // NIGHT, MUCH RAIN EXPECT
2. EAT ONE MORE, ME CAN
3. MOVIE, WE READY GO
4. FIRE ALMOST OUT
5. STAND HERE LINE ONE-HOUR
6. MY VACATION CONTINUE THREE-WEEK MORE
7. HOOK, YOUNG MAN PLACE WORM
8. BASEBALL, MY SON STAND HOME PLATE
9. PUSH CAMERA BUTTON
10. GET ME TOWEL

C. Translate the following discourse into ASL.

Swans are not part of the rabbit family. Rather, they are members of the duck family. They are not smaller than geese, nor are they the same size. Swans are larger. I have never seen a swan that did not have a long neck and short legs. But I can't remember if the feet have webbing. A swan's wing range is no more than eight feet. Swans are not black birds, but they are swimming birds. I never see swans eat food except from the water. Some swans are loud and others are almost silent. Aren't baby swans called cygnets?

D. Diagram the following ASL sentences and then translate them into English.
1. ANSWER, SHE KNOW WILL ̄NEVER̄ (neg)
2. MOVIE, TARA ME SEE NOT // YET (neg)
3. BETTY LIKE MARY MUCH (neg)
4. MY NUMBER HERE (neg)
5. SHERRY FORGET MUSIC LESSON (neg)
6. OPEN FIRE, WE COOK MARSHMALLOWS (neg)
7. MR. BROOK WANT ATTEND (neg)

E. Translate the following sentences into English.
1. LIFE ALWAYS BAD NOT (neg)
2. TERRY GO-TO THERE NOT (neg)
3. BOOK MINE NOT (neg)
4. NEWSPAPER, DEPEND CAN'T (neg)
5. SHOP, YOU GO-TO CAN'T (neg)
6. SATISFY NOT, HE (neg)
7. ME ARRIVE REFUSE THERE (neg)
8. HE REMEMBER NOT (neg)
9. POSTPONE (neg)
10. WRITE, FORGET NOT (neg)
11. TAXI, YOU OUT NOT (neg)
12. HE FORGET NEVER (neg)

F. As you compose ASL dialogue for the following scenarios, play particular attention to the opportunities to create negative communications and the various ways it can be expressed in ASL.

Scenario 1:
You are in a very fine restaurant with a person you hope to impress. When your food comes, it is ill prepared and cold. When you point this out to the waiter, he becomes defensive and accuses you of bad manners. You don't want to cause a commotion, but you also don't want to look weak and unable to handle yourself. What do you say to the waiter?

Scenario 2:
Your best friend has been planning to ask a particular girl (boy) to the upcoming prom. It has taken your friend weeks to get up the nerve to pop the question. The morning when your friend is finally ready to ask the girl (boy) to the prom, that special person asks you to go, right in front of your best friend. What do you do?

Scenario 3:
It is your job to get your roommate to a surprise party in his/her honor. You know s/he is planning to stay in and get a lot of work done because two midterm exams are coming soon, and a ten-page paper is due in three days. How are you going to persuade your roommate to come with you to your friend's house for the party?

14. Stressing a Sentence

American Sign Language uses variations in space and movement to create a wide variety of morphological mechanisms to modify its signs. Although these variations shade the meaning of ASL sentences, they do so without distorting the sign's parameters or identity. Modification of ASL signs is similar to modification of oral delivery in English. An English speaker can convey different meanings by modifying the delivery of an English sentence even though its phonological shape remains constant.

Although there are many different strategies for changing the meaning of an ASL sign, the mechanisms that are preferred are based on relative changes in movement (Klima and Bellugi, 1979). ASL uses relative change in movement to emphasize a sign or an entire message.

In English, such factors as voice tone, voice pitch, and verbal intensity can be used to shade the meaning of words without changing the phonological construction of the sentence. Such elements, along with facial and body language, compose a paralanguage of speaking. "Paralanguage" is the set of nonverbal dimensions that shade meaning on the lexical (word) level. Paralanguage directly influences the meaning of words and longer communications.

Paralanguage in ASL incorporates the signer's facial and body language as well as the delivery style. Paralanguage represents the "tone" of movement and permits the expression of a variety of semantic shadings. A raised eyebrow, widened curious eyes, and a side-to-side head shake are all examples of nonmanual ASL paralanguage.

Delivery Style

A modification in a signer's usual delivery style creates emphasis. It makes certain signs and ideas stand out from the context and spotlights important ideas. Emphasis can also be conveyed by bracketing important ideas with pauses.

There are two strategies for modifying the delivery style. The first strategy is to deliberately exaggerate the relative size of the target sign and to execute it more slowly than the usual signing speed. Slow execution of

219

an enlarged sign blends both adjective and adverb qualities into the sign because it incorporates both size and manner into the sign's execution (Covington, 1973). A slow, exaggerated execution of a sign like FANTASTIC draws attention to it without disrupting either the sign's composition or the sign order of the sentence.

Any amplification of movement, particularly of peripheral-oriented signs, may trespass the spatial boundaries that customarily bound the signing space. It is this trespass that draws special attention to the targeted sign. The effect is to create emphasis. This emphasizing strategy can apply to any sentence pattern. When the sign WOMAN, for instance, is executed with an obviously slow and overstated manner, the question "WOMAN BUY BOOK?" will be interpreted "Did that woman actually buy a book?"

When the command WAIT HERE is signed with ordinary delivery, it means "Just wait here a minute." But when the signer extends the movement of the hands for WAIT out farther than usual and lifts them higher than usual, the same sentence carries the meaning "Wait right here!"

Altering size and manner of delivery in ASL is like altering voice tone in English. If an English speaker prolongs the pronunciation of a word, expresses it in a short explosive manner, or uses a rising voice inflection, the hearer is likely to assign the word three completely different meanings. The word "no," for instance, can mean "yes," can show disbelief, can show surprise, or can even show thoughtfulness. All of these meanings are conveyed by attaching particular voice characteristics to the vocal production of a lexical element.

The second strategy for modifying ASL delivery style is to alter facial expression. Alteration of facial expression can create different semantic shadings of a given sign or key phrase. Depending on the semantic effect the signer wishes to convey, they might accompany sign delivery with such nonmanual behavior as sucking in the breath through tightened lips, clenching the teeth tightly, puffing out the cheeks, or opening the eyes and mouth widely while maintaining direct eye contact with the reader (Hoemann, 1978).

Emphasizing the Question

Some nonmanual mechanisms used for emphasis in ASL apply to questions in particular. One way to intensify a question, for instance, is to perform the final sign farther forward along the sign line than would typically occur in an unstressed question (or declarative sentence). This spatial shift makes that sign or phrase stand out. In the question "Do you really mean that?!" the final sign changes its relative spatial position: YOU MEAN *THAT*?

This strategy of conveying the relative importance of a question by changing the relative spatial orientation is particularly effective when the emphatic information is associated with the final sign. When forward repositioning is used in the question GO YOU WHERE? ("Where are you going?"), the meaning changes to "Where do you think you are going?!" The emphasis is created by the exaggerated proximity toward the reader. The farther forward the final sign or phrase is positioned, the stronger the implied intensity of the question (Hoemann, 1978). When YOU in GO-TO YOU? is emphasized, the question means "Are you really going?"

Both yes/no and interrogative questions can be emphasized. But an additional way to stress the interrogative question is to extend the movement of the interrogative sign. The question YOUR COAT, COST MUCH? ("How much did your coat cost?") expresses an interested but unconcerned curiosity. But when the signer expresses the same question while extending the distance between the hands while forming MUCH, the question is intensified to mean "Just how much money did you really pay for that coat?!"

Emphasis can also be achieved by repeating the movement of the final interrogative sign. Consider the casual inquiry PARDON, YOU SAY WHAT? ("Excuse me, but what did you just say?"). When the interrogative sign (WHAT) is repeated, the interpretation becomes "You said what?!"

Another emphasizing strategy is to use certain interrogative signs twice to bracket the question. This strategy calls attention to the question's significance. The initial sign signals the reader that the question is of particular importance. The question ARRIVE HERE HOW? is translated "How did you come? By car? Taxi? Or did someone give you a ride?" But HOW ARRIVE HERE HOW? means "How in the world did you manage to get here?" Bracketing for emphasis does not apply to WHICH, which uses bracketing for a different purpose, to set off choices.

Sarcasm

The various subtleties conveyed by mannerism and style of delivery are not confined to emphasizing strategies. Nonmanual expression can also be used to convey sarcasm. "Sarcasm" is a form of satirical wit. This expression of ironic language is conveyed not by explicit content, but through delivery. In sarcasm, it is not what you say, but how you say it. Sarcasm is a means of communicating the direct opposite of what the surface units represent. In English, the remark "I really had an exciting time on my blind date," conveyed in a straightforward manner, communicates the idea of a wonderful evening. But when the speaker alters the articulation of the word "exciting" in a certain way, the meaning of the whole sentence can shift either to emphasis (a fantastic date) or to sarcasm (a catastrophically boring date). The delivery of the words (or signs) can change their surface meaning.

One way to express sarcasm in ASL is to miniaturize the movement of a target sign. Imagine a situation where a roommate comes home after a date and tells his friend, TRUE EXCITING TIME // TOGETHER, ME ENJOY, which is interpreted "I really had a good time on my date." This is a literal understanding of the surface meaning of the signs. But if the signer intentionally reduces key signs to a miniaturized size, the effect is opposite to that of an emphatic delivery. Consider the effect of miniaturizing target signs on the above example, TRUE EXCITING TIME // TOGETHER, ME ENJOY. This sentence translates to "I really had a boring time on my date." Restricted, undersized sign delivery removes all importance from the literal meaning, and thus implies the opposite. The word "small" over the target sign(s) is used to mark the miniaturization effect in written form.

Imagine a host who is greeting guests at a party when a guest shows up who is a competitor in business. To make the best of an awkward situation, the host greets the uninvited guest: SEE YOU, ME SURPRISE. INVITE YOU, ME REMEMBER ("I am surprised to see you. I don't remember inviting you."). The small-scale delivery of the sign INVITE tells the guest that she was in fact never invited.

When an ASL signer alters the movement characteristics of a target sign from its ordinary composition, the reader will notice the deviation. Enlarging, repeating, extending, or shrinking a sign's movement will add to — or even reverse — a sign's semantic meaning.

Modifying Signs

Another strategy for adding meaning to an ASL sentence is to incorporate certain modifying signs. In English, the words that qualify the relative degree or intensity of an idea are usually adverbs. "Adverbs" function to modify verbs, adjectives and other adverbs, as in "*thoroughly* satisfied," "*extremely* thirsty," "*highly* regarded," "*marked* improvement," etc. While adverbs tend to fall in several major classes, the two groups most pertinent to our discussion here are adverbs of manner ("highly," "nicely," "thoroughly," "poorly") and adverbs of degree ("extremely," "really," "very," "rather"). Both types of adverbs influence the importance of a sentence.

The usual adverbial mechanism in ASL is the sign TRUE. When added to a verb phrase, TRUE serves as a lexical "stress modifier." The sentence like LOOK SICK, YOU means simply "You look like you're under the weather." But the sentence TRUE SICK, YOU LOOK intensifies the concern to "You look really sick!" When a stress modifier is added to a sentence, it functions to increase the intensity of is target verb.

Serving primarily as an adverb of degree or as an adverb of manner, TRUE is chiefly used to give emphasis to a state of being or condition (Fant, 1983). It qualifies the verb's relative significance. The sentence ME ANGRY conveys the meaning "I am upset." But TRUE ANGRY, ME means "I am really mad!"

In the sentence TRUE UNDERSTAND, YOU, the attention is on the verb: "You are very understanding." But the example TRUE HOT DAY ("It is a very hot day.") illustrates that the stress modifier can influence an adjective as well as a verb. When TRUE qualifies an adjective, it normally tells how much, how many, or what kind. But it can also function as an intensifier, which tells the reader how much of a state of being or condition.

TRUE does not follow all of the rules that are applicable to an adverb in English. A chief difference is that it cannot modify a sign that can function either as an adjective or an adverb, like GREAT, WONDERFUL, AWFUL, CARELESS, SMART, GOOD, and AWKWARD. Since TRUE cannot be used to stress such signs, they have to derive their stress from the dynamics of the delivery style. In fact, delivery rather than additional signing is always the preferred method of emphasizing in ASL—especially when the signer wishes to convey strong emotion, a command, irony, or strong emphasis.

As a stress modifier, TRUE is an independent component that precedes its target verb or adjective. In a diagram, it is placed in front and above its target sign.

ASL: TRUE WANT LEAVE, ME
English: I really want to go.
Diagram:

TRUE
stress modifier (SM)
WANT LEAVE
(T-V)
ME
(S)

ASL	English
TRUE REMEMBER, ME	I sure do remember!
WEATHER TRUE CHANGE	There is a marked change in the weather!
GREAT LOOK, LOOK	You look really great!
TRUE ANXIOUS PLAY, WE-TWO	We were really eager to play!
NOW // TEST TRUE DIFFICULT	This test is awfully hard!
GOOD STUDENT, HE	He is an excellent student!
RANDY TRUE THIRSTY	Randy is definitely thirsty!
LUCK NONE, ME	I don't have any luck at all!

Exercise: Write eight ASL sentences as either statements, commands or questions;
four using the stress modifier and four using other modifiers that function
as adverbs and adjectives.

Positive versus Negative Stress

The stress modifier can also emphasize a verb that expresses a negative
action or state of being. In the sentence TRY STOP TRUE WORRY ("Try
to stop worrying so much."), the stress modifier TRUE draws attention to
the degree of worrying. The sentence TRUE HATE THAT WORK, ME (I
really hate this work!) emphasizes how much the person dislikes the work.
And the sentence TAMMY TRUE ANGRY AT ME ("Tammy is really mad
at me") focuses on relative degree.

In each of these examples, TRUE intensifies a verb. And although each
of these verbs conveys a negative concept, the signs themselves are couched
in positive, declarative sentences. Although the meaning of the verbs has
a negative connotation, the sentences themselves are not grammatically
negative. In ASL, a grammatically negative statement would require a
negating head shake or a negation sign. If a negating signal or negation sign
were added to these declarative sentences, the sentences would then convey
                                                             neg
what is not meant. For example, TRUE HATE THAT WORK, ME means
that the person doesn't really hate the work.

Such verbs as LOSE, ANGRY, MISUNDERSTAND, DISBELIEVE,
and DOUBT convey negative semantic concepts, but grammatically they
function as positive verbs. If the sentences in which they appear do not also
include negation signals or signs, they can be modified by the stress
modifier: ME TRUE DISBELIEVE YOU ("I really don't believe you.").

Training Exercises

A. Translate the following sentences into ASL, and then practice performing
them in an emphatic way through your delivery style only.

1. Can I have some money for lunch?
2. Someone was looking for you.
3. Turn over the keys to the principal.
4. The family will have lunch at Rose's.
5. We went our separate ways.
6. The man standing by the lounge fell asleep.
7. He can take care of himself.
8. You need to work much harder.
9. I signed you up for driving lessons.
10. I sprained my back.

B. Translate the following sentences into ASL. Incorporate stress modifiers whenever possible.

   1. My head is hurting considerably now.
   2. You really should not be hitchhiking.
   3. The green car rides really smoothly.
   4. Your telephone book is thinner than a small button.
   5. Your extra-large party needs additional chairs and tables.
   6. What is your most prized possession?
   7. You have a very important appointment and your ever-trustworthy car won't start.
   8. How do you handle incredibly loud people who sit down next to you?
   9. The very worst season for bad colds seems to be fall.
  10. Place your important papers, extra cash, and jewelry into the safe.

C. Diagram the following sentences.

   1. CAREFUL DROP NOT VASE!
   2. SORRY. ME MEAN NOT HIT YOUR CAR!
   3. TRUE BEAUTIFUL LADY, SHE
   4. SAY PAST YOU, TRUE MEAN?
   5. MEET TRAIN, YOU MUST HURRY!
   6. TRUE FRIEND EVER, YOU!
   7. YOUR MEDICINE DUE SOON
   8. HEAR NEWS NOW, ME
   9. PUT BOOK HERE

D. Perform the following sentences using an ordinary style. Next, practice each of the strategies that can emphasize a target sign. Apply these strategies to the underlined signs. Now shrink the lowercase signs. Translate the emphasized and the miniaturized sentences into English.

   1. *BEST* FRIEND, YOU
   2. ME MAYBE *FAIL* WHAT?
   3. great DRESS, YOU LOOK
   4. TURN LIGHT off
   5. SHE COME-HERE *NOW*
   6. *ALL* FEEL LOSE
   7. MEET MY friend BETTY
   8. WHAT SAY INDEX (PERSON) WHAT?
   9. MAYBE LEE *NOT // WANT* WORK
  10. YOU REMEMBER *ADDRESS*?

E. Translate the following paragraphs in ASL.

   1. A comet is fun to see. Scientists say that comets are made of rock and gases. Their very fast speed makes them hot. The heat creates the very long glowing tail.

   2. Some people are color blind. They cannot see certain colors. The colors most difficult to see are red and green. But some people might be blind to all colors. Most animals see colors, but dogs and cats do not.

F. As you devise the dialogue for the following scenarios, incorporate the various methods that can intensify the importance of a message.

Scenario 1:

Your roommate has just finished typing a forty-page paper due tomorrow morning for his toughest class. He leaves the room for a moment, leaving the paper on his desk. Not noticing the paper, you use his desk to pour a soda and accidentally tip the glass over. The soda spills all over the paper, soaking in and ruining it. As you mop up, your roommate walks in. What do you say?

Scenario 2:

You are an attendant at a casino. One day, one of the slot machines malfunctions and money starts to pour out. A woman walking by notices the pay off and starts to stuff money in her purse. Since the payoff was a malfunction, the woman has no right to this money. Nevertheless, she believes it is her lucky day. Handle this unfortunate situation.

Scenario 3:

You receive an "F" in a course because the school has no record that you took the final exam. You know that you took this exam and received a "B." You go to the professor to say that there has been a mistake. She says she can't recall, that there is nothing she can do about it, and she suggests you take the course over again. But you know how much money and time that will cost you — and all because of the professor's error! Try to convince her to give you the final again.

15. The Complex Sentence

Regardless of the language used, no communicator can communicate an entire complex message all at the same moment. Rather, the main elements of the communication are arranged into chunks of information, and one chunk is arranged after another in a sequence. In this way, one thought is communicated, then another thought, then another, and so on. The communicator (speaker or signer) must determine what sequence best expresses the information he or she wishes to communicate.

In some circumstances, positioning a phrase ahead of the main thought can enhance the meaning of an entire message. Sometimes, for example, a communicator wishes to establish essential information that will better prepare the receiver to understand the main thought. Supplying such information first enhances the richness of the following utterance.

An "introductory phrase" is a group of related lexical items that do not make up a complete, independent thought. Though this major grammatical component is separate, it is directly associated with the main sentence.

An introductory comment in ASL can convey a substantial thought through the delivery of as little as one well-chosen sign. An especially effective one-sign introductory comment is the command, the sentence type that supplies the verb while omitting the subject (understood as "you"). When an unstressed command serves as an introductory ASL comment, it yields a simple request.

Consider an introductory comment such as BEAUTIFUL, expressed with direct eye contact while the signer displays an admiring expression. BEAUTIFUL may either be an idle comment, "You look beautiful," or an introductory comment preparing the reader for the main thought, as in BEAUTIFUL. NOW // NIGHT GO-TO WHERE? ("You look beautiful. So where are you going tonight?").

Another example of an introductory comment is the sign HUNGRY. When expressed with a ravenous facial expression and direct eye contact, it conveys "I am hungry." It might then be followed with the main sentence EAT // NIGHT WHAT? ("What's for dinner?"). Other common introductory comments include WAIT ("Wait here."), SLOW ("Slow down."), STOP ("Stop that."), and CAREFUL ("Be careful.").

Whenever you use an introductory comment in ASL, keep in mind that

227

all comments are economized. To translate the English sentence, "It is for certain, you have won," you must economize the introductory phrase, "It is for certain," into the modifying sign TRUE. The ASL sentence is TRUE. WIN, YOU.

A single-person reference is usually dropped from an introductory comment. If the verb is multidirectional, it will supply the reference, but otherwise, the context of the main sentence is sufficient to imply the person reference. In the sentence "I remember where I put my paper," the introductory comment "I remember" is economized in ASL to REMEMBER. "I" is implied by the direct eye contact and absence of an inquiry expression. The entire ASL message is thus: REMEMBER. WHERE, ME PLACE PAPER.

Although an introductory comment is semantically related to the main sentence, it remains peripheral. In diagramming, the introductory comment is treated as a separate sentence. The relationship to the main sentence is understood.

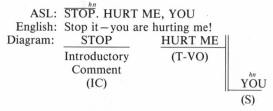

ASL: $\overline{\text{STOP}}^{hn}$. HURT ME, YOU
English: Stop it — you are hurting me!
Diagram:

STOP	HURT ME
Introductory Comment (IC)	(T-VO)

$\overset{hn}{\text{YOU}}$
(S)

ASL	*English*
CORRECT TELL PAST 1 1 2	That's right, I did tell you.
WAIT, INDEX (CHAIR) NOT YOUR	Wait, that's not your chair.
YES, CAN GO-TO CAMP, YOU	Yes, you can go to camp.
NO, GO CAN'T CAMP, YOU	No, you can't go camping.

Exercise: Write four English sentences, two from which the English phrase would be omitted in ASL and two from which the phrase (or part of it) would be expressed.

KNOW Compounds

ASL introductory comments often feature compounds which function as a source sign. Two common introductory compounds are: KNOW // THAT AND KNOW // HOW.

The first compound, KNOW // THAT, is used when the signer believes that the reader is familiar with a particular topic. KNOW // THAT conveys "Did you know?" or "You know such and such?" It is formed by signing KNOW and then moving the open hand forward, up, over, and down again

with the palm finishing down. As an introductory comment, KNOW //
THAT precedes the main sentence.

KNOW // THAT often functions to introduce a rhetorical question by
drawing the reader's attention to a presumably familiar topic. In a phrase
like KNOW // THAT GAIL? for example, a rhetorical question is raised
that states, in effect, "You know Gail, well she. . . ." The signer introduces
the topic GAIL, pauses momentarily, and then follows with the comment,
as in KNOW // THAT GAIL? PAINTING SELL RECENT-PAST ("You
know Gail? Well, she just sold her painting.") KNOW // THAT is usually
performed along with a congruent nonmanual signal of inquiry.

A rhetorical question is always directed to the reader. Because it is
understood that the subject is "you," there is no need for an overt personal
reference. The written expression of this type of rhetorical question might
be expressed (you) KNOW // THAT, to reflect the understood reference.
Since KNOW // THAT is usually tied to the topic, it is diagrammed up and
prior to that grammatical item.

ASL: KNOW // THAT TEST? CANCEL.
English: You know about the test? It was cancelled.
Diagram: KNOW // THAT

    Introductory | TEST(?)
    Phrase (IP) | (T-O)
                          CANCEL
                          (V)

ASL
KNOW // THAT PLANE? LATE
  AGAIN.
KNOW // THAT PARTY? CHRIS
  BECOME DRUNK

English
You know that plane I take?
  It was late again.
You know about the party?
  Chris got really drunk.

Exercise: Write two sentences using the introductory phrase KNOW // THAT to
introduce a rhetorical question.

The second KNOW compound is used when the signer does not know
whether the reader is familiar with the topic. When the signer performs
KNOW // KNOW to raise the topic. The compound KNOW // KNOW is
usually performed as a reduplication of KNOW without a pause, although
it is occasionally exaggerated for emphasis. The nonmanual behavior of
squinting the eyes prompts a response from the reader. The phrase KNOW
// KNOW GAIL? asks the direct question "Do you know Gail?"

After signing KNOW // KNOW GAIL, the signer pauses afterward,
longer than usual, while maintaining direct eye contact. As with any question, the last sign may be held as an additional signal of expectancy. The
signer is waiting for a "yes/no" response to whether the reader is familiar
with the primary topic. If the reader responds "yes," the signer continues

directly with the main sentence. If the reader responds "no," the signer supplies additional identifying information about the topic. Only after the reader understands the topic does the signer proceed with the original message.

To illustrate how KNOW // KNOW serves as an inquiry, the same example regarding "Gail" will be used. The signer begins by communicating KNOW // KNOW GAIL? and then pauses. The squinting eyes and gaze signals a desire for a response.

> A. KNOW // KNOW GAIL?
> Reader: signals affirmative
> Signer: PAINTING SELL RECENT TIME.
> (Well, she just sold her painting.)
> B. KNOW // KNOW GAIL?
> Reader: signals uncertainty or negative
> Signer: PAST-WEEK PARTY, MEET GAIL
> 2

(You met her last week at the party.)

> REMEMBER NOW?
> (Do you remember now?)
> Reader: signals affirmative
> Signer: PAINTING SELL RECENT TIME
> ("She just sold her painting.")

A way to vary the compound KNOW // KNOW is to fuse KNOW to an abbreviated YOU without a pause. The compound KNOW // YOU serves as an alternative in the same question format as KNOW // KNOW. The signer waits for the reader's response and then either continues or provides identifying information about the topic.

When either compound KNOW // THAT or KNOW // KNOW (or its variation KNOW // YOU) is used in an introductory capacity, the topic functions both as the principle theme of the sentence and as the principle point of the question (rhetorical or direct). In the case of KNOW // KNOW, the signer waits for the reader to acknowledge his or her awareness of the topic and then proceeds accordingly.

Post-Sentence Phrases

Certain phrases or comments serve best when they follow the main sentence, supplementing its meaning. The sign FINISH, for instance, has two uses as a post-sentence concept. As a single-sign post-sentence phrase, FINISH conveys the concept "That's all." When used in this capacity, FINISH is placed at the end of the main sentence it refers to it and serves as a secondary comment in and of itself.

All post-sentence phrases are separated from the previous sentence by an intonation break (a natural pause). The use of FINISH can be illustrated by a scenario in which two students are talking about their studies. One of the students brings up a problem and how he went to see his professor regarding it. In explaining to his roommate what happened, he states: TELL PAST TOMORROW MEET EARLY. FINISH. ("She told me to meet her early tomorrow, and that's all she said."). As a post-sentence phrase, FINISH conveys such ideas as "That's all I know," and "That's all that really happened."

A second use of the sign FINISH is as part of the compound ENOUGH // FINISH, meaning "I've had enough," or "Have you had enough?" Differentiating between first- and second-person reference is accomplished by changing the directional movement of FINISH. When the sign is performed with an inward movement, it implies "I have had enough" (ENOUGH // FINISH). When it is performed with a directly outward movement, it asks "Have you had enough?" (ENOUGH // FINISH).

ENOUGH // FINISH follows the main sentence, separated from it by an intonation break. To illustrate both applications of ENOUGH // FINISH consider a scenario in which a family has a guest over for dinner. As they dine, the mother turns and says to her guest:

MOTHER: MORE MEAT
(There is more roast beef here.)
ENOUGH // FINISH?
(Have you had enough to eat?)

GUEST: YES, THANK // YOU
(Yes, thank you.)
TRUE GOOD ALL
(Everything was really good.)
ENOUGH // FINISH
(I have eaten enough.)

Personal comments or impressions such as THINK, BELIEVE, NOTICED, REALIZE, and UNDERSTAND also sometimes follow the main sentence. Since such comments always reflect the signer, the first-person pronoun reference is not overtly supplied. An example of this type of comment is illustrated in a scenario in which the husband is discussing house matters with his wife. He remarks, TOMORROW ME BEGIN PAINT ROOM. THINK. ("I think that I will begin painting the room tomorrow."). If the sentence is topicalized, the person reference is included in the comment portion, and therefore, indirectly serves a dual reference: TOMORROW BEGIN PAINT ROOM, ME. THINK. But because the context has sufficiently limited the associated possibilities of reference, the person reference, "I," is omitted.

Compound Sentences

One of the most common ways to arrange information is to place one information chunk after another in a sequence. The communicator must decide which chunk of information should precede or follow another. Such decisions on sentence arrangement determine how well one communicates a complex message to another person.

In English, the most common vehicle for communicating sequential arrangement of thought is the compound sentence. The "compound sentence" consists of two or more independent sentences joined together by a coordinating word such as "and," "for," "or," "so," or "yet." In essence, a compound sentence consists of at least two sentences linked together functionally. The components of a compound sentence receive relatively equal emphasis. Since each component is an independent sentence, each part of the compound sentence can stand alone.

In American Sign Language, when two sentences are independent, each is expressed separately. The signer relies on implied sentence arrangement to convey relationship. In the sentence "John's bicycle is in the driveway and his mother backed over it with the car," the use of "and" is considered unnecessary in ASL. Thus the ASL version is JOHN BICYCLE (index to establish location) LIE DRIVEWAY. HIS MOTHER DRIVE OVER INDEX (BICYCLE).

ASL sequencing is usually based on the actual chronological order of events. The sentences (main or secondary) are arranged to communicate the events as they are occurring, did occur, or will occur. Chronological order is illustrated in a scenario involving a person who is discussing his plans for the evening. The person comments, "I am going to write a letter as soon as I get home." To communicate this information in ASL, the message must be divided into two sentences: "I will write a letter," "when I return home." The sequence is then arranged according to the actual chronological order of events: RETURN HOME, ME. (pause) WRITE LETTER. ASL economization is evident in this expression. The logical temporal sequence eliminates the need for a connector sign. Because the adjacent sentences or phrases involve a congruent subject, the repeated personal reference is deleted.

ASL	*English*
MY PRIZE, GIVE. WIN KNOW. 　　　　　3　　1	When she gave me my prize, I knew 　I won.
TRUE NOISE, ME HEAR. 　DISCOVER ACCIDENT.	It was not until I heard the noise that 　I discovered the accident.
ME WAIT HERE. YOU 　CALL.	I will wait here until you call.

Another way to arrange a sequence in ASL is to arrange the series of sentences according to their relative importance. In this manner of sequencing, a main thought is established first and then subsequent comments are associated to the first thought by implication. Determining relative importance depends on such factors as subject matter, proximity of timing, type of information, person-reference congruency, and the strategic use of the intonation break (the brief pause of the hands during signing). It also depends on what the signer wants to communicate, what was communicated immediately prior to the present utterance, who is involved in the discussion, and how much further information is yet to be expressed. In other words, this sequencing strategy depends on the scenario already established and what specific information the signer wishes to disclose about it.

The general pattern is to arrange the various chunks of information in a larger-to-smaller sequence, "larger" being more important. This type of arrangement eliminates or at least reduces the need for multiple connector signs. In the English sentence "It rained last Saturday, so the game was delayed," the two thoughts or segments are connected by the word "so." In ASL, the same two thoughts are treated as separate sentences, the sequential arrangement of which is sufficient to imply the communicative conjunction: PAST // SATURDAY RAIN. GAME DELAY. Whenever sentences or phrases are arranged in sequence, either in space or in context, the idea of "and" can be assumed (Hoemann, 1978). The sign AND, therefore, is seldom used in ASL.

To express several thoughts sequentially, as in "I'm going to bed soon after this movie is over to think about this problem," without using a conjunction, an ASL signer must rely either on chronological time order or on priority order. In the latter form, the ASL expression would be: PROBLEM CONTINUE THINK SELF. MOVIE FINISH. BED SOON. ("I am going to think about the problem some more. As soon as the movie is over, I'll be going to bed.").

Another example of a compound message that is arranged according to relative importance is WIN FIRST PLACE, HE. SHE PROUD. ("He won first place, and she was proud of him."). In this sequence, the priority is placed on the accomplishment, and the reaction follows. But when rearranged to yield PROUD, SHE. WIN FIRST PLACE, HE. ("She was proud that he won first place."), the emphasis is on her emotional state, and is followed by the reason for her happy feeling. Either arrangement is acceptable, but the choice of arrangement affects the semantic shading.

Another example is the compound sentence "I think that it is great that you won the contest." To translate this into ASL, the supportive clause "I think it is great" is first economized into the single expressive concept GREAT. If the signer adheres to the event-reaction sequence this phrase follows the main sentence: WIN CONTEST YOU. GREAT. On the other hand, depending on the shade of meaning the signer wishes to convey, the phrase might precede the main sentence to highlight the reaction: GREAT. WIN CONTEST, YOU.

Another way to arrange the various chunks of information is in the order of cause and effect. This order establishes the cause of something first and then follows it by supplying the result. Consider a scenario in which two persons are talking about their summer vacation and one person says, "This summer was so hot that I lost five pounds." The cause SUMMER TRUE HOT is placed before its subsequent effect, 5 POUND, ME LOSE. In ASL, there is no need for a connector: SUMMER TRUE HOT. 5 POUND, LOSE ME. Another example of the cause-effect arrangement is the sentence LIGHT NONE. ME SCARED ("When the lights go out, I get scared.").

Another possibility is the event-reaction arrangement. In this sequence, the main thought is established first, and is then immediately followed by a related reaction or response. Consider a scenario in which a teenager is telling her friend about a man she has just met: "I nearly died when he asked me out." To express this manually, the event is established first and is then followed by the response: DATE, ASK. ALMOST FAINT ME.

A final strategy is governed by the principle of separating emotional states. In American Sign Language, emotion is designated as the sole reaction of the experiencer. Emotional conditions involving two different participants cannot be included in a single manual sentence. The English sentence "He laughed about it but she cried," would be communicated in ASL as two separate thoughts: HE LAUGH. SHE CRY.

To manually convey "I doubt that she will be happy," an ASL signer divides the two emotion components and treats them as separate sentences: ME DOUBT. HAPPY FUTURE, SHE. A single emotion reaction such as "Mary makes me so mad" is a straightforward translation: MARY ANGER ME. Emotions of two separate experiencers can be bundled into the same ASL sentence when the reaction of both participants is the same: HE SHE LAUGH ("They laughed.").

In all of these compound patterns, an intonation break (pause between segments) is used to mark the juncture between sentences. In terms of diagramming, the association between segments is understood, and not grammatical. On the surface level, there is no direct linkage. Each sentence is diagrammed separately.

ASL: MAN START SING. WOMAN CRY.
English: When the man started to sing, the woman cried.

Diagram:	MAN	START SING	WOMAN	CRY
	(S)	(V)	(S)	(V)

ASL	English
OFFICE, HE APPLY. DOUBT ME.	I doubt that he will run for office.
BOOK, BUY PAST ME. THINK GOOD.	I bought a book that I think will be good.
PEOPLE TRUE HURRY RUSH. HAPPY NOT.	When people frantically hurry and rush, they are not very happy.
FEEL BAD, YOU. SORRY.	I'm sorry that you feel that way.
REMEMBER MOVIE "GONE WITH WIND"? ME SEE RECENT-PAST.	Do you remember the movie "Gone With the Wind"? Well, I just saw it.
REMEMBER TOM? RECEIVE NEW JOB.	Remember Tom? Well, he just got a new job.

Complex Sentences

A complex sentence is created when a main idea is combined with a related, secondary idea. A complex sentence contains both an independent clause (a complete sentence) and one or more dependent clauses (a group of related lexical items [signs or words] that conveys a partial thought and relies on other context [a main sentence] to be understood). A major function of a complex sentence is to attach one related idea to another. The more important idea is usually expressed as the complete sentential component, and the supplemental idea is expressed in the dependent clause.

In English, subordinate conjunctions including "if," "since," "as," "until," "when," and "that," link dependent clauses to main sentences. The subordinate conjunction (e.g., "when") introduces the dependent clause (e.g., "His sister tickled him"), which can be positioned either after the main clause (e.g., "John laughed when his sister tickled him.") or before it (e.g., "When his sister tickled him, John laughed"). In either order, the dependent clause relies on the main clause (e.g., "John laughed") for understanding.

When a subordinate conjunction introduces a dependent clause, it tells the reader what relates to what. These connectors enable the speaker to attach various relative clauses to a main clause in order to form longer, more meaningful, and more complicated sentences. The subordinate conjunction "because," for example, introduces causation in the complex English sentence "The bike won't work because it has a flat tire." Used to signal the secondary clause, a subordinate conjunction is a functional grammatical component.

Because a subordinate conjunction is a functional grammatical feature, one might expect that in the interest of economization, ASL would not use it. But such ASL signs as BECAUSE, BUT, FINISH, etc. can and do function as subordinate conjunctions in ASL although their actual frequency is uncertain (Baker and Cokely, 1980; Liddell, 1980). Perhaps they are used because the relationship they convey does, to some extent, add meaning.

The subordinate conjunction, BECAUSE, for example conveys the idea of causation and supplies information on rationale. BECAUSE clauses usually follow the main clause as in CAR WON'T START BECAUSE GAS NONE ("The car won't start because it is out of gas."). For an English sentence that might use the subordinate conjunction "since" to signal the relative clause, as in "We never see each other since you got that new job," the manual equivalent is WE-TWO TOGETHER NEVER BECAUSE YOUR NEW JOB.

Another ASL subordinate conjunction is BUT, which conveys the concept of an exception. BUT clauses also follow the main clause, as in COAT WANT BUY BUT MONEY NONE ("I want to buy the coat, but I don't have the money.").

The sign FINISH can function either as a subordinate or coordinate conjunction. It expresses such concepts as "then," "next in time of order," "in the case," "at another time." When FINISH is placed between two sentences, it establishes a temporal relationship between the two ideas. This can be expressed in written form as the sequence: sentence-FINISH-sentence. In this capacity, FINISH serves as a coordinate conjunction, as in YOU EAT. FINISH. GO-TO SHOP, WE-TWO. ("You finish eating and then we will go shopping."). Because the sign is placed between the two sentences, it remains peripheral to either idea. The activity of the second idea is understood to be conditional on the completion of the initial activity.

But FINISH can do more than link two main independent sentences together, as in EAT. FINISH. GO-TO SCHOOL. ("Once I have eaten I will go to school.") It can also link a dependent clause to a main sentence, as in KISS HIM, SHE. FINISH. FEEL GOOD, SHE. ("She kissed him and then she felt better.").

When diagramming a complex sentence, diagram each clause separately, and position the conjunction sign that links the two segments together between the two base lines.

ASL: ME WANT GO-TO BUT MONEY NONE.
English: I want to go, but I have no money.

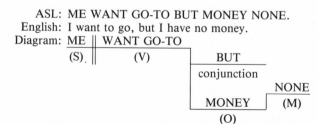

ASL	*English*
PAST // NIGHT ELECTRIC NONE BECAUSE CAR ACCIDENT	We lost our electricity last night because of a car accident.
SPEAK RECENT-PAST BUT WILL AGAIN	I just spoke to her, but I will speak to to her again.

Exercise: Translate the following English sentences into ASL, and the following ASL sentences into English.

1. I was a good ball player when I was young.
2. As long as you are here, you can help me.
3. I had my hair cut because it was too long.
4. If you want to go with us, just say so.
5. The bus will leave soon unless you stop it.
6. The boy who won the contest is my neighbor.
7. The couch is large and comfortable, but worn out.
8. The pilot will land the plane, although not very smoothly.
9. The man will wait, but you'd better hurry.
10. I can't write the notice because it is too late.
11. CAN'T REMEMBER, MAN, ME BUT HE FAMOUS NOW
12. SPEAK RECENT-PAST, ME BUT AGAIN FUTURE
13. HUNGRY, ME BUT EAT RECENT-PAST
14. TEA MY FAVORITE DRINK BECAUSE TASTE
15. SING DANCE ENJOY ME BUT SAME TIME

In English, a verbal (a verb that acts as a noun or an adjective) that is part of the object of a sentence often creates a complex sentence. The infinitive (a verb that combines with the word "to" and is then used as a noun,) for instance, creates a complex sentence in "His transfer prompted her to find a job." This sentence contains both dependent clause ("She found a job.") and an independent clause ("His transfer prompted her action.").

Verbal phrases including infinitive phrases, are like little sentences within sentences. To translate them into ASL, the signer identifies the underlying sentences: "He is transferred," and "She found a job." By reducing this type of complex sentence into its basic components, the signer can manually express each related idea separately: CHANGE JOB, HE. SHE FIND JOB.

Another example of a verbal creating a complex sentence is the sentence "He won by running a good race." In this sentence the gerund "running" is the object of the preposition "by." A gerund is a verb that ends in "ing" and is used as a noun. To translate this sentence into ASL, the signer reduces the sentence into two separate ideas "He won" and "He ran a good race." The sentence pair is then rearranged in order of importance: HE WIN. RUN GOOD RACE.

A participial phrase can also prompt a complex sentence. A participle is a form of a verb that functions as an adjective. In a sentence like "having climbed the hill, she felt good," the participial phrase "having climbed the hill" is an adjectival clause. To translate this sentence in ASL, the signer first divides the sentence into two separate sentences. The two sentences are then arranged chronologically to yield CLIMB HILL, SHE. FEEL GOOD.

To translate English verbals (e.g., infinitives, gerunds, participles) into ASL, the signer first identifies the underlying sentences and then arranges them in a logical order as two separate sentences.

The Conditional Sentence

One kind of complex sentence is a conditional statement, a sentence pattern that establishes an idea and then responds to it. The initial clause of a conditional statement is referred to as the "condition." In English, it is usually introduced by the conjunction "if." The conditional segment is always followed immediately by a "result" segment. In the sentence "If I pass this test, I'm going to take you out for dinner," the conjunction "if" introduces the condition ("If I pass this test"), and the result follows ("I'm going to take you out for dinner.") The result can be expressed in any three forms: (1) in the form of another statement ("I'm going to take you out for dinner"), (2) in the form of a question ("Would you like to go out for dinner?"), or (3) in the form of a command ("Take me out for dinner"). The conditional sentence is arranged in a "cause and effect" order. The speaker establishes a cause and then immediately follows with its resulting effect.

There are two different forms of the conditional sentence: the real condition and the unreal condition. A "real condition" is a situation whose consequences will occur provided the condition is fulfilled. In these cases, the condition portion expresses a statement of fact as in "If I have any money left, you can have it." An "unreal condition" posits conditions that cannot possibly be fulfilled, which means that the subsequent consequences will not actually occur. This type of conditional sentence expresses a wish or a desire, a highly improbable condition, a suggestion, a doubt, or an uncertainty. An example of an unreal condition is "If I had the money, I would buy a gold-plated sports car."

American Sign Language has two ways to express a real or factual conditional sentence. The first way is to mark the sentence with the manual equivalent of the "if" conjunction, SUPPOSE. SUPPOSE is formed with the I hand (small finger extended) oriented with the palm inward. The small finger taps the forehead several times and conveys the concept "on condition that," or "in the event that." To translate the earlier example, "If I have any money left, you can have it," into ASL, the signer will communciate SUPPOSE MONEY REMAIN. GIVE. As in all compound and certain complex sentences, the strategy is to divide the individual thoughts into separate sentences that are joined by semantic association. Conditional sentences are not connected by overt conjunction signs.

Figure 1. SUPPOSE

The second way to express a conditional sentence in ASL is to arrange the condition in the form of a question and then state the consequence as a fact (Hoemann, 1978). The conditional segment represents a rhetorical question, which is immediately followed by its own response. The example could also be expressed: MONEY REMAIN? GIVE.

ASL also has a number of strategies for expressing an unreal conditional sentence. One of the more common methods is to make it clear that the condition cannot be satisfied. Consider the earlier example, "If I had the money, I would buy a gold-plated sports car." To make it apparent that the sentence is hypothetical, the signer might express a precondition statement first to establish the real state of affairs (e.g., "There is no money."). Once reality is established, the conditional sentence is formed as it would be in a real condition: MONEY NONE. SUPPOSE HAVE MONEY? BUY GOLD FANCY CAR.

Another strategy is to begin by informing the reader that the consequence will never be realized. Once this is established, the conditional sentence is formed as a real condition: BUY CAR NONE. HAVE MONEY? BUY GOLD FANCY CAR. ("I am not going to buy a car. But if I had the money? I would like to buy a gold-plated sports car."). In either case, the initial precondition informs the reader of the real state of affairs before the signer expresses the conditional statement. The use of preliminary statement makes it apparent that the conditional sentence is only hypothetical.

ASL	*English*
<u>neg</u> PRESIDENT, ME. BUT ME PRESIDENT. BALANCE BUDGET. BUY HOUSE NONE, PRICE RIGHT. BUY HOUSE.	I am not the president, but if I were, I would balance the budget. I am not going to buy a house now. But if the price was right, I would buy a house.

In the delivery of a conditional sentence in American Sign Language, nonmanual behavior plays a critical role. When the condition is expressed as a statement, it is always accompanied by relaxed eyebrows and direct eye contact, and is followed by an intonation break. The intonation break provides the signer an opportunity to shift sentence type. The pattern of the result segment depends on the signer. It can take the form of a statement, question, or command. But the pattern chosen will be accompanied by different facial markers. If the resulting segment is a statement or command, the eyebrows continue to be relaxed, signaling that the response is not able to be questioned. If the resulting segment is a yes/no question, the eyebrows are raised to signal the basic questioning state. If the resulting segment is an interrogative question, the eyebrows are squinted to signal the seeking of additional information.

A different nonmanual pattern accompanies the conditional sentence that expresses the condition in the form of a question. When the conditional segment is expressed as a rhetorical question it concludes with a raising of the eyebrows to suggest a questioning expectancy, and an intonation break follows to signal the juncture between the sentence segments. The nonmanual pattern now is the same as before. If the resulting segment is a statement or command, the eyebrows relax. If it is a yes/no question the eyebrows momentarily lower and are raised again to resignal the questioning state. If the resulting segment is an interrogative question, the eyebrows squint inward.

The conditional sentence is distinguished from other sentence types by the presence of the condition marker SUPPOSE. In an ordinary pair of statements, for instance, NOW // WEEK-END PARTY. PLAN ATTEND, ME. ("There is a party this weekend. I plan to go to it."), the absence of the condition marker tells the reader that two separate thoughts are being conveyed. But when SUPPOSE precedes the first sentence, the sentence is purposely marked as a conditional sentence: SUPPOSE NOW // WEEK-END PARTY (raised eyebrows). PLAN ATTEND, ME. The marker SUP-POSE is an independent component that precedes the entire conditional sentence and is placed in front of the conditional segment. In a diagram, SUPPOSE is placed above and before the condition segment, and then each sentence is diagrammed separately with a broken line connecting the two segments.

ASL: SUPPOSE WAYNE TRUE ENJOY MARSHA (P) YOU MAD?
English: If Wayne really likes Marsha, will you be mad?
Diagram: SUPPOSE

condition marker (CM)	WAYNE	ENJOY	MARSHA
	(S)	(V)	(O)
		YOU	MAD ?
		(S)	(V)

ASL	*English*
SUPPOSE ALL COST, YOU PAY (P) GO-TO TOGETHER WE-TWO	If you pay all of the cost, then I will go with you.
SUPPOSE HELP (P) AGREE YOU?	I will help you if you want me to.
SUPPOSE ATTEND CAN'T, YOU (P) UNDERSTAND	If you can't make it, I'll understand.
SUPPOSE WANT IMPROVE HIS BEHAVIOR (P) PRAISE HE	If you want him to behave better, then praise him.

Training Exercises

A. Translate the following sentences into equivalent English format.

1. DON EXPLAIN COURSE. DRAW PICTURE.
2. CHOOSE YOUR MAJOR IN SCHOOL; IMPORTANT.
3. FARM, HE LEAVE QUICK.
4. MY ROOM, SHE KEEP BOOK-BOOK.
5. HIS SNORE TRUE BOTHER ME.
6. MY IDEA, WRITE LETTER.
7. WATCH PEOPLE, ENJOY ALL // TIME.
8. LETTER, ME EXPECT WRITE PAST
9. HE TELEPHONE WIFE. TELL HOME SOON.
10. MANY PICTURE, HE DRAW. EXPLAIN NEW PLAN.

B. Translate the various complex English sentences into ASL form.

  1. The boy was carrying a basket of fruit.
  2. The bridge covered with ice was dangerous.
  3. Destroying many homes, storms lashed the country side.
  4. The man, confused by the request, suggested I ask others.
  5. Cars parked in the loading zone will be ticketed.
  6. Walking along the street, he met some friends.
  7. We will have a picnic, weather permitting.
  8. We were delayed because the airport was covered in dense fog.
  9. If you can't make it, should I start the meeting?
  10. The elderly lady went to the store to pick out a dress pattern.
  11. We put on our bathing suits and went for a swim.
  12. When dinner came, I was already full.
  13. On the way home from work, we got caught in rush hour traffic.
  14. If she phones, tell her that I left.
  15. After I swept up the mess, I then mopped the floor.
  16. I saw her. I can't remember where she went.
  17. Mark asked me. Mark wants to know what is your address?
  18. Mother is outside she is working in the garden.
  19. If I go to work tomorrow, I will give you a ride.
  20. Mother checked the cake but it was still not done in the center.
  21. My brother read the newspaper and checked the want ads.
  22. If you give me the money, I'll repay you next week.

C. Diagram the following ASL sentences and then translate into English.

  1. STORE, HE GO-TO. ICE CREAM, BUY HALF GALLON
  2. PAST // MORNING THEIR FATHER CARRY GARBAGE THERE STREET EDGE.
  3. PAST // NIGHT MILD BOTTLE SLIP THROUGH FINGERS. FALL LOOR. CREATE MESS.
  4. SCHOOL CANCEL BUT WE MUST WORK ALL // DAY.
  5. TRY START MY CAR BECAUSE ME $\overset{neg}{\text{CAN}}$.
  6. JOE EAT TOAST EGGS. HURRY GO-TO WORK.
  7. PAST // EVENING HE READ BOOK WATCH TV.
  8. SUPPOSE $\underset{3}{\text{ASK}}$ $\underset{1}{\text{(P)}}$ $\underset{1}{\text{TELL}}$ $\underset{3}{\text{WHAT?}}$

D. As you write dialogues for the following scenarios, pay particular attention to including both compound and complex sentences.

Scenario 1:
      You have a terribly overdue library book and wish to get out of paying the fine. Make up a "fish" story about how you tried to get back to the library in time, but due to a long series of events, could not make it.

Scenario 2:
      You are trying to return an expensive gift you received at the store where your friend told you she bought it. But the clerk is afraid to accept it. This is the clerk's first day on the job, and he is unsure about the store's return policy. In addition, the manager is not in today. The new clerk is pleasant but is afraid to make a decision. You are only visiting the area and may

never get another chance to return the item, so you want your money to-day. Convince the clerk to accept the item.

Scenario 3:

You are traveling late at night and arrive at a small hotel. Since the hotel is not busy, you negotiate a cut-rate price for the room plus a free breakfast. The next morning when you go to have breakfast, you discover no record of your complimentary meal. Furthermore, when you go to pay for your room, the "day" attendant charges you double the agreed price. Straighten out the matter.

References

Adler, Ron, and N. Towne. *Looking Out/Looking In: Interpersonal Communication,* 2d ed. New York: Holt, Rinehart, and Winston, 1978.

Allan, K. "Classifiers." *Language,* 53 (1977): 285–311.

Anthony, David A., ed. *The Seeing Essential English Manual.* Greeley, Colorado: University of Northern Colorado Bookstore, 1974.

Babbini, Barbara E. *Manual Communication: A Course of Study Outline for Instructors.* Urbana: Illinois Institute for Research on Exceptional Children, 1971.

————. *Manual Communication: Fingerspelling and the Language of Signs.* Urbana: University of Illinois Press, 1974.

————. *Manual Communication: Study Outline for Students.* Urbana: University of Illinois Press, 1979.

Baker, Charlotte. "Regulators and Turn-Taking in American Sign Language Discourse." In L. Friedman, ed., *On the Other Hand: New Perspectives on American Sign Language.* New York: Academic Press, 1977.

————. "Sentences in American Sign Language." In C. Baker and R. Battison, eds., *Sign Language and the Deaf Community; Essays in Honor of William C. Stokoe.* Silver Spring, MD: National Association of the Deaf, 1980.

————, and Dennis Cokely. *American Sign Language: A Teacher's Resource Text on Grammar and Culture.* Silver Spring, MD: T.J. Publishers, 1980.

————, and Carol A. Padden. "Focusing on the Nonmanual Components of American Sign Language." In P. Siple, ed., *Understanding Language through Sign Language Research.* New York: Academic Press, 1978.

Battison R.H. "Phonological Deletion in American Sign Language." *Sign Language Studies,* 5 (1974): 1–19.

————, H. Markowicz, and J.C. Woodward. "A Good Rule of Thumb: Variable Phonology in ASL." In R. Shuy and R. Fasold, eds., *Analyzing Variation in Language.* Washington, DC: Georgetown University Press, 1975.

Bellugi, Ursula. "Clues from the Structural Similarity of Sign and Spoken Language." In U. Bellugi, and M. Studdert-Kennedy, eds., *Signed and Spoken Language: Biological Constraints on Linguistic Form.* Weinheim: Verlag Chemic, 1980.

————, and Susan Fischer, "A Comparison of Sign Language and Spoken Language: Rate and Grammatical Mechanisms." *Cognition* 1 (1972): 173–200.

————, and E.S. Klima. "Two Faces of Sign: Iconic and Abstract." In S. Harned, ed., *Origins and Evolution of Language and Speech.* New York: New York Academy of Sciences, 1976.

————, E.S. Klima, and P. Siple. "Remembering in Signs." *Cognition,* 3 (1975): 93–125.

Bess, Fred H., ed. *Childhood Deafness: Causation, Assessment, and Management.* New York: Grune and Stratton, 1977.

245

Blackburn, D.W., J.D. Bonvillian, and R.P. Ashby. "Manual Communication as an Alternative Mode of Language Instruction for Children with Severe Reading Disabilities." *ASHA: Language, Speech and Hearing Services in Schools* 15 (1984): 22-31.

Bonvillian, J.D., and K.E. Nelson. "Sign Language Acquisition in a Mute Autistic Boy." *Journal of Speech and Hearing Disorders* 41 (1976): 339-47.

Bornstein, H. "A Description of Some Current Sign Systems Designed to Represent English." *American Annals of the Deaf* 118 (1973): 454-63.

————, and K.L. Saulnier. "Signed English: A Brief Follow-up to the First Evaluation." *American Annals of the Deaf* 126 (1980): 69-72.

————, ————, and L.B. Hamilton. "Signed English: A First Evaluation." *American Annals of the Deaf* 125 (1980): 467-81.

Bransford, J., J. Barclay, and J. Franks. "Sentence Memory: A Constructive versus Interpretive Approach." *Cognitive Psychology* 3 (1972): 193-209.

Buckout, Robert. "Eyewitness Testimony." *Scientific American* 231 no. 6 (Dec. 1974).

Caccamise, F., et al. "Signs and Manual Communication Systems: Selection, Standardization and Development." *American Annals of the Deaf* 123 (1978): 877-902.

————, N. Hatfield, and L. Brewer. "Manual/Simultaneous Communication (m/sc) Research: Results and Implications." *American Annals of the Deaf* 123 (1978): 803-23.

Chafe, Wallace. "Giveness, Contrastiveness, Subjects and Topics, and Point of View." In N.L. Charles, ed., *Subject and Topic.* New York: Academic Press, 1976.

Clark, John G. "Beyond Diagnosis: The Professional's Role in Education Consultation." *Hearing Journal* (August 1983): 20-25.

Covington, V. "Juncture in American Sign Language." *Sign Language Studies* 2 (1973): 29-38.

Croneberg, C.G. "Sign Language Dialects." In W.C. Stokoe, Jr., D.C. Casterline, and C.G. Croneberg, eds., *A Dictionary of American Sign Language on Linguistic Principles.* Washington, DC, Gallaudet College Press, 1965.

Cross, J.W. "Sign Language and Second Language Teaching." *Sign Language Studies* 16 (1977): 269-82.

Crystal, D., and E. Craig. "Contrived Sign Language." In I.M. Schlesinger and L. Namier, eds., *Sign Language of the Deaf.* New York: Academic Press, 1978.

DeMatteo, A. "Visual Imagery and Visual Analogues in American Sign Language." In L.A. Friedman, ed., *On the Other Hand: New Perspectives on American Sign Language.* New York: Academic Press, 1977.

Edge, V., and L. Herrmann. "Verbs and the Determinant of Subject in American Sign Language." In L.A. Friedman, ed., *On the Other Hand: New Perspectives on American Sign Language.* New York: Academic Press, 1977.

Fant, Louis J., Jr. *Ameslan: An Introduction to American Sign Language.* Silver Spring, MD: National Association of the Deaf, 1972.

————. *Say It with Hands,* Washington, DC: Gallaudet College Press, 1964.

————. *Sign Language.* Northridge, CA: Joyce Media, 1977.

————. *The American Sign Language Phrase Book.* Chicago: Contemporary Books, 1983.

Fillmore, Charles J. "The Case for Case." In E. Bach and R.T. Harms, eds., *Universals in Linguistic Theory.* New York: Holt, Rinehart, and Winston, 1988.

Fischer, Susan D. "Influences on Word-Order Change in American Sign

Language." In C. Li, ed., *Word Order and Word Order Change*. Austin: University of Texas Press, 1975.

————. "Sign Language and Manual Communication." In D.G. Sims, G.G. Walter, and R.L. Whitehead, eds., *Deafness and Communication, Assessment and Training*. Baltimore, MD: Williams and Wilkins, 1982.

————. "Two Processes of Reduplication in the American Sign Language." *Foundations of Language* 9 (1973): 469-80.

————, and Bonnie Gough. "Verbs in American Sign Language." *Sign Language Studies* 18 (1978): 17-48.

Flynn, J., and J. Glaser. *Writer's Handbook*. New York: Macmillan, 1984.

Friedman, L.A. "Formational Properties of American Sign Language." In L.A. Friedman, ed., *On the Other Hand: New Perspectives on American Sign Language*. New York: Academic Press, 1977.

————. "The Manifestation of Subject, Object, and Topic in American Sign Language." In N.L. Charles, ed., *Subject and Topic*. New York: Academic Press, 1976.

————. "Space, Time, and Person Reference in American Sign Language." *Language* 51 (1975): 940-61.

————, ed. *On the Other Hand: New Perspectives on American Sign Language*. New York: Academic Press, 1977.

Frishberg, N. "Arbitrariness and Iconicity: Historical Change in American Sign Language." *Language* 51 (1975): 696-719.

Fromkin, V.A., and R. Rodman. *An Introduction to Language*. New York: Holt, Rinehart and Winston, 1974.

Geers, A., J. Moog, and B. Schick. "Acquisition of Spoken and Signed English by Profoundly Deaf Children." *Journal of Speech and Hearing Disorders* 49 (Nov. 1984): 378-88.

Grosjean, Francois. "The Perception of Rate in Spoken Language and Sign Languages." *Journal of Psycholinguistic Research*. 22 (1977): 408-13.

————, and Harlan Lane. "Pauses and Syntax in American Sign Language." *Cognition* 5 (1977): 101-17.

Gustason, G., D. Pfetzing, and E. Zawol Kow. *Signing Exact English*. Rossmoor, CA: Modern Signs Press, 1972.

Hanson, V., and U. Bellugi. "On the Role of Sign Order and Morphological Structure in Memory for American Sign Language." *Journal of Verbal Learning and Verbal Behavior* 21 (1982): 621-33.

Hodges, J.C., and M.F. Whitten. *Harbrace College Handbook,* 8th ed. New York: Harcourt Brace Jovanovich, 1977.

Hoemann, Harry W. *The American Sign Language: Lexical and Grammatical Notes with Translation Exercises*. Silver Spring, MD: National Association of the Deaf, 1976.

————. *Communicating with Deaf People: a Resource Manual for Teachers and Students of American Sign Language*. Baltimore, MD: University Park Press, 1978.

————, and V.A. Florian. "Order Constraints in American Sign Language: The Effects of Structure on Judgments of Meaningfulness and on Immediate Recall of Anomalous Sign Sequences." *Sign Language Studies* 11 (1976): 121-32.

Hoffmeister, R.J., D.F. Moores, and R.L. Ellenberger. "Some Procedural Guidelines for the Study of the Acquisition of Sign Language." *Sign Language Studies* 7 (1975): 121-37.

Isenhath, J.O. *Signing the Language,* 3 vols. Meadville, PA: Allegheny College, 1983–84.

Jones, M.D., and S.P. Quigley. "The Acquisition of Question Formation in Spoken English and American Sign Language by Two Hearing Children of Deaf Parents." *Journal of Speech and Hearing Disorders* 44 (1979): 196–208.

Klima, Edward. "Sound and its Absence in the Linguistic Symbol. In J. Kavanagh and J. Cutting, eds., *The Role of Speech in Language.* Cambridge, MA: MIT Press, 1975.

_____. *The Signs of Language.* Cambridge, MA: Harvard University Press, 1979.

_____. "The Signs of Language in Child and Chimpanzee." In T. Alloway, L. Krames and P. Pliner, eds., *Communication and Affect: A Comparative Approach.* New York: Academic Press, 1972.

_____. "The Signs of Language." In E. Klima and U. Bellugi, eds. *The Structured Use of Space and Movement: Morphological Processes.* Cambridge, MA: Harvard University Press, 1979.

_____, and Ursula Bellugi. "Exception and Production in a Visually Based Language." In D. Aaronson and R.W. Rieber, eds., *Developmental Psycholinguistics and Communication Disorders.* New York: New York Academy of Sciences, 1975.

Lawrence, Edger D. *Sign Language Made Simple.* Springfield, MO: Gospel Publishing House. 1974.

Liberman, A.M. "The Grammars of Speech and Language." *Cognitive Psychology* 1 (1970): 301–23.

Liddell, Scott K. *American Sign Language Syntax.* New York: Mouton, 1980.

_____. "Nonmanual Signals and Relative Clauses in American Sign Language." In P. Siple, ed., *Understanding Language through Sign Language Research.* New York: Academic Press, 1978.

_____. "Think and Believe: Sequentiality in ASL Signs." *Language* 60 (1984): 372–99.

Lloyd, L.L., and J.E. Doherty. "The Influence of Production Mode on the Recall of Signs in Normal Adult Subjects." *Journal of Speech and Hearing Research* 26 (1983): 595–600.

A Look at American Sign Language. Public Service Programs, book 1. Washington, DC: Gallaudet College.

A Look at Fingerspelling. Public Service Programs, book 2. Washington, DC: Gallaudet College.

Madsen, W.J. *Conversational Sign Language II: An Intermediate-Advanced Manual.* Washington, DC: Gallaudet College, 1972.

Markowicz, H. *American Sign Language: Fact and Fancy.* Washington, DC: Gallaudet College, Public Service Programs, 1977.

Martin, J. "Rhythmic (Hierarchical) versus Serial Structure in Speech and Other Behavior." *Psychological Review* 79 (1972): 487–509.

Matthews, P.H. *Morphology: An Introduction to the Theory of Word Structure.* Cambridge, England: Cambridge University Press, 1974.

Mattingly, I.G. "Reading, the Linguistic Process, and Linguistic Awareness." In J.F. Kavanagh and Ignatius G. Mattingly, eds., *Language by Ear and by Eye: the Relationships Between Speech and Reading.* Cambridge, MA: MIT Press, 1972.

Mayberry, Rachel. "If a Chimp Can Learn Sign Language, Surely My Nonverbal Client Can Too." *ASHA* 18 (April 1976): 223–28.

_____. "Manual Communication." In H. Davis and S.R. Silverman, eds., *Hearing and Deafness*. New York: Holt, Rinehart and Winston, 1964.

Monsen, Randall B. "Toward Measuring How Well Hearing-Impaired Children Speak." *Journal of Speech and Hearing Journal* 21 (1978): 197–219.

Muller, G.H. *The American College Handbook of Contemporary English*. New York: Harper and Row, 1985.

Norman, Donald A. "The Role of Memory in the Understanding of Language." In J.F. Kavanagh and Ignatius G. Mattingly, eds., *Language by Ear and by Eye: the Relationships between Speech and Reading*. Cambridge, MA: MIT Press, 1972.

Northern, J.L., and M.P. Downs. *Hearing in Children*. Baltimore, MD: Williams and Wilkins, 1974.

Orlansky, M.D., and J.D. Bonvillian. "The Role of Iconicity in Early Sign Language Acquisition." *Journal of Speech and Hearing Disorders* 49 (1984): 287–92.

O'Rourke, T.J. *A Basic Course in Manual Communication,* rev. ed. Silver Spring, MD: National Association of the Deaf, 1972.

Padden, Carol. "Some Arguments for Syntactic Patterning in American Sign Language." *Sign Language Studies* 32 (1981): 239–59.

Page, Judith L. "Relative Translucency of ASL Signs Representing Three Semantic Classes." *Journal of Speech and Hearing Disorders* 50 (1985): 241–47.

Raffin, M.J.M., J.M. Davis, and L.A. Gilman. "Comprehension of Inflectional Morphemes by Deaf Children Exposed to a Visual English Sign System." *Journal of Speech and Hearing Research* 21 (1977): 387–400.

Riekehof, L. Lottie. *Talk to the Deaf*. Springfield, MO: Gospel Publishing House, 1963.

_____. *The Joy of Signing: The New Illustrated Guide for Mastering Sign Language and the Manual Alphabet*. Springfield, MO: Gospel Publishing House, 1978.

Romski, M.A., and K.F. Ruder. "Effects of Speech and Speech and Sign Instruction on Oral Language Learning and Generalization of Action and Object Combinations by Down's Syndrome Children." *Journal of Speech and Hearing Disorders* 49 (1984): 293–302.

Sanders, Derek A. *Aural Rehabilitation*. Englewood Cliffs, NJ: Prentice Hall, 1971.

Schein, Jerome D. *Speaking the Language of Sign: The Art and Science of Signing*. Garden City, NY: Doubleday, 1984.

Schlesinger, I. "Grammar of Sign Language." In I. Schlesinger and Namir, eds., *Sign Language of the Deaf*. New York: Academic Press, 1978.

_____, and Lila Namir, eds. *Sign Language of the Deaf; Psychological, Linguistic, and Sociological Perspectives*. New York: Academic Press, 1978.

Shulman, H.G. "Similarity Effects in Short-Term Memory." *Psychological Bulletin* 75 (1971): 399–415.

Siple, P., ed. *Understanding Language through Sign Language Research*. New York: Academic Press, 1978.

Stokoe, William C. *Semiotics and Human Sign Languages*. The Hague: Mouton, 1972.

_____. "Sign Language Structure: An Outline of the Visual Communication Systems of the American Deaf." *Studies in Linguistics, Occasional Papers* 8. Buffalo, NY: University of Buffalo Press, 1960. Reprint Silver Spring, MD: Linstok Press, 1978.

_____, D. Casterline, and C. Croneberg. *A Dictionary of American Sign Language on Linguistic Principles*. Washington, DC: Gallaudet College Press, 1965.

Supalla, T., and E.L. Newport. "How Many Seats in a Chair? The Derivation of Nouns and Verbs in American Sign Language." In P. Siple, ed., *Understanding Language through Sign Language Research*. New York: Academic Press, 1978.

Tervoort, Bernard T. "Bilingual Interference." In, I.M. Schlesinger and L. Namir eds., *Sign Language of the Deaf: Psychological, Linguistic, and Sociological Perspectives*. New York: Academic Press, 1978.

Thompson, Henry. "The Lack of Subordination in American Sign Language." In L.A. Friedman, ed., *On the Other Hand: New Perspectives on American Sign Language*. New York: Academic Press, 1977.

Tweney, R.D., and H.W. Hoemann. "Back Translation: A Method for the Analysis of Manual Languages." *Sign Language Studies* 2 (1973): 51–72, 77–80.

Wilbur, R.B. *American Sign Language: Linguistic and Applied Dimensions* (second edition). Boston, MA: Little, Brown and Company, 1987.

_____. *American Sign Language and Sign Systems*. Baltimore, MD: University Park Press, 1979.

_____. "The Linguistics of Manual Languages and Manual Systems." In L.L. Lloyd, ed., *Communication Assessment and Intervention Strategies*. Baltimore: University Park Press, 1976.

_____, M.E. Berstein, and R. Kantor. "The Semantic Domain of Classifiers in American Sign Language." *Sign Languge Studies* 46 (1985): 1–38.

Wilentz, Joan S. *The Senses of Man*. New York: Thomas Y. Crowell, 1968.

Woodward, J.C., Jr. "Facing and Handling Variation in American Sign Language Phonology." *Sign Language Studies* 11 (1976): 43–51.

_____. "Implication Variation in American Sign Language: Negative Incorporation." *Sign Language Studies* 5 (1974): 20–30.

_____. "Signs of Change: Historical Variation in American Sign Language." *Sign Language Studies* 10 (1976): 81–94.

_____, and C. Erting. "Synchronic Variation and Historical Change in American Sign Language." *Language Science* 37 (1975): 9–12.

_____, and S. Oliver. "Facing and Handling Variation in ASL Phonology" *Sign Language Studies* 11 (1976): 43–51.

Index

Entries in all capital letters refer to ASL signs. The entry's page number will be in boldface when there is an illustration of the sign.

251